Praise for **CRITIQUE OF BLACK REASON**

Winner of the 2015 Geschwister-Scholl-Preis
Winner of Le Prix FETKANN! de la Mémoire 2013

"A captivating and simultaneously vexing mixture of historical lecture and political-philosophical manifesto."
　　　　　　　—Andreas Eckert, *Frankfurter Allgemeine Zeitung*

"Achille Mbembe is one of those paradoxical optimists who predict the worst without ever losing their faith in the future. . . . Admittedly, slavery has been abolished and colonialism is a thing of the past. But today new forms of alienation have arisen, the Other continues to be stigmatized, and the monster of capitalism reaches for its dream of a limitless horizon. An inevitability? Not necessarily, shoots back this thinker, who invites us to reimagine the geography of the world."
　　　　　　　—Maria Malagardis, *Libération*

". . . a book that you want to shout about from the rooftops, so that all your colleagues and friends will read it. My copy, only a few months old, is stuffed with paper markers at many intervals, suggesting the richness of analysis and description on nearly every page. . . . This is certainly one of the outstanding intellectual contributions to studies of empire, colonialism, racism, and human liberation in the last decade, perhaps decades. . . . A brilliant book."
　　　　　　　—Elaine Coburn, *Decolonization: Indigeneity, Education & Society*

CRITIQUE OF
BLACK REASON

CRITIQUE OF BLACK REASON

ACHILLE MBEMBE

Translated by

LAURENT DUBOIS

Duke University Press
Durham and London
2017

© 2017 Duke University Press
"CRITIQUE DE LA RAISON NÈGRE" by Achille Mbembe
© Editions LA DÉCOUVERTE, Paris, France, 2013.
All rights reserved
Printed in the United States of America on acid-free paper ∞
Cover designed by Matthew Tauch
Typeset in Arno Pro by Westchester Publishing Services

Library of Congress Cataloging-in-Publication Data
Names: Mbembe, Achille, [date] author. |
Dubois, Laurent, [date] translator.
Title: Critique of black reason / Achille Mbembe ;
translated by Laurent Dubois.
Other titles: Critique de la raison nègre. English
Description: Durham : Duke University Press, 2017. |
"A John Hope Franklin Center Book." | Originally published
as "Critique de la raison nègre": Paris : La Decouverte, [2013] |
Includes bibliographical references and index.
Identifiers: LCCN 2016043545 (print)
LCCN 2016046043 (ebook)
ISBN 9780822363323 (hardcover : alk. paper)
ISBN 9780822363439 (pbk. : alk. paper)
ISBN 9780822373230 (ebook)
Subjects: LCSH: Blacks—Race identity. | Whites—Race
identity. | Race—Philosophy. | Race—Social aspects. |
Race awareness—Moral and ethical aspects. | Slavery—Moral
and ethical aspects. | Racism. | Difference (Philosophy)
Classification: LCC HT1581 .M3313 2017 (print) |
LCC HT1581 (ebook) | DDC 305.8001—dc23
LC record available at https://lccn.loc.gov/2016043545

CONTENTS

TRANSLATOR'S INTRODUCTION

If a language is a kind of cartography, then to translate is to transform one map into another. It is a process of finding the right symbols, those that will allow new readers to navigate through a landscape. What Mbembe offers us here is a cartography in two senses: a map of a terrain sedimented by centuries of history, and an invitation to find ourselves within this terrain so that we might choose a path through it—and perhaps even beyond it.

What is "Black reason"? Mbembe's sinuous, resonant answer to that question is that it is what constitutes reason as we know it—the reason of state, the reason of capital, the reason of history. To understand the category of Blackness, one must understand the history of the modern world, its forms of conquest and exploitation, the manifold responses to its systems of oppression, the forms of resistance and voicing, the totality and its fragments. But the only way to make sense of that broader history is to begin from the category itself, from its power to condense and crystallize these broader processes. The critique offered here is one of remarkable historical and philosophical breadth. But it is also always attentive to the labyrinths and multiplicities of individual experience as shaped by social and conceptual worlds. "'Black' is first of all a word," Mbembe writes. "But the word has its own weight, its own density." "There are words that wound," he notes, notably this "name that was given to me by someone else." "To be Black is to be stuck at the foot of a wall with no doors, thinking nonetheless that everything will open up in the end" (pp. 151, 152).

With a voice that is conceptually percussive and often deeply poetic, Mbembe offers an account that is also always a theorization, sometimes puncturing what seems solid, at other times offering us vistas, openings, through a poetic evocation of possibilities unfulfilled. His voice and perspective are unique for the way he brings together African-American and Caribbean history, European imperial history, and multiple histories of Africa, notably South Africa. This is a painful story but also one that pulses with energy—the energy of the actors and thinkers that have guided Mbembe through this cartography, whose ideas in turn take on new meaning as they are assembled and analyzed here through his unique vision.

This book offers a powerful and at times beautifully sardonic critique of existing discourses about Blacks and Africa. "Still today," Mbembe writes, "as soon as the subject of Blacks and Africa is raised, words do not necessarily represent things," and "the true and the false become inextricable" (p. 13). He explores the historical process through which Blackness and Africa became a concatenation of symbols and narratives, with the African continent coming to serve as "the mask as well as the hollow sun." "When Africa comes up," he notes, "correspondence between words, images, and the thing itself matters very little. It is not necessary for the name to correspond to the thing, or for the thing to respond to its name." There has always been a remarkable freedom surrounding talk about Africa and Blackness, a "total abdication of responsibility" that allows people, again and again, to conveniently end up "with a tale with which we are already familiar" (pp. 49, 51–52).

How are we to navigate through this landscape constituted largely out of deeply consequential fantasizing? Partly, as Mbembe does here, by both analyzing and puncturing the genealogy, by mapping it out but also by seeking to look at the map it has constituted for itself. Race, he writes, is "image, form, surface, figure, and—especially—a structure of the imagination." And racism, a "site of a rupture, of effervescence and effusion," is a way of "substituting what *is* with something else, with another reality" (p. 32). And it is, as Mbembe insists throughout the work, a force that infuses and haunts global thought, practice, and possibility in ways we must fully confront and understand if we are to move beyond.

His book seeks to lucidly account for the historical foundations for this haunting, to provide categories through which to simultaneously apprehend and unravel it. "The Black Man is in effect the ghost of modernity," he writes (p. 129). That modern history is "the product of a process that transforms people of African origin into living *ore* from which *metal* is extracted" (p. 40). The history of the Atlantic slave trade, of the fundamental links between the creation of the plantation complex of the Americas and the constitution of modern Europe, is retold here as the foundation for the global order, and the order of thought itself. But Mbembe's chronology is never a stable one, for the present is shot through with the past, and the structures of labor, migration, surveillance, and capital in our contemporary world are presented here as deeply connected with and alarmingly close to older slaving and colonial orders. And they are sustained, too, by the continuing deployment of the form of thought Mbembe seeks to analyze historically and confront philosophically and analytically.

The history of slavery and colonialism constituted the term "Black" as the name "of the slave: *man-of-metal, man-merchandise, man-of-money*" (p. 47). The word "designated not human beings *like all others* but rather a *distinct* humanity—one whose very humanity was (and still is) in question." Blackness came to "represent *difference in its raw manifestation*—somatic, affective, aesthetic, imaginary." Symbiotically, Whiteness "became the mark of a certain mode of Western presence in the world, a certain figure of brutality and cruelty, a singular form of predation with an unequaled capacity for the subjection and exploitation of foreign peoples" (pp. 45, 46). Mbembe explores the structural drivers and consequences for this process but also its affective and psychological dimensions, the ways it constituted subjects the world over. To be Black, he writes, was to become "the prototype of a poisoned, burnt subject" and "a being whose life is made of ashes" (p. 40).

The creation of these categories was central to the "process of accumulation that spanned the globe" in the era of plantation slavery and the slave trade (p. 47). The Middle Passage; the creation of brutal, thriving colonies in the Caribbean; and the long history of colonialism in Africa are recounted here but not so much through a traditional chronology as through a narrative that connects various periods, showing how different pasts—and the present—are shot through with one another. For the legacies of this giant process of destruction are everywhere: "Racial capitalism is the equivalent of a giant necropolis. It rests on the traffic of the dead and human bones" (pp. 136–137). This history has created race and given it the power to shape meaning, experience, the past, and the future. Race, "at once image, body, and enigmatic mirror," writes Mbembe, is "the expression of resistance to multiplicity" and "an act of imagination as much as an act of misunderstanding" (pp. 110, 112).

Our contemporary confrontation with the legacies of this history must nourish itself from, find illumination and inspiration in, the work of many who have come before—those who resisted enslavement, those who crafted dreams of alternative worlds, the poets and activists whose presence is as old as the configuration of plantation slavery, the slave trade, and colonialism itself. The enslaved, he writes, were "fertilizers of history and subjects beyond subjection." Always sustaining the "possibilities for radical insurgency," they represented a "kind of silt of the earth, a silt deposited at the confluence of half-worlds produced by the dual violence of race and capital" (pp. 36–37), because, always, there was creation in the midst of destruction, as those subjected to these barbarous systems "produced ways of thinking and languages that were truly their own. They invented their own literatures, music, and ways of celebrating the divine" (p. 48). The worlds of meaning and possibility they created through religious and political practice as well as through literature and art are taken up throughout the work and infuse it with the sense of alternative histories and futures. Mbembe shows here how categories can be challenged and remade, sometimes from within. In the hands of those who resisted, Blackness could be transformed "into a symbol of beauty and pride" and "a sign of radical defiance, a call to revolt, desertion, or insurrection" (p. 47). The category itself could even become "an island of repose in the midst of racial oppression and objective dehumanization" (p. 48).

From the eighteenth century to the present day, this process was partly about the reconstitution of history, the "foundation of an archive," a project in which Mbembe's work participates. The goal has been "to create community, one forged out of debris from the four corners of the world," while grappling with a history that meant that this was "a community whose blood stains the entire surface of modernity." Mbembe crystallizes the work of generations of writers and historians who have struggled to write the past in a way that can open up a different future. As he notes, their work has always been challenging, for the "historical experiences of Blacks did not necessarily leave traces," and therefore the history can be "written only from fragments brought together to give an account of an experience that itself was fragmented." But this act of historical reconstruction was and remains, at its core, a necessary act of "moral imagination" (pp. 28–29).

In dialogue with the work of Fabien Eboussi Boulaga, Mbembe reflects luminously on the way in which both Christianity and Islam were encountered, absorbed, transformed, and reconfigured in Africa, as people used them as an "immense field of signs" through which to interpret and act within the world. The history of these religious reconfigurations, he writes, highlights the "heretical genius" out of which "flows the capacity of Africans to inhabit several worlds at once and situate themselves simultaneously on both sides of an image" (p. 102). All of these worlds of religious practice, of art, are central in the project to "awaken slumbering powers" in the pursuit of new worlds, allowing for an experience of a "plenitude of time" and serving as "the metaphor for a future to come" (pp. 174, 175).

Mbembe's book is rooted in and engages with the writings of a wide range of other thinkers. He writes of Marcus Garvey's search for an Africa that was "the name of a promise—the promise of a reversal of history," and of the "volcanic thought" of Aimé Césaire (p. 156). He delves into the work of African novelists Amos Tutuola and Sony Labou Tansi and shows how they offer powerful readings of slavery and political oppression. He writes inspiringly of Nelson Mandela, "a man constantly on the lookout, a sentinel at the point of departure," who "lived intensely—as if everything were to begin again, and as if every moment was his last" (pp. 170, 171). And he writes of Édouard Glissant and his search for a new world to be born from the "underside of our history," from the silt that has been "deposited along the banks of rivers, in the midst of archipelagos, in the depths of oceans" (p. 181).

But the greatest guide throughout is Frantz Fanon, whose writings Mbembe has engaged with throughout much of his work. Fanon's "*situated thinking*, born of a lived experience that was always in progress, unstable, and changing," provides a model of "critical thought" that was "aimed at smashing, puncturing, and transforming" colonialism and racism. His was always a "*metamorphic thought*," and as such an ever-present and ever-relevant guide through the ruins of the present (pp. 161, 162).

All of these thinkers were the products of a "polyglot internationalism" through which writings, practices, and ideas "circulated within a vast global network, producing the modern Black imaginary." Following Paul Gilroy, he argues that their work offers "the foundation for an alternative genealogy of human rights" (p. 30). Mbembe's own book is also meant to offer an alternative genealogy—of a category, "Black," that has been made by the world and made the world—in order to find what Glissant calls the "*reservoirs of life*" (p. 181). "The path is clear: on the basis of a critique of the past, we must create a future that is inseparable from the notions of justice, dignity, and the *in-common*." This book is for those "to whom the right to have rights is refused, those who are told not to move," and "those who are turned away, deported, expelled"—the "new 'wretched of the earth'" (p. 177).

Mbembe's book is at once a global history, a philosophical intervention, and a call for the creation of new futures. Because the book's language here often serves as a conceptual and historical cartography, my task has been to create a new map in a new language. The problem has been that the existing cartography of terms, particularly those dealing with race, is quite different in French and English. The same symbols can mean different things in the two languages, resonating with vastly different histories of interpretation and sensibility.[1]

Perhaps the most difficult challenge in the translation was a question raised from the title page forward: how should I translate the French word *Nègre*? It is a particularly capacious and shifting term in French, layered with uses and counteruses, shot through in a sense with centuries of struggle over its very meaning. I knew the title had to be *Critique of Black Reason*, which inspired my first attempt, in which I translated directly from "le Nègre" to "the Black," which had the benefit of seeming accuracy but the disadvantage that it sounded weird to most readers. Using "the Negro," following a tradition of twentieth-century African-American thought, worked for some parts but not others: and calling the book *Critique of Negro Reason* just didn't quite work.

It was, ultimately, a particular spiral of illuminated conversation that led to a solution that, once found, seemed perfectly clear and obvious. It is a strategy with pleasingly theological resonances. Here, the unity of "le Nègre" becomes a trinity of words: sometimes "Blacks," sometimes "Blackness," and at others "the Black Man." This allowed me to map, in particular, correspondences that moved from the multiplicity of meanings in the French term to words that pointed and flowed well in English. Something is lost, of course, and perhaps things are added too: the limiting masculinism of the term "the Black Man" worried me, but in fact most of the passages where I translated using this term are articulated in a gendered way, often as a result of that tendency in the works of the thinkers (like Fanon) who so deeply guide much of the text.

In fact, *Critique of Black Reason* itself is, from one perspective, one winding, layered, and detailed definition of the term "Nègre," an illustration of precisely how complex the term is, and how central it is to the very constitution of modern thought, politics, ideology, and social life. Once embarked in the text, readers will understand that the term—or, in the translation, the trinity of terms—is always insufficient, always just a bit to the side, approaching but not arriving. And this is, in a sense, precisely the point. Mbembe here offers nothing less than a map of the world as it has been constituted through colonialism and racial thinking, an archive of entrapment that also serves, perhaps, as a guide for escape—or at least the beginnings of a reparation through recognition, the first hint of the constitution of a beyond.

ACKNOWLEDGMENTS

This work of translation is what it is partly because it is the result of a friendship: I have taught and collaborated closely with Achille Mbembe for several years, and also co-led the Francophone Postcolonial Studies Playgroup with him, during which visits to museums, ice cream parlors, and playgrounds have served as the backdrop for ongoing conversations. Aniel, Anton, and Lea, the other participants in this group, are perhaps those who deserve the greatest acknowledgment, among many who have helped create this translation. Perhaps I can attribute to them the sense of freedom that I brought to this project, in which the goal was to somehow transmit the poetic nature of Mbembe's prose into the right pacing, imagery, and openness in English.

There are, of course, many others who made this project possible. Ken Wissoker of Duke University Press had the idea of having me translate the work. Eliza Dandridge, a doctoral student at Duke University, expertly re-read and critiqued a full draft of the translation. And the Franklin Humanities Center funded a translation manuscript workshop, which allowed us to gather a remarkable array of colleagues to discuss an early draft of a few translated chapters, providing guidance and inspiration: Srinivas Aravamudan, Sandie Blaise, J. Kameron Carter, Roberto Dainotto, Ainehi Edoro, Michael Hardt, Azeen Khan, Ranjana Khana, Adriane Lentz-Smith, Anne-Maria B. Makhulu, Emma Monroy, Mark Anthony Neal, Sarah Nutall, Charlie Piot, Rachel Rothendler, and Anne-Gaëlle Saliot. Finally, two anonymous reviewers for Duke University Press provided encouragement and thoughtful critique that made the final version of this what it is.

INTRODUCTION
THE BECOMING BLACK
OF THE WORLD

These heads of men, these collections of ears, these burned houses, these Gothic invasions, this steaming blood, these cities that evaporate at the edge of the sword, are not to be so easily disposed of.

—AIMÉ CÉSAIRE, *Discourse on Colonialism*

I envision this book as a river with many tributaries, since history and all things flow toward us now. Europe is no longer the center of gravity of the world. This is the significant event, the fundamental experience, of our era. And we are only just now beginning the work of measuring its implications and weighing its consequences.[1] Whether such a revelation is an occasion for joy or cause for surprise or worry, one thing remains certain: the demotion of Europe opens up possibilities—and presents dangers—for critical thought. That is, in part, what this essay seeks to examine.

To capture the precise contours of these dangers and possibilities, we need first to remember that, throughout its history, European thought has tended to conceive of identity less in terms of mutual belonging (cobelonging) to a common world than in terms of a relation between similar beings—of being itself emerging and manifesting itself in its own state, or its own mirror.[2] But it is also crucial for us to understand that as the direct consequence of the logic of self-fictionalization and self-contemplation, indeed of closure, Blackness and race have played multiple roles in the imaginaries of European societies.[3] Primary, loaded, burdensome, and unhinged, symbols of raw intensity and repulsion, the two have always occupied a central place—simultaneously, or at least in parallel—within modern knowledge and discourse about man (and therefore about humanism and humanity). Since the beginning of the eighteenth century, Blackness and race have constituted the (unacknowledged and often denied) foundation, what we might call the nuclear power plant, from which the modern project of knowledge—and of governance—has been deployed.[4] Blackness and race, the one and the other, represent twin figures of the delirium produced by modernity (chapters 1 and 2).

What are the reasons for the delirium, and what are its most basic manifestations? It results, first, from the fact that the Black Man is the one (or the thing) that one sees when one sees nothing, when one understands nothing, and, above all, when one wishes to understand nothing. Everywhere he appears, the Black Man unleashes impassioned dynamics and provokes an irrational exuberance that always tests the limits of the very system of reason. But delirium is also caused by the fact that no one—not those who invented him, not those who named him thus—would want to be a Black Man or to be treated as one. As Gilles Deleuze observed, "there is always a Black person, a Jew, a Chinese, a Grand Mogol, an Aryan in the midst of delirium," since what drives delirium is, among other things, race.[5] By reducing the body and the living being to matters of appearance, skin, and color, by granting skin and color the status of fiction based on biology, the Euro-American world in particular has made Blackness and race two sides of a single coin, two sides of a codified madness.[6] Race, operating over the past centuries as a foundational category that is at once material and phantasmic, has been at the root of catastrophe, the cause of extraordinary psychic devastation and of innumerable crimes and massacres.[7]

Vertiginous Assemblage

There are three critical moments in the biography of the vertiginous assemblage that is Blackness and race. The first arrived with the organized despoliation of the Atlantic slave trade (from the fifteenth through the nineteenth century), through which men and women from Africa were transformed into human-objects, human-commodities, human-money.[8] Imprisoned in the dungeon of appearance, they came to belong to others who hated them. They were deprived of their own names and their own languages. Their lives and their work were from then on controlled by the others with whom they were condemned to live, and who denied them recognition as cohumans. And yet they nevertheless remained active subjects.[9] The second moment corresponded with the birth of writing near the end of the eighteenth century, when Blacks, as beings-taken-by-others, began leaving traces in a language all of their own and at the same time demanded the status of full subjects in the world of the living.[10] The moment was punctuated by innumerable slave revolts and the independence of Haiti in 1804, by the battle for the abolition of the slave trade, by African decolonization, and by the struggle for civil rights in the United States. The second era culminated in the dismantling of apartheid during the last decades of the twentieth century. The third moment—the early twenty-first century—is one marked by the globalization of markets, the privatization of the world under the aegis of neoliberalism, and the increasing imbrication of the financial markets, the postimperial military complex, and electronic and digital technologies.

By "neoliberalism" I mean a phase in the history of humanity dominated by the industries of the Silicon Valley and digital technology. In the era of neoliberalism, time passes quickly and is converted into the production of the money-form. Capital, having reached its maximal capability for flight, sets off a process of escalation. The vision that defines the neoliberal moment is one according to which "all events and situations in the world of life can be assigned a market value."[11] The process is also characterized by the production of indifference; the frenzied codification of social life according to norms, categories, and numbers; and various operations of abstraction that claim to rationalize the world on the basis of corporate logic.[12] Capital, notably finance capital, is haunted by a baneful double and defines itself as unlimited in terms of both ends and means. It does more than just dictate its own temporal regime. Having taken as its responsibility the "fabrication of all relations of filiation," it seeks to reproduce itself "on its own" in an infinite series of structurally insolvent debts.[13]

There are no more workers as such. There are only laboring nomads. If yesterday's drama of the subject was exploitation by capital, the tragedy of the multitude today is that they are unable to be exploited at all. They are abandoned subjects, relegated to the role of a "superfluous humanity." Capital hardly needs them anymore to function. A new form of psychic life is emerging, one based on artificial and digital memory and on cognitive models drawn from the neurosciences and neuroeconomics. With little distinction remaining between psychic reflexes and technological reflexes, the human subject becomes fictionalized as "an entrepreneur of the self." This subject is plastic and perpetually called on to reconfigure itself in relation to the artifacts of the age.[14]

This new man, subject to the market and to debt, views himself as the simple product of natural luck. He is a kind of "ready-made abstract form," characteristic of the civilization of the image and of the new relationships that it establishes between fact and fiction, and capable of absorbing any content.[15] He is now just one animal among others, lacking an essence of his own to protect or safeguard. There are no longer any limits placed on the modification of his genetic, biological structure.[16] The new subject differs in many ways from the tragic and alienated figure of early industrialization. First and foremost, he is a prisoner of desire. His pleasure depends almost entirely on his capacity to reconstruct his private life publicly, to turn it into viable merchandise and put it up for sale. He is a neuroeconomic subject absorbed by a double concern stemming from his animal nature (as subject to the biological reproduction of life) and his thingness (as subject to others' enjoyment of the things of this world). As a *human-thing, human-machine, human-code,* and *human-in-flux,* he seeks above all to regulate his behavior according to the norms of the market. He eagerly instrumentalizes himself and others to optimize his own pleasure. Condemned to lifelong apprenticeship, to flexibility, to the reign of the short term, he must embrace his condition as a soluble, fungible subject to be able to respond to what is constantly demanded of him: to become another.

Moreover, in the era of neoliberalism, capitalism and animism—long and painstakingly kept apart from each other—have finally tended to merge. The cycle of capital moves from image to image, with the image now serving as an accelerant, creating energy and drive. The potential fusion of capitalism and animism carries with it a number of implications for our future understanding of race and racism. First, the systematic risks experienced specifically by Black slaves during early capitalism have now become the norm for, or at least the lot of, all of subaltern humanity. The emergence of new imperial practices is then tied to the tendency to universalize the Black condition. Such practices borrow as much from the slaving logic of capture and predation as from the colonial logic of occupation and extraction, as well as from the civil wars and raiding of earlier epochs.[17] Wars of occupation and counterinsurgency aim not only to track and eliminate the enemy but also to create a partition in time and an atomization of space. In the future, part of the task of empire will consist in transforming the real into fiction, and fiction into the real. The mobilization of airpower and the destruction of infrastructure, the strikes and wounds caused by military action, are now combined with the mass mobilization of images, a key part of the deployment of a violence that seeks purity.[18]

Capture, predation, extraction, and asymmetrical warfare converge with the rebalkanization of the world and intensifying practices of zoning, all of which point to a new collusion between the economic and the biological. Such collusion translates in concrete terms into the militarization of borders, the fragmentation and partitioning of territories, and the creation of more or less autonomous spaces within the borders of existing states. In some cases such spaces are subtracted from all forms of national sovereignty, operating instead under the informal laws of a multitude of fragmented authorities and private armed forces. In other cases they remain under the control of foreign armies or of international organizations operating under the pretext of, or on behalf of, humanitarianism.[19] Zoning practices are linked in general to transnational networks of repression whose tools and methods include the imposition of ideological grids on populations, the hiring of mercenaries to fight local guerrillas, the formation of "hunt commandos," and the systematic use of mass imprisonment, torture, and extrajudicial execution.[20] This "imperialism of disorganization," which feeds on anarchy, leverages practices of zoning to manufacture disasters and multiply states of exception nearly everywhere.

Foreign corporations, powerful nations, and local dominant classes all in turn present themselves as helping with reconstruction or use the pretext of fighting insecurity and disorder in order to help themselves to the riches and raw materials of countries thrown into chaos through zoning practices. The age has seen the massive transfer of wealth to private interests, increasing dispossession of the riches wrested from capital during previous struggles, and indefinite payments of massive debt. Even Europe, struck by the violence of capital, has witnessed the emergence of a new class of structurally indebted people.[21]

The potential fusion of capitalism and animism presents a further implication: the very distinct possibility that human beings will be transformed into animate things made up of coded digital data. Across early capitalism, the term "Black" referred only to the condition imposed on peoples of African origin (different forms of depredation, dispossession of all power of self-determination, and, most of all, dispossession of the future and of time, the two matrices of the possible). Now, for the first time in human history, the term "Black" has been generalized. This new fungibility, this solubility, institutionalized as a new norm of existence and expanded to the entire planet, is what I call the *Becoming Black of the world.*

Race in the Future Tense

Although this fact has always been denied, Euro-American discourse on man depends on the two central figures of Blackness and race. Does the demotion of Europe to the rank of a mere world province signal the extinction of racism? Or must we instead understand that as humanity becomes fungible, racism will simply reconstitute itself in the interstices of a new language on "species," inserting itself as a kind of sand, molecular and in fragments? In posing the question in these terms, we uphold the idea that neither Blackness nor race has ever been fixed (chapter 1). They have, on the contrary, always belonged to a chain of open-ended signifiers. The fundamental meanings of Blackness and race have always been existential. For ages, the term "Black" in particular flowed with incredible energy, at times connoting inferior instincts and chaotic powers, at others serving as the luminous sign of the possibility that the world might be redeemed and transfigured (chapters 2 and 5). In addition to designating a heterogeneous, multiple, and fragmented world—ever new fragments of fragments—the term "Black" signaled a series of devastating historical experiences, the reality of a vacant life, the fear felt by the millions trapped in the ruts of racial domination, the anguish at seeing their bodies and minds controlled from the outside, at being transformed into spectators watching something that was, but also was not, their true existence.[22]

This is not all. The term "Black" was the product of a social and technological machine tightly linked to the emergence and globalization of capitalism. It was invented to signify exclusion, brutalization, and degradation, to point to a limit constantly conjured and abhorred. The Black Man, despised and profoundly dishonored, is the only human in the modern order whose skin has been transformed into the form and spirit of merchandise—the living crypt of capital. But there is also a manifest dualism to Blackness. In a spectacular reversal, it becomes the symbol of a conscious desire for life, a force springing forth, buoyant and plastic, fully engaged in the act of creation and capable of living in the midst of several times and several histories at once. Its capacity for sorcery, and its ability to incite hallucination, multiplies tenfold. Some saw in the Black Man the salt of the earth, the vein of life through which the dream of a humanity reconciled with nature, and even with the totality of existence, would find its new face, voice, and movement.[23]

Europe's twilight has arrived, and the Euro-American world has not yet figured out what it wants to know about, or do with, the Black Man. "Racism without races" is now surfacing in many countries.[24] To practice racism today even as it is rendered conceptually unthinkable, "culture" and "religion" have replaced "biology." Republican universalism is presented as blind to race, even as non-Whites are locked in their supposed origins. Racialized categories abound, most of them feeding into everyday practices of Islamophobia. But who among us can doubt that the moment has finally arrived for us to begin-from-ourselves? While Europe goes astray, overtaken by the malaise of not knowing where it is within and with the world, is it not time to lay the foundation for something absolutely new? To do so, will we have to forget Blackness? Or perhaps, on the contrary, must we hold on to its false power, its luminous, fluid, and crystalline character—that strange subject, slippery, serial, and plastic, always masked, firmly camped on both sides of the mirror, constantly skirting the edge of the frame? And if, by chance, in the midst of this torment, Blackness survives those who invented it, and if all of subaltern humanity becomes Black in a reversal to which only history knows the secret, what risks would a Becoming-Black-of-the-World pose to the promise of liberty and universal equality for which the term "Black" has stood throughout the modern period (chapter 6)?

The fierce colonial desire to divide and classify, to create hierarchies and produce difference, leaves behind wounds and scars. Worse, it created a fault line that lives on. Is it possible today to craft a relationship with the Black Man that is something other than that between a master and his valet? Does the Black Man not insist, still, on seeing himself through and within difference? Is he not convinced that he is inhabited by a double, a foreign entity that prevents him from knowing himself? Does he not live in a world shaped by loss and separation, cultivating a dream of returning to an identity founded on pure essentialism and therefore, often, on alterity? At what point does the project of a radical uprising in search of autonomy in the name of difference turn into a simple mimetic inversion of what was previously showered with malediction?

These are some of the questions I ask in this book. It is neither a history of ideas nor an exercise in sociological history, but it uses history to propose a style of critical reflection on our contemporary world. By privileging a sort of reminiscence, half solar and half lunar, half day and half night, I have in mind a single question: how can we think through difference and life, the similar and the dissimilar, the surplus and the *in-common*? This kind of questioning is familiar to the Black experience, which knows so well how to occupy the place of a fleeing limit within contemporary consciousness, serving as a kind of mirror in perpetual motion. But we must wonder why the mirror never stops turning. What prevents it from stopping? What explains the infinite refraction of divisions, each more sterile than the last?

—*Johannesburg, 2 August 2013*

This essay was written during my long stay at the Witwatersrand Institute for Social and Economic Research at the University of Witwatersrand (in Johannesburg, South Africa). It is part of a cycle of reflections first opened up in *On the Postcolony* (2000), then pursued in *Sortir de la grande nuit* (2010), and concluded by my teaching in a course on Afropolitanism.

During this cycle we sought to inhabit several worlds at the same time, not in an easy gesture of fragmentation, but in one of coming and going, able to authorize the articulation, from Africa, of *a thinking of circulation and crossings*. Along this path it was not useful to seek to "provincialize" European traditions of thought. They are, of course, not at all foreign to us. When it comes to speaking the world in a language for everyone, however, there exist relations of power at the heart of these traditions, and part of the work consisted in weighing in on these internal frictions, inviting them to a decentering, not in order to deepen the distance between Africa and the world, but rather to make possible the emergence, relatively lucidly, of the new demands of a possible universalism.

Throughout my time at the institute I benefited from the support of my colleagues Deborah Posel, Sarah Nutall, John Hyslop, Ashlee Neeser, Pamila Gupta, and, recently, Cathy Burns and Keith Breckenridge. The pages that follow owe a great deal to the friendship of David Theo Goldberg, Arjun Appadurai, Ackbar Abbas, Françoise Vergès, Pascal Blanchard, Laurent Dubois, Eric Fassin, Ian Baucom, Srinivas Aravamudan, Charlie

Piot, and Jean-Pierre Chrétien. Paul Gilroy, Jean Comaroff, John Comaroff, and the much-missed Carol Breckenridge were enormous sources of inspiration. I also thank my colleagues Kelly Gillespie, Julia Hornberger, Leigh-Ann Naidoo, and Zen Marie of the Johannesburg Workshop in Theory and Criticism of the University of Witwatersrand.

My editor, François Gèze, and his team (Pascale Iltis and Thomas Deltombe in particular) were, as always, a steady source of support.

I thank the journals *Le Débat*, *Politique Africaine*, *Cahiers d'Études Africaines*, *Research in African Literatures*, *Africulture*, and *Le Monde Diplomatique*, which welcomed the exploratory texts that form the basis for this essay.

For reasons there is no reason to repeat here, this book is dedicated to Sarah, Léa, and Aniel, as well as Jolyon and Jean.

ONE
THE SUBJECT
OF RACE

The pages that follow deal with "Black reason." By this ambiguous and polemical term I mean to identify several things at once: forms of knowledge; a model of extraction and depredation; a paradigm of subjection, including the modalities governing its eradication; and, finally, a psycho-oneiric complex. Like a kind of giant cage, Black reason is in truth a complicated network of doubling, uncertainty, and equivocation, built with race as its chassis.

We can speak of race (or racism) only in a fatally imperfect language, gray and inadequate. Let it suffice to say, for now, that race is a form of primal representation. Unable to distinguish between the outside and the inside, between envelopes and their contents, it sends us, above all, back to surface simulacra. Taken to its limit, race becomes a perverse complex, a generator of fears and torments, of disturbed thoughts and terror, but especially of infinite sufferings and, ultimately, catastrophe. In its phantasmagoric dimensions, it is a sign of neurosis—phobic, obsessive, at times hysterical. Otherwise, it is what reassures itself by hating, deploying dread, and practicing altruicide: the constitution of the Other not as similar to oneself but as a menacing object from which one must be protected or escape, or which must simply be destroyed if it cannot be subdued.[1] As Frantz Fanon has noted, "race" is also the name for bitter resentment and the irrepressible desire for vengeance. "Race" is the name for the rage of those who, constrained by subjection, suffer injuries, all manner of violations and humiliations, and bear countless wounds.[2] We will therefore ask, in this book, about the nature of this resentment. We will provide an account of what race does, of its depth, at once real and fictive, and of the relationships through which it expresses itself. And we will examine the gesture of race that, notably in the case of people of African origin, consists in dissolving human beings into things, objects, and merchandise.[3]

Fantasy and the Closing of the Spirit

It may seem surprising to resort to the concept of race, at least in the way that it is sketched out here. In fact, race does not exist as a physical, anthropological, or genetic fact.[4] But it is not just a useful fiction, a phantasmagoric construction, or an ideological projection whose function is to draw attention away from conflicts judged to be more real—the struggle between classes or genders, for example. In many cases race is an autonomous figure of the real whose force and density can be explained by its characteristic mobility, inconstancy, and capriciousness. It wasn't all that long ago, after all, that the world was founded on an inaugural dualism that sought justification in the old myth of racial superiority.[5] In its avid need for myths through which to justify its power, the Western world considered itself the center of the earth and the birthplace of reason, universal life, and the truth of humanity. The most "civilized" region of the world, the West alone had invented the "rights of the people." It alone had succeeded in constituting a civil society of nations understood as a public space of legal reciprocity. It alone was at the origin of the idea that to be human was to possess civil and political rights that allowed individuals to develop private and public powers as citizens of the human race who, as such, were shaped by all that was human. And it alone had codified a range of customs accepted by different peoples that included diplomatic rituals, the rules of engagement, the right of conquest, public morality and polite behavior, and practices of business, religion, and government.

The Remainder—the ultimate sign of the dissimilar, of difference and the pure power of the negative—constituted the manifestation of existence as an object. Africa in general and Blackness in particular were presented as accomplished symbols of a vegetative, limited state. The Black Man, a sign in excess of all signs and therefore fundamentally unrepresentable, was the ideal example of this other-being, powerfully possessed by emptiness, for whom the negative had ended up penetrating all moments of existence— the death of the day, destruction and peril, the unnameable night of the world.[6] Georg Wilhelm Friedrich Hegel described such figures as statues without language or awareness of themselves, human entities incapable of ridding themselves definitively of the animal presence with which they were mixed. In fact, their nature was to contain what was already dead.

Such figures, he wrote, were the province of "a host of separate, antagonistic national Spirits who hate and fight each other to the death," dismembering and destroying themselves like animals—a kind of humanity staggering through life, confusing becoming-human and becoming-animal, and all along "unconscious of their universality."[7] Others, more charitable, admitted that such entities were not completely devoid of humanity. They were, rather, in a state of slumber and had not yet become engaged in the adventure of what Paul Valéry called the "leap of no return." It was possible, they claimed, to raise them up to our level, and shouldering that burden did not grant the right to take advantage of their inferiority. On the contrary, it was Europe's duty to help and protect them.[8] This made the colonial enterprise a fundamentally "civilizing" and "humanitarian" enterprise. The violence that was its corollary could only ever be moral.[9]

European discourse, both scholarly and popular, had a way of thinking, of classifying and imagining distant worlds, that was often based on modes of fantasizing. By presenting facts, often invented, as real, certain, and exact, it evaded what it claimed to capture and maintained a relationship to other worlds that was fundamentally imaginary, even as it sought to develop forms of knowledge aimed at representing them objectively. The essential qualities of the imaginary relationship remain to be elucidated, but the procedures that enabled the work of fantasy to take shape, as well as the violence that resulted from it, are now sufficiently well known. At this point, there are very few things we can add. But if there is one space in which the imaginary relationship and the fictional economy undergirding it existed in their most brutal, distinct, and obvious form, it is in the sign that we call Blackness and, as if by ricochet, in the seeming outer zone that we call Africa, both of which are fated to be not common nouns, or even proper nouns, but rather mere indicators of an absence of achievement.

Clearly, not all Blacks are Africans, and not all Africans are Blacks. But it matters little where they are located. As objects of discourse and objects of knowledge, Africa and Blackness have, since the beginning of the modern age, plunged the theory of the name as well as the status and function of the sign and of representation into deep crisis. The same was true of the relation between being and appearance, truth and falsehood, reason and unreason, even language and life. Every time it confronted the question of Blacks and Africa, reason found itself ruined and emptied, turning constantly in on itself, shipwrecked in a seemingly inaccessible place where language was destroyed and words themselves no longer had memory. Language, its ordinary functions extinguished, became a fabulous machine whose power resided in its vulgarity, in its remarkable capacity for violation, and in its indefinite proliferation. Still today, as soon as the subject of Blacks and Africa is raised, words do not necessarily represent things; the true and the false become inextricable; the signification of the sign is not always adequate to what is being signified. It is not only that the sign is substituted for the thing. Word and image often have little to say about the objective world. The world of words and signs has become autonomous to such a degree that it exists not only as a screen possessed by its subject, its life, and the conditions of its production but as a force of its own, capable of emancipating itself from all anchoring in reality. That this is the case must be attributed, to a large extent, to the law of race.

It would be a mistake to believe that we have left behind the regime that began with the slave trade and flourished in plantation and extraction colonies. In these baptismal fonts of modernity, the principle of race and the subject of the same name were put to work under the sign of capital. This is what distinguishes the slave trade and its institutions from indigenous forms of servitude.[10] Between the fourteenth and the nineteenth centuries, the spatial horizon of Europe expanded considerably. The Atlantic gradually became the epicenter of a new concatenation of worlds, the locus of a new planetary consciousness. The shift into the Atlantic followed European attempts at expansion in the Canaries, Madeira, the Azores, and the islands of Cape Verde and culminated in the establishment of a plantation economy dependent on African slave labor.[11]

The transformation of Spain and Portugal from peripheral colonies of the Arab world into the driving forces of European expansion across the Atlantic coincided with the flow of Africans into the Iberian Peninsula itself. They contributed to the reconstruction of the Iberian principalities in the wake of the Black Death and the Great Famine of the fourteenth century. Most were slaves, but certainly not all. Among them were freemen. Slaves had previously been supplied to the peninsula via trans-Saharan routes controlled by the Moors. Around 1440 the Iberians opened up direct contact with West and Central Africa via the Atlantic Ocean. The first public sale of Black victims captured in a raid took place in Portugal in 1444. The number of "captives" increased substantially between 1450 and 1500, and the African presence grew as a consequence. Thousands of slaves disembarked in Portugal each year, destabilizing the demographic equilibrium of certain Iberian cities. Such was the case in Lisbon, Seville, and Cádiz, where nearly 10 percent of the population was African at the beginning of the sixteenth century.[12] Most were assigned to agricultural and domestic work.[13] Once the conquest of the Americas began, Afro-Iberians and African slaves could be found among ship's crews, at commercial outposts, on plantations, and in the urban centers of the empire.[14] They participated in different military campaigns (in Puerto Rico, Cuba, and Florida) and in 1519 were among Hernán Cortés's regiments when they invaded Mexico.[15]

 After 1492 the triangular trade transformed the Atlantic into an entangled economy connecting Africa, the Americas, the Caribbean, and Europe. Relatively autonomous regions became interconnected, part of a vast Oceanic-Continental formation. The new multi-hemispheric ensemble engendered a series of transformations without parallel in the history of the world. People of African origin were at the heart of new and frenzied dynamics of coming and going, from one side to the other of the same ocean, from the slave ports of West and Central Africa to those in the Americas and Europe. The economy on which the new structure of circulation was based required colossal capital. It also involved the transfer of metals, agricultural products, and manufactures, alongside the dissemination of knowledge, the circulation of cultural practices that were previously unknown, and the development of insurance, accounting, and finance. The increasing traffic of religions, languages, technologies, and cultures set in motion new processes of creolization. Black consciousness during early capitalism emerged in part within this dynamic of movement and circulation. It was the product of a tradition of travel and displacement, one rooted in a logic that denationalized the imagination. Such processes of denationalization continued through the middle of the twentieth century and marked most of the great movements of Black emancipation.[16]

Between 1630 and 1780, far more Africans than Europeans disembarked in Great Britain's Atlantic colonies.[17] In this sense the height of Black presence within the British Empire was at the end of the eighteenth century. Ships leaving the slave forts and ports of West Africa and the Bay of Biafra with human cargoes deposited their wares in Jamaica and the United

States. But alongside the macabre commerce in slaves, whose only objective was profit, was the movement of free Africans, the new colonists—the "black poor" in England, or refugees from the War of Independence in the United States who left Newfoundland, Virginia, or Carolina to settle in the new colonies of Africa itself, such as Sierra Leone.[18]

The transnationalization of the Black condition was therefore a constitutive moment for modernity, with the Atlantic serving as its incubator. The Black condition incorporated a range of contrasting states and statuses: those sold through the transatlantic slave trade, convict laborers, subsistence slaves (whose lives were spent as domestics), feudal slaves, house slaves, those who were emancipated, and those who were born slaves. Between 1776 and 1825, Europe lost most of its American colonies as a result of revolutions, independence movements, and rebellions. Afro-Latins played an eminent role in the constitution of the Iberian-Hispanic empires. They served not only as servile laborers but also as ship's crewmen, explorers, officers, settlers, property owners, and, in some cases, freemen who owned slaves.[19] In the anticolonial uprisings of the nineteenth century that resulted in the dissolution of empire, they played diverse roles as soldiers and leaders of political movements. The collapse of the imperial structures of the Atlantic world and the rise of new nation-states transformed the relationships between metropoles and colonies. A class of Creole Whites asserted and consolidated their influence.[20] Old questions of heterogeneity, difference, and liberty were once again posed, with new elites using the ideology of *mestizaje* to deny and disqualify the racial question. The contribution of Afro-Latins and Black slaves to the historical development of South America has been, if not erased, at least severely obscured.[21]

The case of Haiti was crucial from this standpoint. The country's declaration of independence came in 1804, only twenty years after that of the United States, and it marked a turning point in the modern history of human emancipation. Over the course of the eighteenth century—the age of Enlightenment—the colony of Saint-Domingue was the classic example of a plantocracy, a hierarchical social, political, and economic order led by a relatively small number of rival White groups ruling in the midst of freemen of color and those of mixed heritage and over a large majority of slaves, more than half of them born in Africa.[22] In contrast to other independence movements, the Haitian Revolution was the result of an insurrection of the enslaved. It resulted, in 1805, in one of the most radical constitutions of the New World. It outlawed nobility, instituted freedom of religion, and attacked the two concepts of property and slavery, something that the American Revolution had not dared to do. Not only did the new Haitian Constitution abolish slavery. It also authorized the confiscation of lands belonging to French settlers, decapitating most of the dominant class along the way. It abolished the distinction between legitimate and illegitimate birth and pushed then-revolutionary ideas of racial equality and universal liberty to their ultimate conclusion.[23]

In the United States, the first Black slaves disembarked in 1619. On the eve of the revolution against the English, there were more than 500,000 slaves in the rebel colonies. In 1776 about five thousand enlisted as soldiers on the side of the Patriots, even though most of them were not considered citizens. The struggle against British domination and the fight against the slave system went hand in hand for most. Yet nearly ten thousand slaves in Georgia and South Carolina deserted plantations to join the English troops. Others fought for their own liberation by escaping into swamps and forest. At the end of the war, roughly fourteen thousand Blacks, some of them now free, were evacuated from Savannah, Charleston, and New York and transported to Florida, Nova Scotia, Jamaica, and, later, Africa.[24]

The anticolonial revolution against the English gave rise to a paradox: on the one hand, the expansion of the spheres of liberty for Whites and, on the other, an unprecedented consolidation of the slave system. To a large extent, the planters of the South had bought their freedom with the labor of slaves. Because of the existence of servile labor, the United States largely avoided class divisions within the White population, divisions that would have led to internal power struggles with incalculable consequences.[25]

Over the course of the Atlantic period briefly described here, the small province of the planet that is Europe gradually gained control over the rest of the world. In parallel, particularly during the eighteenth century, there emerged discourses of truth relating to nature, the specificity and forms of the living, and the qualities, traits, and characteristics of human beings. Entire populations were categorized as species, kinds, or races, classified along vertical lines.[26]

Paradoxically, it was also during this period that people and cultures were increasingly conceptualized as individualities closed in upon themselves. Each community—and even each people—was considered a unique collective body endowed with its own power. The collective also became the foundation for a history shaped, it was thought, by forces that emerged only to destroy other forces, and by struggle that could result only in liberty or servitude.[27] The expansion of the European spatial horizon, then, went hand in hand with a division and shrinking of the historical and cultural imagination and, in certain cases, a relative closing of the mind. In sum, once genders, species, and races were identified and classified, nothing remained but to enumerate the differences between them. The closing off of the mind did not signify the extinction of curiosity itself. But from the High Middle Ages to the Enlightenment, curiosity as a mode of inquiry and a cultural sensibility was inseparable from the work of fantasy, which, when focused on other worlds, constantly blurred the lines between the believable and the unbelievable, the factual and the marvelous.[28]

By the time Georges-Louis Buffon attempted the first great racial classification, the language on other worlds was suffused with naive and sensualist prejudices. Extremely complex forms of life had been reduced to mere epithets.[29] We can call this the gregarious phase of Western thinking. The period represented the Black Man as the prototype of a prehuman figure incapable of emancipating itself from its bestiality, of reproducing itself, or of raising itself up to the level of its god. Locked within sensation, the Black Man struggled to break the chains of biological necessity and for that reason was unable to take a truly human form and shape his own world. He therefore stood apart from the normal existence of the human race. During this gregarious moment of Western thinking, and propelled by imperialist impulse, the act of capturing and grasping ideas became gradually detached from the effort to know deeply and intimately. Hegel's *Reason in History* represents the culmination of the gregarious period.[30] For several centuries the concept of race—which we know referred initially to the animal sphere—served to name non-European human groups.[31] What was then called the "state of race" corresponded, it was thought, to a state of degradation and defect of an ontological nature. The notion of race made it possible to represent non-European human groups as trapped in a lesser form of being. They were the impoverished reflection of the ideal man, separated from him by an insurmountable temporal divide, a difference nearly impossible to overcome. To talk of them was, most of all, to point to absence—the absence of the same—or, rather, to a second presence, that of *monsters* and *fossils*. If the fossil, as Michel Foucault writes, is "what permits resemblances to subsist throughout all the deviations traversed by nature," and functions primarily "as a distant and approximative form of identity," the monster, in contrast "provides an account, as though in caricature, of the genesis of differences."[32] On the great chart of species, genders, races, and classes, Blackness, in its magnificent obscurity, represented the synthesis of these two figures. But Blackness does not exist as such. It is constantly produced. To produce Blackness is to produce a social link of subjection and a *body of extraction*, that is, a body entirely exposed to the will of the master, a body from which great effort is made to extract maximum profit. An exploitable object, the Black Man is also the name of a wound, the symbol of a person at the mercy of the whip and suffering in a field of struggle that opposes socioracially segmented groups and factions. Such was the case for most of the insular plantocracies of the Caribbean, those segmented universes in which the law of race depended as much on conflict between White planters and Black slaves as between Blacks and "free people of color" (often manumitted mulattoes), some of whom owned slaves themselves.

The Blacks on the plantation were, furthermore, diverse. They were hunters of maroons and fugitives, executioners and executioners' assistants, skilled slaves, informants, domestics, cooks, emancipated slaves who were still subjugated, concubines, field-workers assigned to cutting cane, workers in factories, machine operators, masters' companions, and occasionally soldiers. Their positions were far from stable. Circumstances could change, and one position could become another. Today's victim could tomorrow become an executioner in the service of the master. It was not uncommon for a slave, once freed, to become a slave owner and hunter of fugitive slaves.

Moreover, Blacks of the plantation were socialized into the hatred of others, particularly of other Blacks. The plantation was characterized by its segmented forms of subjection, distrust, intrigue, rivalry, and jealousy, ambivalent tactics born out of complicity, arrangements of all kinds, and practices of differentiation carried out against a backdrop of the reversibility of positions. But it was also defined by the fact that the social links defined by exploitation were never stable. They were constantly challenged and had to be produced and reproduced through violence of a molecular kind that sutured and saturated the master–slave relationship.

From time to time that relationship exploded in uprisings, insurrections, and slave plots. A paranoid institution, the plantation lived under a perpetual regime of fear. It combined aspects of a camp, a pen, and a paramilitary society. The slave master could deploy one form of coercion after another, create chains of dependence between him and his slaves, and alternate between terror and generosity, but his existence was always haunted by the specter of extermination. The Black slave, on the other hand, was constantly on the threshold of revolt, tempted to respond to the insistent call of liberty or vengeance, or else pulled into a form of maximum degradation and radical self-abdication that consisted in protecting his life by participating in the project of subjection.

Furthermore, between 1620 and 1640, the forms of servitude remained relatively fluid, particularly in the United States. Free labor coexisted with indentured labor (a form of impermanent servitude, or servitude of a predetermined length) and slavery (both hereditary and nonhereditary). There were profound class divisions within the settler population as well as between settlers and the mass of the enslaved. Slaves were furthermore a multiracial group. Between 1630 and 1680, a bifurcation took place that gave birth to plantation society as such. The principle of lifelong servitude for people of African origin stigmatized because of their color gradually became the rule. Africans and their children became slaves for life. The distinctions between White servants and Black slaves became much sharper. The plantation gradually took shape as an economic, disciplinary, and penal institution in which Blacks and their descendants could be bought for life.

Throughout the seventeenth century a massive legislative effort sealed their fate. The construction of subjects of race on the American continent began with their civic destitution and therefore their exclusion from the privileges and rights guaranteed to the other inhabitants of the colonies. From then on they were no longer humans *like all others*. The process continued with the extension of lifetime slavery to their children and their descendants. This first phase marked the completion of a long process aimed at establishing their legal incapacity. The loss of the right to appear in court turned the Black individual into a nonperson from a juridical standpoint. To this judicial mechanism was added a series of slave codes, often developed in the aftermaths of slave uprisings. Around 1720, with legal codification complete, what we might call the *Black structure of*

the world, which already existed in the West Indies, officially appeared in the United States, with the plantation as its core structure. As for Blacks, they were nothing more than pieces of property, at least from a strict legal perspective. The pressing question from 1670 on was how to deploy large numbers of laborers within a commercial enterprise that spanned great distances. The answer was the invention of Blackness. It was the cog that made possible the creation of the plantation—one of the period's most effective forms of wealth accumulation—and accelerated the integration of merchant capitalism with technology and the control of subordinated labor. The plantation developed over this period represented an innovation in scale, through the denial of liberty, the control of worker mobility, and the unlimited deployment of violence. The invention of Blackness also opened the way for crucial innovations in the areas of transportation, production, commerce, and insurance.

Not all of the Blacks in the Caribbean or the United States were slaves, however. The racialization of servitude in the United States pushed Whites, and especially the "poor Whites" who did all kinds of labor, to distinguish themselves as much as possible from the Africans reduced to the state of slavery. Freemen had one great fear: that the wall separating them from the slaves was not sturdy enough. At one point or another, societies across the hemisphere included freemen of color, some of whom were owners of slaves and land, in addition to indentured Whites. The population of free people of color gradually grew as a result of waves of manumission and mixed unions between Black slaves and free Whites or between White women and Blacks. In the Caribbean in particular, the phenomenon of Whites with Black concubines became relatively widespread. Even with racial segregation officially in place, interracial libertinage and concubinage with women of color, whether free or enslaved, were commonplace among White elites.[33]

Recalibration

The twenty-first century is, of course, not the nineteenth century. That period was marked by the linked processes of colonial expansion in Africa and the deliberate biologization of race in the West. It was also, with the help of Darwinian and post-Darwinian evolutionary thought, the period that saw the spread of eugenicist strategies in many countries and rising obsessions with degeneration and suicide.[34] Yet, encouraged by processes of globalization and the contradictory effects they provoke, the problematic of race has once again burst into contemporary consciousness.[35] The fabrication of racial subjects has been reinvigorated nearly everywhere.[36] Alongside anti-Semitic racism, the colonial model of comparing humans to animals, and color prejudice inherited from the slave trade and translated through institutions of segregation (as with Jim Crow laws in the United States and the apartheid regime in South Africa), new patterns of racism have emerged that reconstruct the figure of the intimate enemy within mutated structures of hate.[37] After a brief intermission, the end of the twentieth century and the beginning of the twenty-first have witnessed the return to biological understandings of the distinctions between human groups.[38] Genomics, rather than marking the end of racism, has instead authorized a new deployment of race.[39] Whether through the exploration of the genomic bases of illnesses within certain groups or genealogical efforts to trace roots or geographic origins, recourse to genetics tends to confirm the racial typologies of the nineteenth century (White Caucasians, Black Africans, Yellow Asiatics).[40] The same racial syntax is present in discourses on reproductive technologies involving the manipulation of ovaries and sperm and in those concerning reproductive choice through the selection of embryos, or in languages related to the planning of life in general.[41]

The same is true of the different ways in which living things can be manipulated, including the hybridization of organic, animal, and artificial elements. In fact, there is good reason to believe that in a more or less distant future genetic techniques will be used to manage the characteristics of populations to eliminate races judged "undesirable" through the selection of trisomic embryos, or through theriomorphism (hybridization with animal elements) or "cyborgization" (hybridization with artificial elements). Nor is it impossible to believe that we will arrive at a point where the fundamental role of medicine will be not only to bring a sick organism back to health but to use medical techniques of molecular engineering to refashion life itself along lines defined by racial determinism. Race and racism, then, do not only have a past. They also have a future, particularly in a context where the possibility of transforming life and creating mutant species no longer belongs to the realm of fiction.

Taken on their own, the transformations of the capitalist mode of production during the second half of the twentieth century cannot explain the reappearance and various metamorphoses of the Beast. But they—along with major discoveries in technology, biology, and genetics—do undeniably constitute its background.[42] A new political economy of life is emerging, one irrigated by international flows of knowledge about cells, tissues, organs, pathologies, and therapies as well as about intellectual property.[43] The reactivation of the logic of race also goes hand in hand with the increasing power of the ideology of security and the installation of mechanisms aimed at calculating and minimizing risk and turning protection into the currency of citizenship.

This is notably the case in regard to the management of migration and mobility in a context in which terrorist threats are believed to increasingly emanate from individuals organized in cells and networks that span the surface of the planet. In such conditions the protection and policing of territory becomes a structural condition for securing the population. To be effective, such protection requires that everyone remain at home, that those living and moving within a given national territory be capable of proving their identities at any given moment, that the most exhaustive information possible be gathered on each individual, and that the control of foreigners' mobility be carried out not only along borders but also from a distance, preferably within their countries of departure.[44] The massive expansion of digitization under way nearly everywhere in the world partly adheres to this logic, with the idea that optimal forms of securitization necessarily require the creation of global systems of control over individuals conceived of as biological bodies that are both multiple and in motion.

Protection itself is no longer based solely on the legal order. It has become a question of biopolitics. The new systems of security build on various elements of prior regimes (the forms of punishment used within slavery, aspects of the colonial wars of conquest and occupation, legal-juridical techniques used in the creation of states of exception) and incorporate them, on a nanocellular level, into the techniques of the age of genomics and the war on terror. But they also draw on techniques elaborated during the counterinsurgency wars of the period of decolonization and the "dirty wars" of the Cold War (in Algeria, Vietnam, Southern Africa, Burma, and Nicaragua), as well as the experiences of predatory dictatorships put into power throughout the world with the direct encouragement, or at least complicity, of the intelligence agencies of the West.

The increasing power of the security state in the contemporary context is, furthermore, accompanied by a remodeling of the world through technology and an exacerbation of forms of racial categorization.[45] Facing the transformation of the economy of violence throughout the world, liberal democratic regimes now consider themselves to be in a nearly constant state of war against new enemies who are in flight, both mobile and reticular. The theater of this new form of war is both external and internal. It requires a "total" conception of defense, along with greater tolerance for legal exceptions and special dispensations. The conduct of this type of war depends on the creation of tight, panoptic systems that enable increasing control of individuals, preferably from a distance, via the traces they leave behind.[46] In place of the classic paradigm of war, in which opposing sides meet on a well-defined battlefield and the risk of death is reciprocal, the logic is now vertical. There are two protagonists: prey and predator.[47] The predator, with nearly complete control of the airspace, selects the targets, locations, times, and nature of the strikes.[48] The increasingly vertical character of war and the more frequent use of unpiloted drones means that killing the enemy looks more and more like a video game, an experience of sadism, spectacle, and entertainment.[49] And, even more important, these new forms of warfare carried out from a distance require an unprecedented merging of the civil, police, and military spheres with those of surveillance.

The spheres of surveillance, meanwhile, are also being reconfigured. No longer mere state structures, and operating as chains linked in form only, they function by cultivating private-sector influence, by expanding into those corporate entities responsible for gathering the data necessary for mass surveillance. As a result, the objects of surveillance become daily life, the space of relationships, communication (notably through electronic technologies), and transactions. There is not, of course, a total concatenation of the mechanisms of the market and those of the state. But in our contemporary world the liberal state is transformed into a *war power* at a time when, we now realize, capital not only remains fixed in a phase of primitive accumulation but also still leverages *racial subsidies* in its pursuit of profit.

In this context the citizen is redefined as both the subject and the beneficiary of surveillance, which now privileges the transcription of biological, genetic, and behavioral characteristics through digital imprints. In a new technetronic regime characterized by miniaturization, dematerialization, and the fluid administration of state violence, imprints (fingerprints, scans of the iris and retina, forms of vocal and facial recognition) make it possible to measure and archive the uniqueness of individuals. The distinguishing parts of the human body become the foundations for new systems of identification, surveillance, and repression.[50] The security state conceives of identity and the movement of individuals (including its own citizens) as sources of danger and risk. But the generalized use of biometric data as a source of identification and for the automation of facial recognition constitutes a new type of populace, one predisposed toward distancing and imprisonment.[51] So it is that, in the context of the anti-immigration push in Europe, entire categories of the population are indexed and subjected to various forms of racial categorization that transform the immigrant (legal or illegal) into an essential category of difference.[52] This difference can be perceived as cultural or religious or linguistic. It is seen as inscribed in the very body of the migrant subject, visible on somatic, physiognomic, and even genetic levels.[53]

War and race have meanwhile become resurgent problems at the heart of the international order. The same is true of torture and the phenomenon of mass incarceration. It is not only that the line between war and peace has been blurred. War has become a "gigantic process of labor," while the military regime seeks to impose its own model on the "public order of the peace state."[54] While some citadels have collapsed, other walls have been strengthened.[55] As has long been the case, the contemporary world is deeply shaped and conditioned by the ancestral forms of religious, legal, and political life built around fences, enclosures, walls, camps, circles, and, above all, borders.[56] Procedures of differentiation, classification, and hierarchization aimed at exclusion, expulsion, and even eradication have been reinvigorated everywhere. New voices have emerged proclaiming, on the one hand, that there is no such thing as a universal human being or, on the other, that the universal is common to some human beings but not to all. Others emphasize the necessity for all to guarantee the safety of their own lives and homes by devoting themselves—and their ancestors and their memories, in one way or another—to the divine, a process that only subtracts them from historical interrogation and secures them completely and permanently within the walls of theology. Like the beginning of the nineteenth century, the beginning of the twenty-first constitutes, from this perspective, a significant moment of division, universal differentiation, and identity seeking.

The Noun "Black"

In these conditions the noun "Black"—which serves as the anchor for this book—is less polemical than it seems. In resuscitating a term that belongs to another era, that of early capitalism, I mean to question the fiction of unity that it carries within it. Already in his own time, James Baldwin had suggested that the Black Man (what he and other writers of his day called the Negro) was not at all easy to define in the abstract. Beyond ancestral links, there was very little evidence of an automatic unity between the Blacks of the United States, the Caribbean, and Africa. The presence of Blacks from the Caribbean in the United States, for example, dates from as early as the seventeenth century. During that period slaves arriving from Barbados represented a significant portion of the population of Virginia. Likewise, South Carolina was in many ways a subcolony of Barbados until the beginning of the eighteenth century. The number of Blacks from the Caribbean increased significantly after the Civil War, from 4,067 to 20,236 between 1850 and 1900. Most of the new arrivals were artisans, teachers, and preachers, but they also included lawyers and doctors.[57] Afro-Caribbeans made a key contribution to Black internationalism and the rise of radicalism in the United States and Africa. But the various conflicts that accompanied these processes laid bare the distance that often separated the Blacks of North America and those of the islands.[58]

The Blacks of North America and the Caribbean came to know Africa first as a form of difference.[59] Most of the Black thinkers of the period claimed both their Africanness and their Americanness. There were very few separatists.[60] Even though they constituted an undesirable minority in the country of their birth, the Blacks of the United States belonged to an American "we," to a subculture that was at once fundamentally American and *lumpen*-Atlantic. This led to the development of the motif of double consciousness, which among authors like Ralph Ellison could lead to a refusal to recognize any filiation with Africa.[61] Africa was a drypoint print of a reality that was unknowable—a hyphen, a suspension, a discontinuity. And those who traveled to Africa or chose to live there never felt at home, assailed as they were by the continent's strangeness, by its devouring character.[62] Their encounters with the Blacks of Africa from the first constituted an encounter with *another's other*.[63]

That said, a long tradition of coidentification and of *mutual concern* characterized the relationship of Blacks beyond their dispersion.[64] In his "letter" concerning "the Relations and Duties of Free Colored Men in America to Africa," Alexander Crummell started from the principle of a community of kinship linking Africa to its "children" and "sons" living in "foreign lands." By virtue of a relationship of kinship and filiation, he called on them to take advantage of their rights as inheritors. In his eyes at least, the right to inherit the cradle of their ancestors in no way contradicted their desire to belong fully to the "land of their birth," the United States. Claiming kinship with Africa and contributing to its regeneration was an act of self-love and self-respect. It was, he said, a way to get rid of the shroud that Blacks had carried from the depths of the tomb of slavery. Crummell's Africa had two characteristics. On the one hand, it was an amputated member of humanity. Prostrated in idolatry and darkness, it lived awaiting revelation. On the other hand, Africa was the land of unfathomable natural riches. Its mineral riches were colossal. With the race to capture its treasures under way, its faraway sons should not exclude themselves from sharing in the spoils. Africa would emerge from its cave, out into the light of the world, through trade and evangelization. Its salvation would come from outside, through its transformation into a Christian state.[65]

Because of this mutual concern, the encounter between the Blacks of the United States, the Caribbean, and Africa was not only an encounter with another's other but also, in many cases, an encounter with *others of my kind*—a castrated humanity, a life that must at all costs be pulled out of the dungeon and that needed to be healed. In this encounter Africa was a transformative force, almost mythico-poetic—a force that referred constantly to a "time before" (that of subjection), a force that, it was hoped, would make it possible to transform and assimilate the past, heal the worst wounds, repair losses, make a new history out of old events, and, according to the words of Friedrich Nietzsche on another topic, "[rebuild] shattered forms out of one's self."[66]

But just beneath the surface of this constellation there was always another, carried by those who believed that Blacks would never find peace, rest, or liberty in America. For their own genius to flourish, they had to emigrate.[67] This constellation saw liberty and territory as indivisible. It was not enough to build one's own institutions in the context of worsening segregation, to acquire expertise and gain respectability, when the right to citizenship was fundamentally contested, fragile, and reversible. It was necessary to have one's own state and to be able to defend it.[68] The vision of exodus was consolidated in particular between 1877 and 1900, within three different projects. The first was that of colonization, which had a racist dimension to the extent that it aimed, largely through the American Colonization Society, to rid America of its Black population by deporting Blacks to Africa. The second consisted of free emigration, spurred by the rise in violence and racial terrorism, particularly in the South. The third developed in the context of American expansionism between 1850 and 1900. Henry Blanton Parks, for example, considered that American Blacks and Africans formed two distinct races. As a result of their prolonged contact with civilization, American Blacks were more evolved than the natives of Africa.[69] The latter had, on the other hand, preserved a primal power. Combined with what American Blacks brought home to Africa from their centuries of accommodation with civilization, this power would reanimate the virility of the Black race as a whole.[70]

On one level, then, Black reason consists of a collection of voices, pronouncements, discourses, forms of knowledge, commentary, and nonsense, whose object is things or people "of African origin." It is affirmed as their name and their truth (their attributes and qualities, their destiny and its significance as an empirical portion of the world). Composed of multiple strata, this form of reason dates at least from the time of antiquity. Numerous works have focused on its Greek, Arab, Egyptian, and even Chinese roots.[71] From the beginning, its primary activity was fantasizing. It consisted essentially in gathering real or attributed traits, weaving them into histories, and creating images. The modern age, however, was a decisively formative moment for Black reason, owing, on the one hand, to the accounts of travelers, explorers, soldiers, adventurers, merchants, missionaries, and settlers and, on the other, to the constitution of a "colonial science" of which "Africanism" is the last avatar. A range of intermediaries and institutions—scholarly societies, universal exhibitions, museums, amateur collections of "primitive art"—contributed to the development of this reason and its transformation into common sense and a habitus.

Black reason was not only a system of narratives and discourses with academic pretensions but also the reservoir that provided the justifications for the arithmetic of racial domination. It was, admittedly, not completely devoid of a concern for the truth. But its function was first and foremost to codify the conditions for the appearance and the manifestation of a *racial subject* that would be called the Black Man and, later, within colonialism, the Native (*L'indigène*). ("Who is he?" "How does one recognize him?" "What differentiates him from us?" "Can he become like us?" "How should we govern him and to what end?")[72] In this context "Black reason" names not only a collection of discourses but also practices—the daily work that consisted in inventing, telling, repeating, and creating variations on the formulas, texts, and rituals whose goal was to produce the Black Man as a racial subject and site of savage exteriority, who was therefore set up for moral disqualification and practical instrumentalization. We can call this founding narrative the *Western consciousness of Blackness*. In seeking to answer the question "Who is he?" the narrative seeks to name a reality exterior to it and to situate that reality in relationship to an *I* considered to be the center of all meaning. From this perspective, anything that is not identical to that *I* is abnormal.

This founding narrative was in reality a constellation in perpetual reconfiguration over time. It always took on multiple, contradictory, and divergent forms. In response came a second narrative, one that saw itself as a gesture of self-determination, a way of being present to oneself and looking inward, and as a form of utopian critique. The second narrative answered a series of questions of a new kind, again posed in the first person singular: "Who am I?" "Am I, in truth, what people say I am?" "Is it true that I am nothing more than *that*—what I appear to be, what people see me as and say of me?" "What is my real social status, my real history?"[73] If the Western consciousness of the Black Man is an *identity judgment*, this second narrative is, in contrast, a *declaration of identity*. Through it the Black Man affirms of himself that he is that which cannot be captured or controlled; the one who is not where they say he is, and even less where they are looking for him. Rather, he exists where he is not thought.[74]

The written work of the second narrative had a series of distinctive traits that are worth briefly recalling. It sought, above all, to create an archive. If Blacks were to reclaim their history, the foundation of an archive was the first step. The historical experiences of Blacks did not necessarily leave traces, and where they were produced, they were not always preserved. How could one write history in the absence of the kinds of traces that serve as sources for historiographical fact? Very early, it became clear that the history of Blacks could be written only from fragments brought together to give an account of an experience that itself was fragmented, that of a pointillist people struggling to define itself not as a disparate composite but as a community whose blood stains the entire surface of modernity.

Such writing sought, furthermore, to create community, one forged out of debris from the four corners of the world. In the Western Hemisphere, the reality was that a group of slaves and free people of color lived for the most part in the gray zones of a nominal citizenship, within states that celebrated liberty and democracy but remained foundationally slave states. Across the period, the writing of history had a performative dimension. The structure of the performance was in many ways theological. The goal was, in effect, to write a history for the descendants of slaves that reopened the possibility for them to become agents of history itself.[75] During the period of Emancipation and Reconstruction, the act of writing history was conceived more than ever as an act of moral imagination. The ultimate historical gesture consisted in enacting the journey from the status of a slave to that of a citizen *like all others*. The new community of freed peoples saw itself as linked by common faith and certain ideas of work and respectability, by moral duty, solidarity, and obligation.[76] Yet this moral identity took shape in the context of segregation, extreme violence, and racial terror.[77]

The declaration of identity that is characteristic of the second narrative was, however, based on profound ambiguity. Although its authors wrote in the first person and in a mode of self-possession, they, as subjects, were haunted by the idea that they had become strangers to themselves. They nevertheless sought to assume their responsibility to the world by creating a foundation for themselves.[78] On the horizon was full and complete participation in the empirical history of liberty, an indivisible liberty at the heart of "global humanity."[79] That is the other side of Black reason—the place where writing seeks to exorcise the demon of the first narrative and the structure of subjection within it, the place where writing struggles to evoke, save, activate, and reactualize original experience (tradition) and find the truth of the self no longer outside of the self but standing on its own ground.

There are profound disjunctures but also undeniable solidarities between the second narrative and the first narrative it sought to refute. The second was traversed by the traces, marks, and incessant buzzing of the first and, in certain cases, its dull injunction and its myopia, even where the claim of rupture was most forceful. Let us call this second narrative the *Black consciousness of Blackness*. It nevertheless had its own characteristics. Literary, biographical, historical, and political, it was the product of a polyglot internationalism.[80] It was born in the great cities of the United States and the Caribbean, then in Europe, and later in Africa. Ideas circulated within a vast global network, producing the modern Black imaginary.[81] The creators of the imaginary were often people in motion, crossing constantly from one continent to another. At times involved in American and European cultural and political life, they participated in the intellectual globalization of their epoch.[82]

Black consciousness of Blackness was also the fruit of a long history of radicalism, nourished by struggles for abolition and against capitalism.[83] Over the course of the nineteenth century in particular, this resistance was to a large extent driven by international anarchism, the principal vehicle for opposition movements against capitalism, slavery, and imperialism. But it was also carried forward by a number of humanitarian and philanthropic currents in whose struggles, as Paul Gilroy reminds us, lay the foundation for an alternative genealogy of human rights.[84] The content of the second narrative was most of all marked by the efforts of people subjected to colonization and segregation who sought to free themselves from racial hierarchy. The intelligentsia among them developed forms of collective consciousness that, even as they embraced the epistemology of class struggle itself, attacked the ontological assumptions that resulted from the production of racial subjects.[85]

The notion of Black reason, then, refers to different sides of the same framework, the same constellation. It refers, moreover, to a dispute or a conflict. Historically, the conflict over blackness has been inseparable from the question of our modernity. The name raises a question that has to do, first of all, with the relationship of what we call "man" with animals, and therefore the relationship of reason to instinct. The expression "Black Reason" refers to a collection of deliberations concerning the distinction between the impulse of the animal and the *ratio* of man, the Black Man being living proof of the impossibility of such a separation. For, if we follow a certain tradition of Western metaphysics, the Black Man is a "man" who is not really one of us, or at least not like us. Man distinguishes himself from animality, but this is not the case for the Black Man, who maintains within himself, albeit with a certain degree of ambiguity, animal possibility. A foreign body in our world, he is inhabited—under cover—by the animal. To debate Black reason is therefore to return to the collection of debates regarding the rules of how to define the Black Man: how he is recognized, how one identifies the animal spirit that possesses him, under which conditions the *ratio* penetrates and governs the *animalitas*.

Second, the expression "Black Reason" turns our attention to the technologies (laws, regulations, rituals) that are deployed—as well as the devices that are put in place—with the goal of submitting animality to measurement. Such calculation aims ultimately to inscribe the animal within the circle of extraction. Yet the attempt at inscription is inevitably paradoxical. On the one hand, it requires that the price of that which simply *is* (facticity)— but which carries no price, or only ever a potential price, since it has been emptied of value—be measured and calculated. On the other hand, the operation makes clear how difficult it is to measure the incalculable. The difficulty flows partly from the fact that the *thing* that must be calculated is part of the ontological—what thought itself cannot think, even as it demands to be thought, as if in a vacuum. Finally, the term refers to what, in principle, requires no explanation because it is off the books, unaccountable, part of an antieconomy. There is no need to justify it because it creates nothing. Moreover, there is no need to offer an account of it since, strictly speaking, it is not based on law, and no calculation as such can ever guarantee its exact price or value.

Appearances, Truth, and Simulacrum

When we say the word "race," what do we really mean? It is not enough to say that race itself has no essence; that it is nothing more than "the effect, profile, or cut" of a perpetual process of power, of "incessant transactions" that modify, displace, and shift its meaning; or that, having no guts because it has no insides, it consists only of the practices that constitute it as such.[86] It is not enough, furthermore, to affirm that it is a complex of microdeterminations, an internalized effect of the Other's gaze and a manifestation of secret, unfulfilled beliefs and desires.[87] On the one hand, race and racism are part of the fundamental process of the unconscious. In that respect they relate to the impasses of human desire—to appetites, affects, passions, fears. They symbolize above all the memory of a lost original desire, or of a trauma whose causes often have nothing to do with the person who is the victim of racism. On the other hand, race is not only the result of an optical effect. It is not only a part of the world of the senses. It is also a way of anchoring and affirming power. It is above all a specular reality and impulsive force. For it to operate as affect, impulse, and speculum, race must become image, form, surface, figure, and—especially—a structure of the imagination. And it is as a structure of the imagination that it escapes the limitations of the concrete, of what is sensed, of the finite, even as it participates within and manifests itself most immediately through the senses. Its power comes from its capacity to produce schizophrenic objects constantly, peopling and repeopling the world with substitutes, beings to point to, to break, in a hopeless attempt to support a failing *I*.

Race and racism also have the fundamental characteristic of always inciting and engendering a double, a substitute, an equivalent, a mask, a simulacrum. A real human face comes into view. The work of racism consists in relegating it to the background or covering it with a veil. It replaces this face by calling up, from the depths of the imagination, a ghost of a face, a simulacrum of a face, a silhouette that replaces the body and face of a human being. Racism consists, most of all, in substituting what *is* with something else, with another reality. It has the power to distort the real and to fix affect, but it is also a form of psychic derangement, the mechanism through which the repressed suddenly surfaces. When the racist sees a Black person, he does not see that the Black person is not there, does not exist, and is just a sign of a pathological fixation on the absence of a relationship. We must therefore consider race as being both beside and beyond being. It is an operation of the imagination, the site of an encounter with the shadows and hidden zones of the unconscious.

I have emphasized that racism is a site of reality and truth—the truth of appearances. But it is also a site of rupture, of effervescence and effusion. The truth of individuals who are assigned a race is at once elsewhere and within the appearances assigned to them. They exist behind appearance, underneath what is perceived. But they are also constituted by the very act of assigning, the process through which certain forms of infralife are produced and institutionalized, indifference and abandonment justified, the part that is human in the other violated or occulted through forms of internment, even murder, that have been made acceptable. Foucault, dealing with racism and its inscription in the mechanisms of the state and power, noted in this regard that "the modern State can scarcely function without becoming involved with racism at some point, within certain limits and subject to certain conditions." Race or racism, "in a normalizing society," he noted, "is the precondition that makes killing acceptable." He concludes, "Once the State functions in the biopower mode, racism alone can justify the murderous functions of the State."[88]

The people to whom race is assigned are not passive. Imprisoned in a silhouette, they are separated from their essence. According to Fanon, one of the reasons for their unhappiness is that their existence consists in inhabiting the separation as if it were their real being, in hating what they are and seeking to be what they are not. The critique of race is, from this perspective, more than a simple critique of separation. The *racial theater* is a space of systematic stigmatization. The call to race or the invocation of race, notably on the part of the oppressed, is the emblem of an essentially obscure, shadowy, and paradoxical desire—the desire for community.[89] Such a desire is obscure, shadowy, and paradoxical because it is doubly inhabited by melancholia and mourning, and by a nostalgia for an archaic *that* which is always doomed to disappear. The desire is at once worry and anxiety—linked to the possibility of extinction—and a project. Moreover, it is the language of bemoaning, and of a mourning that rebels in its own name. It articulates itself around, and creates itself by circumventing, a terrible memory, the memory of a body, a voice, a face, and a name that, if not completely lost, have at least been violated and dirtied, and that must at all costs be rescued and rehabilitated.[90]

For Blacks confronted with the reality of slavery, loss is first of a genealogical order. In the New World, the Black slave is legally stripped of all kinship. Slaves are, in consequence, "without parents." The condition of *kinlessness* is imposed on them through law and power. And eviction from the world of legal kinship is an inherited condition. Birth and descent afford them no right to any form of social relationship or belonging as such.[91] In such conditions the invocation of race or the attempt to constitute a racial community aims first to forge ties and open up space in which to stand, to respond to a long history of subjugation and biopolitical fracturing. Aimé Césaire and the poets of Negritude, for example, made the exaltation of the "Black race" a tremendous cry whose function was to save from total decay what had been condemned to insignificance.[92] As conjuration, announcement, and protest, the cry expressed the will of the enslaved and the colonized to escape resignation, to *form a body*, to produce themselves as a free and sovereign community, ideally through their own work and achievements. They sought to make themselves their own points of origin, their own certainty, and their own destination in the world.[93]

We can therefore say of the invocation of race that it is born from a feeling of loss, from the idea that the community has suffered a separation, that it is threatened with extermination, and that it must at all costs be rebuilt by reconstituting a thread of continuity beyond time, space, and dislocation.[94] From this perspective, the call to race (which is different from racial assignation) is a way of resurrecting the immolated corpse that had been buried and severed from the links of blood, soil, institutions, rites, and symbols that made it a living being. During the nineteenth and early twentieth centuries, this was the meaning of the call to race in Black discourse. At times the call became a search for original purity or a desire for absolute separation. Such was the case for Marcus Garvey, for example. At other times it was more the expression of a will to escape the principle of immolation and sacrifice. And in other cases it was a response to a desire for protection in the face of the threat of disappearance, an instinct for survival and preservation. The goal was to imagine and create a different space, where isolation would guarantee protection. Safety would require a redistribution of feeling and affect, of perception and speech. Whatever the case, the racial community was a community founded on the memory of a loss—a community of the kinless. It was a "community of loss" in the way that Jean-Luc Nancy, dealing with community in general, has defined it: a space inseparable from death, since it is precisely through death that community reveals itself.[95]

Finally, race is one of the raw materials from which difference and *surplus*—a kind of life that can be wasted and spent without limit—are produced. It does not matter that race does not actually exist as such, and not only because of the extraordinary genetic homogeneity of human beings. It continues to produce its effects of mutilation because from the beginning it is, and always will be, that for which and in whose name the hyphens at the center of society are created, warlike relationships established, colonial relationships regulated, and people distributed and locked up. The lives and presence of such people are considered symptoms of a delimited condition. Their belonging is contested because, according to the classifications in place, they represent a surplus. Race is an instrumentality that makes it possible both to name the surplus and to commit it to waste and unlimited spending. It is what makes it acceptable to categorize abstractly in order to stigmatize, disqualify morally, and eventually imprison or expel. It is the mechanism through which a group is reified. On the basis of this reification, someone becomes their master, determining their fate in a way that requires neither explanation nor justification. We can therefore compare the work of race to a sacrificial cut, the kind of act for which one does not have to answer. A dead-letter address—this is precisely what in our modern world the principle of race oversees, producing its targets as complete signs of radical exteriority.

The Logic of Enclosure

Historically, race has always been a more or less coded way of dividing and organizing a multiplicity, of fixing and distributing it according to a hierarchy, of allocating it to more or less impermeable spaces according to a *logic of enclosure*. Such was the case under the regimes of segregation. It does not much matter that, in the age of security, race is expressed through the sign of religion or culture. Race is what makes it possible to identify and define population groups in a way that makes each of them carriers of differentiated and more or less shifting risk.

In this context the processes of racialization aim to mark population groups, to fix as precisely as possible the limits within which they can circulate, and to determine as exactly as possible which sites they can occupy—in sum, to limit circulation in a way that diminishes threats and secures general safety. The goal is to sort population groups, to mark them simultaneously as "species," "classes," and "cases" through a generalized calculation of risk, chance, and probability. It is all to prevent the dangers inherent in their circulation and, if possible, to neutralize them in advance through immobilization, incarceration, or deportation. Race, from this perspective, functions as a security device based on what we can call the principle of the biological rootedness of the species. The latter is at once an ideology and a technology of governance.

This was the case under the regime of the plantation, at the time of apartheid, and in the colony. In each case, race served to assign living beings characteristics that permitted their distribution into such and such a box on the great chart of human species. But it also participated in a *bioeconomy*. Race reconciled masses, classes, and populations, respectively the legacies of natural history, biology, and political economy. Work and the production of wealth were inseparable from the problems specific to life and population, the regulation of movement and displacement—in short, the processes of circulation and capture. And the processes of circulation and capture constituted a central dimension of both the technologies of security and the mechanisms that inscribed people within differentiated juridical systems.

As phenomena, racism and the phobia of others share a great deal. Racist logic supports a high degree of baseness and stupidity. As Georges Bataille noted, it implies a form of cowardice—that of the man who "attributes to some external sign a value that has no meaning other than his own fears, his guilty conscience and his need to burden others, through hatred, with the deadweight of horror inherent in our condition"; he added that men "hate, it would seem, to the same extent that they are themselves to be hated."[96] It is false to think that racist logic is only a symptom of class warfare, or that class struggle is the final word regarding the "social question." Race and racism are certainly linked to antagonisms based on the economic structure of society. But it is not true that the transformation of the structure leads ineluctably to the disappearance of racism. For a large part of modern history, race and class have coconstituted one another. The plantation and colonial systems were the factories par excellence of race and racism. The "poor Whites" in particular depended on cultivating differences that separated them from Blacks to give themselves the sense of being human. The racist subject sees the humanity in himself not by accounting for what makes him similar to others but by accounting for what makes him different. The logic of race in the modern world cuts across social and economic structures, impacts the movements within them, and constantly metamorphoses.

As a slave, the Black Man represents one of the troubling figures of our modernity, and in fact constitutes its realm of shadow, of mystery, of scandal. As a human whose name is disdained, whose power of descent and generation has been foiled, whose face is disfigured, and whose work is stolen, he bears witness to a mutilated humanity, one deeply scarred by iron and alienation. But precisely through the damnation to which he is condemned, and because of the possibilities for radical insurgency that he nevertheless contains and that are never fully annihilated by the mechanisms of servitude, he represents a kind of silt of the earth, a silt deposited at the confluence of half-worlds produced by the dual violence of race and capital. The enslaved, fertilizers of history and subjects beyond subjection, authored a world that reflects this dark contradiction. Operating in the bottoms of slave ships, they were the first coal shovelers of our modernity. And if there is one thing that haunts modernity from beginning to end, it is the possibility of that singular event, the "revolt of the slaves." A slave uprising signals not only liberation but also radical transformation, if not of the system of property and labor itself, then at least of the mechanisms of its redistribution and so of the foundations for the reproduction of life itself.

TWO
THE WELL
OF FANTASIES

"Africa" and "Blackness": these two notions took shape together. To speak of one is to invoke the other. Each consecrates the other's value. As we have noted, not all Africans are Blacks. But if Africa has a body, and if it is a body, a *thing*, it gets it from the Black Man—no matter where he finds himself in the world. And if the term "Black" is a nickname, if it is *that thing*, it is because of Africa. Both of these—*the thing* and *that thing*—refer to the purest and most radical difference and the law of separation. They mix with and burden each other as a sticky weight, at once shadow and matter. As this chapter demonstrates, both are the result of a long historical process that aimed at producing racial subjects. This chapter examines how Africa and the Black Man have become signs of an alterity that is impossible to assimilate; they are a vandalism of meaning itself, a happy hysteria.

A Humanity on Reprieve

But what do we mean by "Black" (*Nègre*)? It is commonly accepted that the term "Nègre" is of Iberian origin and appeared in the French language only at the beginning of the sixteenth century. But it was only in the eighteenth century, at the zenith of the slave trade, that it entered definitively into common use.[1] On a phenomenological level, the term first designates not a significant reality but a field—or, better yet, a coating—of nonsense and fantasies that the West (and other parts of the world) have woven, and in which it clothed people of African origin long before they were caught in the snares of capitalism as it emerged in the fifteenth and sixteenth centuries. A lively human of a strange shape, roasted by the rays of the celestial fire, endowed with an excessive petulance, captive to the empire of joy, and abandoned by intelligence, the Black Man is above all a body—gigantic and fantastic—member, organs, color, a smell, flesh, and meat, an extraordinary accumulation of sensations.[2] If he is movement, it can only be a movement of contraction while stuck in one place, as a crawling or spasm, the quivering of a bird, the sound of the hooves of the beast.[3] And if it is strength, it can be only the brute strength of the body, excessive, convulsive, spasmodic, and resisting thought: a wave, rage, nervousness all at once, whose domain is to incite disgust, fear, and dread.

So it is in the scene of the little boy and the Negro described by Frantz Fanon: "The Negro is an animal, the Negro is bad, the Negro is wicked, the Negro is ugly; look, a Negro, it's cold, the Negro is trembling, the Negro is trembling because he is cold, the small boy is trembling because he's afraid of the Negro, the Negro is trembling with cold, that cold that chills the bones, the lovely little boy is trembling because he thinks that the Negro is quivering with rage, the little white boy runs to his mother's arms: Mama, the Negro's going to eat me up."[4] Through a process of dissemination but especially of inculcation—one that has been the subject of many studies—this massive coating of nonsense, lies, and fantasies has become a kind of exterior envelope whose function has since then been to stand as substitute for the being, the life, the work, and the language of Blacks. What began on the surface became stratified, transformed into a framework and over time a *calcified shell*—a second ontology—and a canker, a living wound that eats at, devours, and destroys its victim. Fanon, for example, in *Black Skin, White Masks*, deals with the wound and the conditions under which it can be healed. James Baldwin, comparing the wound to a poison, asks what it produces in the person who makes and distills it and in the person to whom it is systematically administered.

Starting in the nineteenth century, the shell and canker took on a quasiautonomous existence, at times functioning as an ornamental motif, at others as the image of a double, and in an even more sinister way as a *carcass*, what is left of the body after it has been dismembered and stripped of its flesh. From a strictly historical perspective, the word "Black" refers first and foremost to a phantasmagoria. Studies of the phantasmagoria hold interest not only for what they can tell us about those who produced it but also for what they say about the timeworn problematic of the status of appearances and their relation to reality (the reality of appearances and the appearance of reality), and about the symbolism of color. The process of transforming people of African origin into Blacks, that is, into bodies of extraction and subjects of race, largely obeys the triple logic of ossification, poisoning, and calcification. Not only is the Black Man the prototype of a poisoned, burnt subject. He is a being whose life is made of ashes.

The noun "Black" is in this way the name given to the product of a process that transforms people of African origin into living *ore* from which *metal* is extracted. This is its double dimension, at once metaphorical and economic. If, under slavery, Africa was the privileged site for the extraction of ore, the New World plantation was where it was cast, and Europe where it was converted into financial currency.[5] The progression from *man-of-ore* to *man-of-metal* to *man-of-money* was a structuring dimension of the early phase of capitalism. Extraction was first and foremost the tearing or separation of human beings from their origins and birthplaces. The next step involved removal or extirpation, the condition that makes possible the act of pressing and without which extraction remains incomplete. Human beings became objects as slaves passed through the mill and were squeezed to extract maximum profit. Extraction not only branded them with an indelible stamp but also produced the Black Man, or, in the case that will preoccupy us throughout this book, the subject of race, the very figure of what could be held at a certain distance from oneself, of a *thing* that could be discarded once it was no longer useful.

Summons, Interiorization, and Reversal

The term "Black," taken up by European avant-garde movements and then poets of African origin at the beginning of the twentieth century, became the object of a radical reversal. The crisis of conscience that swallowed up the West at the turn of the century was linked to a reevaluation of the African contribution to the history of humanity. Colonial propaganda, spurred on by European military excursions, dwelled on supposed practices of cannibalism and ancestral hatreds that it claimed had always pitted natives against each other. From the 1920s on, however, discourse on aesthetics, notably among the avant-garde, viewed Africa as a land of difference, a reservoir of mysteries, and the ultimate kingdom of catharsis and the magico-religious.[6] For Picasso, African masks were "objects that men have created with a sacred and magical goal, so that they can serve as intermediaries between them and unknown and hostile forces, in the process attempting to overcome their fear by giving it color and form." The meaning of painting, he claimed, could be found in the commerce between the made object and the universe of immaterial forms. "It is not an aesthetic process," he concluded. "It is a form of magic that interposes itself between us and the hostile universe, a way of seizing power by imposing a form on our terrors as well as our desires."[7]

During the first half of the twentieth century, the increasing interest in so-called exotic cultures was shaped decisively by materialism in politics and the sciences and by positivism in philosophy. The epoch was shadowed by fear and anxiety incited by the world wars, but above all by the reality of the death of God, which Friedrich Nietzsche and the Marquis de Sade, among others, had long since proclaimed. In this context African art—and to some extent jazz—appeared as a celestial path of return to one's origins, a kind of grace by which sleeping powers could be awakened, myths and rituals reinvented, tradition rerouted and undermined, and time reversed. The figure of Africa as a reservoir of mysteries corresponded with a certain desire within Western discourse—a desire that infused postwar Europe—for a celebration both joyous and savage, without limits or guilt, in search of a vitalism that had no awareness of evil.

The renewal of an anticolonial critique within aesthetics and politics shaped the reevaluation of Africa's contribution to the project of a humanity to come. The surrealist movement and the proponents of primitivism were key contributors to the critique. André Breton in the 1920s declared that surrealism was connected to "people of color" and that there were affinities between so-called primitive thinking and surrealist thinking. Both, he argued, aimed to eliminate the hegemony of the conscious.[8] The project was to travel upriver to lost headwaters in order to escape a history that offered promises of eternity but brought only decadence and death. From this perspective, "the Black model" opened the way for a new kind of writing, one that hoped to rediscover the savage character of language and resuscitate the word.[9] It was only through the flexibility of idiom that the fullness of language could be obtained.[10]

In the wake of World War II, surrealists and libertarian and Trotskyist militants forged ties with anticolonial activists.[11] Their aesthetic criticism, a blend of anarchism and avant-gardism, nevertheless had an ambiguous quality. On the one hand, it depended heavily on reflections about the "African soul" and the supposed essence of "the Black Man" that were fashionable at the time. But such speculative constructions were inherited directly from Western ethnographies and philosophies of history that dominated the second half of the nineteenth century. They were based on the idea that two forms of human society existed: primitive societies, which were governed by the "savage mentality," and civilized societies governed by reason and endowed with, among other things, the power that came from writing. The so-called savage mentality was not adapted to the processes of rational argumentation. It was not logical but rather "prelogical." Unlike us, the savage lived in a universe of its own making, impervious to experience and inaccessible to our ways of thinking.[12] Only the White race possessed a will and a capacity to construct life within history. The Black race in particular had neither life, nor will, nor energy of its own. Consumed by ancient ancestral hatreds and unending internal struggles, it turned endlessly in circles. It was nothing but inert matter, waiting to be molded in the hands of a superior race.[13]

The roots of the racial unconscious that subtends the politics of Blackness in the contemporary world can be found in this primitive psychology about peoples and emotions, and other false knowledge inherited from the nineteenth century. In it we encounter a prostrate Africa trapped in the world of childhood from which the other peoples of the earth have long since escaped. In it we also find the Black Man, a naturally prehistoric figure struck by a kind of blind consciousness, incapable of distinguishing between history and mystery, or between history and the marvelous. His life exhausts and consumes itself, lost in the great, undifferentiated night of those who have no names.

Moreover, the aesthetic critique of colonialism never fully departed from the myth of the existence of "superior peoples," and therefore the danger or fear of degeneration, or the possibility for regeneration. It did not distance itself enough from the idea that "Black blood" could play a central role in the awakening of the imagination and artistic genius. In many ways the conceptions of art developed between 1890 and 1945 were deeply shaped by the idea that civilization had exhausted itself. They drew a contrast between the supposed vigor of savages and the exhausted blood of the civilized. There were indigenous qualities inscribed in the blood of each race. In the blood of the Black race ran instinct, irrational impulses, and primal sensuality. The universal power of the imagination was linked to a "melanin principle," which provided an explanation for why the blood of the Blacks disguised the spring from which the arts could burst forth. Arthur Gobineau in particular believed that within the Black race resided a profusion of fire, "flames, sparks, drives, thoughtlessness." Sensuality, imagination, and "all forms of appetite for the material" were reflected in the Black Man and primed him to "experience the impressions produced by art to a degree of intensity totally unknown among other human families."[14]

Anticolonial critique of an aesthetic, avant-gardist, and anarchist bent largely drew on the very colonial myths and stereotypes that it sought to invert. It did not call into question the existence of the cannibal or of a fundamentally irrational and savage Black world. It sought to embrace all the symptoms of degeneration—like sparks of fire—with the idea that the ardent power of the Black Man, his furious love of forms, rhythms, and colors, was the product of that very degeneration.[15]

Many of the poets of the Negritude movement took a similar approach. For them, the noun "Nègre" no longer referred to an experience of emptiness that had to be filled. Through the creative work of Black poets it became what Aimé Césaire called a "miraculous weapon." They sought to turn the name into an active power that would enable Blacks to see themselves in all their specificity, to discover the deepest springs of life and liberty. A noun turned into a concept, "Blackness" became the idiom through which people of African origin could announce themselves to the world, show themselves to the world, and draw on their own power and genius to affirm themselves as a world. This great moment of irruption into universal life—the "great midday," as Césaire would call it—was triply an annunciation, a transfiguration, and a denunciation. "I no longer search: I've got it!" Césaire proclaimed; "my revolt / my name"; "I a man! just a man! . . . I want only the pure treasure, / the one which endlessly generates others."[16]

The Black of the White and the White of the Black

Fanon was right, however, when he suggested that the Black Man was a figure, an "object," invented by Whites and as such "fixed" by their gaze, gestures, and attitudes. He was woven "out of a thousand details, anecdotes, and stories."[17] We should add that Whiteness in turn was, in many ways, a fantasy produced by the European imagination, one that the West has worked hard to naturalize and universalize. Fanon himself said of the two that Blackness did not exist any more than Whiteness did. In reality, there exists no human being whose skin color can be strictly described as white—at least in the sense that one speaks of the white of paper, chalk, lime, or a shroud. But if both categories refer ultimately to a lack, from where does this absence—and therefore the fantasy of Whiteness—draw its strength?

In settler colonies like the United States, "White" was a racial category constructed over time as the institutionalization of legal rights encountered the regimes of labor extortion. Nearly half a century after the creation of the colony of Virginia in 1607, for example, the distinctions between the Africans and Europeans subjected to similarly brutal conditions of exploitation remained relatively fluid. The Europeans were captive labor, temporary and exploitable, considered "superfluous" in the metropole. Their status was similar to that of Africans, with whom they shared certain practices of sociability: alcohol, sex, marriage. Some emancipated Africans gained a right to portions of land. On this basis they demanded rights, including the right to own slaves. The subaltern community, then, went beyond race. From the 1660s on, it was responsible for a series of revolts, including the Indentured Servants' Plot of 1661, Bacon's Rebellion in 1676, and the Tobacco Riots of 1682.

The Royal African Company was reorganized in 1685 in response to the threat of ongoing insurrections carried out by subaltern classes united across race. With a steady supply of African slaves, more and more of the workforce in the colony was composed of enslaved people. During the last years of the seventeenth century, the figure of the slave became increasingly racialized. By 1709 the composition of the labor force had shifted, so that Africans enslaved for life far outnumbered indentured laborers of European origin, who were forced to work only temporarily and freed at the end of their terms of captivity.

The process of racialization was accompanied by a massive regulatory effort meant to establish clear distinctions between laborers of European origin and Africans, both indentured and enslaved. Beginning in 1661, systems of punishment were structured according to an explicitly racial logic. Indentured laborers of European origin who joined Africans in marronage (running away from plantations) were punished with extended periods of captivity. Sexual relations between races were outlawed. The mobility of slaves was drastically reduced, and the "low Whites" were given the task of patrolling them. Blacks were prohibited from carrying weapons, while each former indentured laborer of European origin was given a musket.

Three historical determinants, then, explain the power of the fantasy of Whiteness. First of all, there were many who believed in it. But far from being spontaneous, the belief was cultivated, nourished, reproduced, and disseminated by a set of theological, cultural, political, economic, and institutional mechanisms whose evolution and implications over the centuries have been carefully analyzed by critical theorists of race. In several regions of the world, a great deal of work went into transforming Whiteness into a dogma and a habitus. Such was notably the case in the United States, in other countries with slavery, in most settler colonies, and until recently in South Africa. There, racial segregation became a semiotic that was simultaneously a right, a faith, and a doctrine, any transgression of which could result in a range of punishments, including death.

Second, such mechanisms often functioned to transform Whiteness into common sense as well as a form of desire and fascination. As long as a belief does not become desire and fascination, terrifying to some, mere dividend to others, it cannot operate as an autonomous and internalized power. In this view the fantasy of Whiteness involves a constellation of objects of desire and public signs of privilege that relate to body and image, language and wealth. Fantasy, we know, seeks to anchor itself in the real in the form of an effective social truth. In this, the fantasy of Whiteness succeeded, for, in the end, it became the mark of a certain mode of Western presence in the world, a certain figure of brutality and cruelty, a singular form of predation with an unequaled capacity for the subjection and exploitation of foreign peoples.

Such power manifested itself in various ways across historical epochs and geographic contexts: in the exterminations and genocides of the New World and Australia; in the Atlantic triangle trade based on the slave trade; in the colonial conquests in Africa, Asia, and South America; in apartheid in South Africa; in the dispossession, depredation, expropriation, and pillage carried out in the name of capital and profit almost everywhere; and, as a crowning achievement, in the vernacularization of alienation. The fantasy of Whiteness draws part of its self-assurance from structural violence and the ways in which it contributes on a planetary scale to the profoundly unequal redistribution of the resources of life and the privileges of citizenship. But that assurance comes also from technical and scientific prowess, creations of the mind, forms of political organization that are (or at least seem to be) relatively disciplined, and, when necessary, from cruelty without measure, from what Césaire identified as a propensity for murder without reason.

For Fanon, the term "Black" is more a mechanism of attribution than of self-designation. I am not Black, Fanon declares, any more than I am a Black Man. Black is neither my last name nor my first name, even less my essence or my identity. I am a human being, and that is all. The Other can dispute this quality, but they can never rob me of it ontologically. The fact of being a slave or of being colonized—of being the object of discrimination and bullying, privation and humiliation, because of the color of my skin—changes absolutely nothing. I remain a complete human being no matter how violent are the efforts aimed at making me think that I am not one. This *uneliminable surplus* escapes all attempts at capture and fixation within a particular social or legal status. Even death cannot interrupt it. It cannot be erased by any name or administrative measure, by any law or summons, or by any doctrine or dogma. "Black" is therefore a nickname, a tunic that someone else has dressed me in, seeking to trap me within it. But a separation always exists between the intended meaning of the nickname and the human person who is asked to shoulder it. It is this distance that the subject is called on to cultivate, even radicalize.

In fact, the noun "Black" has served three functions in modernity: those of summoning, internalization, and reversal. It first designated not human beings *like all others* but rather a *distinct* humanity—one whose very humanity was (and still is) in question. It designated a particular kind of human: those who, because of their physical appearance, their habits and customs, and their ways of being in the world, seemed to represent *difference in its raw manifestation*—somatic, affective, aesthetic, imaginary. The so-called Blacks appeared subsequently as individuals who, because of the fact of their ontological difference, represented a caricature of the *principle of exteriority* (as opposed to the principle of inclusion). It therefore became very difficult to imagine that they were once like us, that they were once of us. And precisely because they were not either like us or of us, the only link that could unite us is—paradoxically—the *link of separation*. Constituting a world *apart*, the *part apart*, Blacks cannot become full subjects in the life of our community. Placed *apart*, put to the side, piece by piece: that is how Blacks came to signify, in their essence and before all speech, the injunction of segregation.

Some of those who were enclosed in the nickname—and who, in consequence, were placed *apart* or to the side—have, at certain moments in history, ended up inhabiting it. The name "Black" ("Nègre") has passed into common use. But does that make it more authentic? Some, in a conscious gesture of reversal that at times is poetic and carnivalesque, inhabit the name only to rebel against its inventors and its reviled heritage as a symbol of abjection. They instead transform the name into a symbol of beauty and pride and use it as a sign of radical defiance, a call to revolt, desertion, or insurrection. As a historical category, Blackness exists only within these three moments: of attribution, of return and internalization, and of reversal or overthrow. The latter inaugurates the full and unconditional recuperation of the status of the human, which irons and the whip had long denied.

The Black Man, however, has also always been the name par excellence of the slave: *man-of-metal, man-merchandise, man-of-money.* The complex of Atlantic slavery, centered around the plantation system in the Caribbean, Brazil, and the United States, was key to the constitution of modern capitalism. The types of societies and the types of slaves that were produced within the Atlantic complex differed from the Islamic trans-Saharan slave-trading complex and from those connecting Africa to the Indian Ocean. The indigenous forms of slavery in precolonial African societies were never able to extract from their captives a surplus value comparable to that obtained within the regimes of Atlantic slavery in the New World. The slave of African origin in the New World therefore represents a relatively singular figure of the Black Man, one fated to become an essential mechanism in a process of accumulation that spanned the globe.

Through the triple mechanism of capture, removal, and objectification, the slave was forcibly locked within a system that prevented him from freely making of his life—and from his life—something true, something with its own consistency that could stand on its own. Everything produced by the slave was taken from him: the products of his labor, offspring, the work of his mind. He authored nothing that fully belonged to him. Slaves were considered mere merchandise, objects of luxury or utility to be bought and sold to others. At the same time, however, they were human beings endowed with the ability to speak, capable of creating and using tools. Often deprived of family ties, they were deprived as well of inheritance and of the enjoyment of the fruits of their own labor. Those to whom they belonged, and who extracted their unpaid labor, denied them their full humanity. Yet, on a purely ontological level at least, their humanity was never entirely erased. They constituted, by the force of things, a *supplemental humanity* engaged in constant struggle to escape imprisonment and repetition, and driven by a desire to return to the place where autonomous creation had once been possible.

The suspended humanity of the slave was defined by the fact that he was condemned to reconstitute himself perpetually, to announce his radical, unsinkable desire, and to seek liberty or vengeance. This was especially true when the enslaved refused the radical abdication of the subject that was demanded of them. Although legally defined as movable property, slaves always remained human, despite the cruelty, degradation, and dehumanization directed at them. Through their labor in service of the master, they continued to create a world. Through gesture and speech, they wove relationships and a universe of meaning, inventing languages, religions, dances, and rituals and creating "community."[18] Their destitution and the abjection to which they were subjected never entirely eliminated their capacity to create symbols. By its very existence, the *community of the enslaved* constantly tore at the veil of hypocrisy and lies in which slave-owning societies clothed themselves. The slaves were capable of rebellion and at times disposed of their own lives through suicide, thus dispossessing their masters of their so-called property and de facto abolishing the link of servitude.

Those who were burdened with the name "Black" were forcibly placed in a world apart, yet they retained the characteristics that made them human beyond subjection. Over time they produced ways of thinking and languages that were truly their own. They invented their own literatures, music, and ways of celebrating the divine. They were forced to found their own institutions—schools, newspapers, political organizations, a public sphere different from the official public sphere. To a large extent, the term "Black" is the sign of minoritization and confinement. It is an island of repose in the midst of racial oppression and objective dehumanization.

The Paradoxes of a Name

The term "Africa" generally points to a physical and geographic fact—a continent. But the geographic fact of Africa in turn signifies not only a state of things but a collection of attributes and properties—and a racial condition. Over time, different points of reference became attached to a series of images, words, enunciations, and stigmas, all meant to establish physical, geographic, and climactic conditions, the supposed attributes of local populations, their states of poverty, their desperation, and, above all, their commerce with a form of life whose length was never certain, since superstition, death, and ugliness always lay close by. "Africa," then, is the word through which the modern age seeks to designate two things. First, it identifies a certain litigious figure of the human as an emptiness of being, walled within absolute precariousness. Second, it points to the general question of the inextricability of humans, animals, and nature, of life and death, of the presence of one in the other, of the death that lives in life and gives it the rigidity of a corpse. Africa is the mask as well as the hollow sun, reminding us of the persistence of death in life through the play of doubling and repetition.

In modern consciousness, "Africa" is the name generally given to societies that are judged impotent—that is, incapable of producing the universal and of attesting to its existence. Such societies are easy to recognize by the ways in which they are governed. They are led by high-flying clowns, covered in fetishes and bird's feathers, dressed up like hooded monks, drinking the best of wines in gold vases, unashamed to seek out prostitutes even on Holy Friday. The leaders of such potentates took on an autonomous animal existence long ago, and they carry in their heads nothing except the corpses of real or imagined enemies, killed instantly and left for crows on a plaza. They are, at their core, superstitious societies, impotent societies whose world is subjected to, and ruined by, tribal war, debt, sorcery, and pestilence. They are the underside of the world, in essence the symbol of the awkward gesture and of the disruption and corruption of time. One can speak of such a reality only anecdotally and from a distance. Like gray parentheses, an invisible cave of inaccessible things, everything there is empty, deserted, and animal, virgin and savage, piled high in surprising disarray.[19]

As the living figure of difference, the term "Africa" sends us to a world apart, to that for which we are hardly responsible and with which many of our contemporaries have difficulty identifying. A world overwhelmed by harshness, violence, and devastation, Africa is the simulacrum of an obscure and blind power, walled in a time that seems pre-ethical, and in a sense prepolitical.[20] We have difficulty feeling links of affinity with it. In our eyes, life down there is not just human life. It appears always as someone else's life, as others in some other place, far from us, in an else-where. They and we both lack the ability to share a common world, so that the African politics of our world cannot be a *politics of the similar*. It can only be a politics of difference—the politics of the Good Samaritan, nourished by a sense of guilt, resentment, or pity, but never by an obliga-tion to justice or responsibility. Say what you will, there is little similarity in humanity between them and us. The link that connects us is not one between similar beings. We do not share a common world. All of this is what the term "Africa" certifies.

But what would Africa be without its fetishes and mysteries? At first glance, they are symbols of petrification, erosion, and fossilization, the doorway to a "land of fifty degrees of shadow, of convoys of slaves, canni-bal festivals, empty skulls, of all the things that are eaten, corroded, lost."[21] Through fetish and mystery, for the first time, myth and reality seem to co-incide. And once the impassable threshold has been crossed, the dream of a freeing, cathartic elsewhere becomes possible. Writing as well. Possessed by Africa, one can finally transform one's identity, shatter the barriers of difference, overcome the feeling of disintegration, the desire for suicide and anxiety about death. But the journey has meaning only because it leads to a mountain of signs. Only through dance and trance, via the music of heal-ing, in the midst of cries, gestures, movements—by way of voice, breath, and a new idea of man—can the mountain be penetrated. To find Africa is to experience the loss of identity authorized by possession. It is to submit oneself to the violence of the fetish that possesses us and, through loss and the mediation of the fetish, to experience a pleasure beyond symboliza-tion. It is in this condition that one can declare, as did Michel Leiris fac-ing Gondar in Abyssinia: "I am a man. I exist."[22] For, in the end, the fetish reveals its true nature: the becoming-form of power and the becoming-power of the form. Since the metamorphosis of form into power and power into form is categorically incomplete, and can never be achieved, every relationship to Africa will on principle be agnostic, a mix of desire, disappointment, and, incidentally, regret—unless, following Leiris, one comes to understand that archaic existence is not to be found in an else-where, far away, but within oneself, and that in the end the Other is noth-ing else but ourselves.

The polemical dimension of the term "Africa" flows precisely from the strange power that resides within it, the terrible ambiguity that it con-

critical

ceals like a mask. One of the functions of a mask, as we know, is to hide the face by doubling it. The mask is the power of the double, the crossing of being with appearance. But the person wearing the mask can also see others without being seen, and see the underneath of things, like a hidden shadow. But if being and appearance combine in the mask, it is true as well that, because of the impossibility of seeing the face hidden by the mask, of peering through the miniscule gap, the mask always denounces itself as a mask. The name "Africa" plays the role of the mask in the drama of contemporary existence. Each invocation of the name covers the body of the individual in a sea of opaque fabric. It is the very essence of the name that invites such a foundational process of erasure and veiling, one that compromises any possibility of language. Worse still, is not Africa the very tomb of the image, a massive sarcophagus in which light cannot turn, nor the members of the body move?

The polemical dimension of the term "Africa" flows from the fundamental fact that it refers to an empty form that, in the strictest sense, escapes the criteria of truth and falsehood. Truth, writes Gilles Deleuze, "signifies that a denotation is effectively filled by the state of affairs.... 'False' signifies that the denotation is not filled, either as a result of a defect in the selected images or as a result of the radical impossibility of producing an image which can be associated with words."[23] When it comes to the term "Africa," everything stems from the extraordinary difficulty in producing a true image that can be associated with a word that is also true. The subject who speaks or expresses himself does not, in fact, matter very much. When Africa comes up, correspondence between words, images, and the thing itself matters very little. It is not necessary for the name to correspond to the thing, or for the thing to respond to its name. For that matter, the thing itself at any moment can lose its name, and the name its referent, with no consequence for the statement itself, or for what is said and what is produced, or for who says it and produces it. All that matters is the power of falsehood.

The name "Africa," then, directs us not only to what nothing is meant to respond to but also to a kind of primordial arbitrariness, the arbitrariness of designations to which nothing in particular seems to need to respond, except for inaugural prejudice in its infinite regression. When one says the word "Africa," one generally abdicates all responsibility. The concept of wrongdoing is evacuated on principle. It is presupposed as well that nonsense is constitutive, from the beginning, of the word itself. In other words, to say "Africa" always consists in constructing figures and legends—it matters little which ones—on top of an emptiness. One must only choose words and images that are nearly alike and add to them similar images and words with slightly different meanings, and we end up, every time, with a tale with which we are already familiar. This is what makes Africa the ultimate proliferating aggregate, a power that is all the more voracious because it rarely secretes its own oneiric quality, tending instead in most cases to point to the dreams of others. Here, the name becomes the object of a new name, which in turn can designate something totally different from the first object. We can therefore say of Africa that it is the *symbol of what is as much outside life as beyond life*. It is given over to repetition and reduction, to death repeated in life, and life that inhabits the mask of death, at the border of the impossible possibility that is language.

It is an impossible possibility for two reasons. First, as Michel Foucault says, language—and, mutatis mutandis, life itself—offers itself to be read "as a sun." Language, in effect, does not only constitute the locus of forms. It is the very system of life. It is meant to offer up things to our gaze, but with a visibility so stunning that it actually shields what language itself has to say and what life has to offer. It separates "appearance and reality, the face and the mask with a thin sliver of light." Foucault adds, "The sun of language is hidden within the secret; but at the heart of this night where it is maintained, it is marvelously fecund, causing machines and automaton corpses, incredible inventions and careful imitations." In the meantime, life takes the form of an "imminent afterlife."[24] Second, language is an impossible possibility because, as Deleuze explains, it is constituted by a paradox with "the highest power of language" on the one hand and, on the other, "the impotence of the speaker" to "state the sense of what I say, to say at the same time something and its meaning."[25] For, as Foucault puts it, "language speaks only from something essential that is lacking."[26] When you look closely, the term "Africa" has the same characteristics as those that Deleuze and Foucault believe to have identified in language—an essential gap, or, to use Foucault's words again, a "solar hollow" that blinds us but, since it is its own mirror, always keeps a nocturnal underside that the gaze struggles to penetrate. Life itself, and not just words, constantly trips up against the underside. Fanon in any case understood this well: for him, any examination of the conditions surrounding the production of the self in a colonial context had to start with a critique of language.[27] The critique of life as a critique of language is, then, precisely what the term "Africa" invites us to undertake.

The *Kolossos* of the World   *life and death*

The Black Man serves as witness to this process. He serves as the very kolossos of the world, the double of the world, its cold shadow. As Jean-Pierre Vernant explains, in ancient Greece the term "kolossos" designated, first of all, a gigantic effigy. But the effigy is buried in an empty tomb, next to objects belonging to a dead person. In the night of the tomb, the kolossos serves as a substitute for the absent corpse. It occupies the place of the deceased. Its role is not, says Vernant, "to reproduce the traits of the deceased, to give the illusion of their physical appearance. It does not incarnate and fix in stone the image of the dead. It is, rather, its life in the beyond, life that is opposed to that of the living, just as the world of night is opposed to the world of light. The *kolossos* is not an image; it is a 'double,' just as the dead man himself is a double of the living."[28]

The Black Man serves as the kolossos of our world to the extent that our world can be understood as a giant tomb or cave. In this immense and empty tomb, to say "Black" is to evoke the absent corpses for which the name is a substitute. Each time we invoke the word "Black," we bring out into the light of day all the waste of the world, the excess whose absence within the tomb is as strange as it is terrifying. As the kolossos of the world, the Black Man is the fire that illuminates the things of the cave—the things of the empty tomb that is our world—as they really are. He is the shadowy axis of the world, like Homer's Hades, a kingdom of perishable things, where human life is both fleeting and extraordinarily fragile. The term "Black" is a kind of *mnèma*, a sign for how life and death, within the politics of our world, have come to be defined so narrowly in relation to one another that it is nearly impossible to delimit the border separating the order of life from the order of death. Within the philosophical horizon of our time, then, the term "Africa" signifies nothing more than a way of posing the political question of the desiccation of life—a manner of examining the harshness, dryness, and roughness of life, or the visible but opaque and blind forms that death has assumed within the commerce of the living.

Behind the word—what it says and what it hides, or else what it cannot say, or perhaps what it says without being able to *be heard*—there is a certain figure of our world, of its body and spirit, as well as some of the most squalid realities of our time—there is the *scandal of humanity*. It is the living witness, certainly the most worrying, of the violence of our world and the iniquity that is its mainspring. As we ponder the world and its future, the scandal of humanity confronts us with the most urgent of demands, beginning with responsibility and justice. For the word "Africa" stands as a fundamental negation of these very terms.

This negation is the result of the work of race—the very negation of the idea of the common, or of common humanity. Race contradicts the idea of a single humanity, of an essential human resemblance and proximity. Africa, in geographic and human terms, has certainly not been the sole object of this negation. In fact, other parts of the world are currently undergoing a process of "Africanization." There is consequently something in the name "Africa" that *judges* the world and calls for reparation, restitution, and justice. Its spectral presence in the world can be understood only as part of a critique of race.

The Partition of the World

In the not-too-distant past, race was the privileged language of social conflict, if not the mother of all law. It was the unit of measure of difference and enmity, the main criterion in the struggle for life, and the principle of elimination, segregation, and purification within society. "Modernity" is in reality just another name for the European project of unlimited expansion undertaken in the final years of the eighteenth century. The expansion of European colonial empires was one of the most important political questions, both then and at the beginning of the nineteenth century. The nineteenth century saw the triumph of European imperialism. Given the technical development, military conquests, commerce, and propagation of Christianity that marked the period, Europe exercised a properly despotic power over other peoples throughout the world—the sort of power that one can exercise only outside of one's own borders and over people with whom one assumes one has nothing in common.

The question of race and of the absence of a community of destiny occupied European political thought for half a century, until about 1780. It profoundly marked the reflections of thinkers such as Jeremy Bentham, Edmund Burke, Emmanuel Kant, Denis Diderot, and the Marquis de Condorcet. European liberalism was forged in parallel with imperial expansion. It was in relation to expansion that liberal political thought in Europe confronted such questions as universalism, individual rights, the freedom of exchange, the relationship between ends and means, the national community and political capacity, international justice, the nature of the relationship between Europe and extra-European worlds, and the relationship between despotic governance beyond national borders and responsible representative governance within them.

In many ways our world remains a "world of races," whether we admit it or not. Although this fact is often denied, the racial signifier is still in many ways the inescapable language for the stories people tell about themselves, about their relationships with the Other, about memory, and about power. Our critique of modernity will remain incomplete if we fail to grasp that the coming of modernity coincided with the appearance of the *principle of race* and the latter's slow transformation into the privileged matrix for techniques of domination, yesterday as today. In order to reproduce itself, the principle of race depends on an assemblage of practices whose immediate and direct target is the body of the Other and whose scope is life in general. These practices, at first prosaic, disparate, and more or less systematic, were subsequently solidified as customs and embodied in institutions, laws, and techniques whose historical development we can trace and whose effects we can describe. We must understand the principle of race as a spectral form of division and human difference that can be mobilized to stigmatize and exclude, or as a process of segregation through which people seek to isolate, eliminate, or physically destroy a particular human group.

It has recently been established that the sociobiological transcription of race dates essentially from the nineteenth century. But it was anticipated by the multisecular discourse of racial war, which historically preceded the discourse of class war. During the era of the slave trade and colonialism, however, a new link emerged between, on the one hand, the biological discourse on race (although the meaning of the biological has always been quite unstable) and, on the other, a discourse that viewed race metaphorically within a broader approach to age-old questions of division and subjection, resistance and the fragility of the political, of the tenuous but nevertheless inseparable links between politics and life, politics and the power to kill, power and the thousands of ways in which to kill or enable people to live, or at least survive.

According to Hannah Arendt, race first became a core principle of the political body (a substitute for the nation) and of bureaucracy as a technique of domination in the modern age, specifically during the "scramble for Africa." Although racism and bureaucracy were conceived of and developed separately, it was in Africa that they first revealed themselves to be tightly linked.[29] The link afforded new potentialities for the accumulation of power—the power to dispossess, produce, and manage an exploited humanity. But the combination of race and bureaucracy also led to the multiplication of potentialities for destruction, to massacres and forms of administration that served—as they did in South Africa and in colonies in southwestern Africa—to create political communities governed by the principle of race. Race, writes Arendt, "was the emergency explanation of human beings whom no European or civilized man could understand and whose humanity so frightened and humiliated the immigrants that they no longer cared to belong to the same human species."[30]

As a result of colonization, groups of people who did not claim the same origin and who did not share the same language, much less the same religion, were forced to live together in the midst of territorial entities forged by the iron of conquest. The entities were not, strictly speaking, political bodies, at least not at first. The violence of war and subjection served most often as the common link between groups. Such links were maintained through an exercise of power, one of whose functions was literally to invent races, to classify them, and to establish the necessary hierarchies among them. The state then took on the task of assuring the integrity and purity of each, or, rather, of maintaining them all within permanent relations of hostility.

The most extreme application of the differentiation of species, of the idea that races are locked in a biological struggle for life in which the strongest triumphs, took place in South Africa during the long period that stretched from the eighteenth century into the twentieth century. It culminated in apartheid, when the state leveraged race in a generalized social struggle meant both to infuse the entire social body and to sustain a particular relationship to rights and the law. But to comprehend the paradoxes of what became apartheid by 1948, we must go back to the period stretching from the fifteenth to the nineteenth century and take into account the massive appropriation of land and the partitioning of the world that took place. To a large extent, the historical and spatial consciousness of the planet that we have today is rooted in events that began in the fifteenth century and that led, by the nineteenth century, to the division and partitioning of the entire world.

The events were themselves the consequence of a considerable migration of peoples across the period. Migration occurred for four different reasons. The first was the extermination of entire peoples, notably in the Americas. The second was the deportation, in inhuman conditions, of cargoes of millions of Blacks to the New World, where an economic system founded on slavery contributed in a decisive manner to the raw accumulation of transnational capital and to the formation of Black diasporas. The third was the conquest, annexation, and occupation of immense lands until then unknown in Europe, and the subjection of their populations to the law of the foreigner. Before the arrival of the Europeans, local societies had been self-governed through diverse political forms. The fourth has to do with the formation of racist states and the logic of the "indigenization" of colonists, of which the Afrikaners in South Africa are an example.

The brutal stampede out of Europe came to be known as *colonization* or *imperialism*. Colonization was one of the central mechanisms through which the European pretension of universal domination was made manifest. It was a form of constitutive power whose relationship to land, populations, and territory brought together the three logics of race, bureaucracy, and commerce (*commercium*) in a way that was new in the history of humanity. In the colonial order, race operated as a principle of the political body. Race made it possible to classify human beings in distinct categories supposedly endowed with specific physical and mental properties. Bureaucracy emerged as a tool of domination, and the network linking death and commerce operated as the fundamental matrix of power. Power henceforth made the law, and the content of the law was power.

During this same period, European powers devoted themselves to fierce competition outside Europe. Meanwhile, within, they engaged in a complex process of the secularization of politics. By the end of the sixteenth century, this led, notably in France, to the end of civil war between religious groups and to the birth of a state that was both legally sovereign and conscious of its sovereignty. Two factors tempered intra-European competition and the rivalries that it engendered. On the one hand, the "Christian nations" of Europe defined themselves as "creators and representatives of an order applicable to the whole earth."[31] They confused "civilization" with Europe itself, persuaded that their continent was the center of the earth. Athens, Jerusalem, and Rome were part of its ancient world. Islam was an old enemy. Only later, with the emergence of the United States, did Europe's pretension to world centrality diminish.

There was increasing interest in foreign peoples starting in the eighteenth century. But most European powers gradually adhered to racial thinking, which by the nineteenth century was a constitutive part of the spirit and sensibility of the Western world. As Arendt has shown, the politics of race during the period presented multiple objectives. It sought—notably in Germany—to unite people against foreign domination by awakening a consciousness of a common origin within them. This led to the emergence of nationalisms that accorded vital importance to links of blood, family attachments, tribal unity, and the cult of unmixed origin. The conviction was that each race exists as a complete and distinct totality. Human laws were therefore conceived of as equivalent to the laws of the animal world. The politics of race, then, also operated as an instrument for creating internal divisions. In this regard race became a weapon of civil war before it became a weapon of international war.

There was another current of racial thinking, one that found its most consequential translation in South Africa. At its center was the idea of a superhuman endowed with exceptional rights, a superior genius, and a universal mission—that of governing the world. This current resisted the concept of the unity of the human species and the equality of all people, founded on a common ancestry. It insisted instead on physical difference and convinced itself that non-European peoples had never been able to develop on their own a form of expression adequate to human reason. This current nourished the proud language of conquest and racial domination. As Arendt reminds us, it did not exercise a monopoly on the political life of European nations. In fact, it "would have disappeared in due time together with other irresponsible opinions of the nineteenth century, if the 'scramble for Africa' and the new era of imperialism had not exposed Western humanity to new and shocking experiences."[32]

All of these currents of thought shared in the conviction that a state of nature, one in which neither faith nor law governed, reigned outside of the European enclosure. Peace, friendship, and the treaties that codified intra-European relations were applicable only to Europe and Christian states. Such being the case, each power could legitimately carry out far-off conquests, even at the expense of its neighbors and rivals. It was accepted that the world order was divided into spheres that separated interior and exterior. The interior sphere was governed by law and justice, the conditions not only of social life but also of an international life that had to be traced, marked out, and cultivated. It was here, it was thought, that all ideas of property, payment for work, and the rights of people were developed. It was here that cities, empires, and commerce—in short, human civilization—were built. But there was also, elsewhere, a free zone of lawlessness, a place without rights, where one could pillage and ransack in good conscience, and where the work of pirates, privateers, buccaneers, adventurers, criminals, and all sorts of "elements outside the pale of normal, sane society" had free reign, their actions justified by the two principles of free trade and the freedom to evangelize.[33] This free zone had no borders as such. There were no fences, no sanctuaries that one could, a priori, violate.

The line separating Europe and this "World-outside" could be recognized by the fact that war had no limits there. On the other side of the line, writes Carl Schmitt, was a zone where only the law of the most powerful counted, since there were no legal limits imposed on war. From the beginning, whenever Europe referred to the principle of liberty in relation to the World-outside, what was really meant was an absence of law and organized civil society, which authorized the free and unscrupulous use of force. The assumption was this: the World-outside was the space in which there operated no principle of conduct other than the right of the most powerful, whether in relation to indigenous peoples or rivals. In other words, everything that happened outside of the walls of Europe was situated "outside the legal, moral and political values recognized on this side of this line." If one did find law or justice there, it could only be law that "the European conquerors imported and established, either in their Christian missions or in the accomplished fact of a European system of justice and administration."[34]

The World-outside was therefore beyond the line, a frontier that was always re-created. It was a free space of unrestricted conflict, open to free competition and free exploitation, where men were free to confront one another as savage beasts.[35] There, the only way to judge war legally or morally was to ask whether it was effective. The World-outside was not only a border but also an enclosure. "In the beginning was the fence," explains Jost Trier, quoted by Schmitt. "Fence, enclosure, and border are deeply interwoven in the world formed by men, determining its concepts. The enclosure gave birth to the shrine by removing it from the ordinary, placing it under its own laws, and entrusting it to the divine." "The enclosing ring," Schmitt adds, "the fence made by men's bodies, the man-ring, is a primeval form of ritual, legal and political cohabitation."[36] Such is the case for two reasons. First, there is nothing that is common to human beings in general. The common is shared only among men endowed with reason. And, second, war can never be abolished and can therefore not be the object of limitations. Permanent war is the central problem of the legal order. One way to limit war is to build fortified citadels, to classify and differentiate between those who are protected within the walls of the citadel and those who have no right to it. The latter, as a consequence, cannot enjoy the protection of weapons and the law.

The next question surrounds occupation and the taking of land. Here the problem has always been to know whether the Other, the native, is a human being in the same way that those who are taking his land are. According to what principle can the native be deprived of all rights? From the beginning one line of argument has focused on the realm of belief, insisting that the savages worship idols. Their gods are not real gods. They practice human sacrifice, cannibalism, and other types of inhuman crimes that an evolved person would not commit and that are proscribed even by nature itself. The savage therefore stands simultaneously against humanity and against nature, and is therefore a stranger to the human condition in two ways. In this view the World-outside is the equivalent of a zone outside humanity, outside of the space where humans exercise their rights. It is a space where human rights can be exercised only through the supremacy of humans over those who are not completely human. For if there are indeed humans in these territories, they are fundamentally inhuman.

Their subjection is justified through the allegation that they are slaves by nature and, therefore, enemies. War against non-Christians, according to the ideas of the time, was different from war against Christians. Sharp distinctions were therefore drawn among different kinds of enemies and different kinds of war. Such distinctions themselves referred to other distinctions drawn among humans to highlight their differences and varied status. Not all humans had the same rights. The civilized had a right to dominate the noncivilized, to conquer and subjugate the barbarians because of their intrinsic moral inferiority, to annex their lands, to occupy them and make them subjects. The original legal right of intervention was considered part of "just law," which could be applied equally to wars of extermination and to wars of subjugation. Out of the just law of war was born the just law of property. Schmitt writes,

> Just as in international law the land-appropriating state could treat the public property (*imperium*) of appropriated colonial territory as leaderless, so it could treat private property (*dominium*) as leaderless. It could ignore native property rights and declare itself to be the sole owner of the land; it could appropriate indigenous chieftains' rights and could do so whether or not that was a true legal succession; it could create private government property, while continuing to recognize certain native use rights; it could initiate public trustee-ownership of the state; and it also could allow native use rights to remain unchanged, and could rule over indigenous peoples through a kind of *dominium eminens* [eminent domain]. All these various possibilities were undertaken in the praxis of the 19th and 20th century colonial land appropriations.[37]

In this case, then, law was a method for creating a juridical foundation for a certain idea of humanity that upheld distinctions between the race of conquerors and the other of slaves. Only the race of conquerors could legitimately attribute the quality of being human to itself. The quality of being human was not given to all from the beginning. And even if it had been, this would not abolish difference. In a way, the differentiation between the soil of Europe and the soil of the colonies was the logical consequence of the distinction between Europeans and savages. Until the nineteenth century, despite colonial occupation, colonial soil was not identified as part of the European territory of the occupying state. It was always distinct from it, no matter the type of colony—plantation, extraction, or settler. Only near the end of the nineteenth century did some colonial states attempt to sketch out ways to integrate colonial territories into the systems of government and administration of the colonizing states.

National Colonialism

To become a habitus, the logic of races had to be coupled with the logic of profit, the politics of power, and the instinct for corruption, which together precisely define colonial practice. In this view the example of France reveals the weight of race in the formation of imperial consciousness and the immense work that had to be carried out so that the racial signifier—which is inseparable from any colonial project—could penetrate the soft fibers of French culture.

We can never sufficiently emphasize the complexity and heterogeneity of the colonial experience. There were remarkable variations from one period to another and from one territory to another. That said, the racial signifier was always an essential and even constitutive structure of what would become the imperial project. If there was one form of subjectivity that defined colonial relations, race was its symbolic matrix and primal scene. Take the case of France. The consciousness of empire was the result of a singular political and psychic investment in which race was at once the currency of exchange and the use value. Near the end of the 1870s, France consciously sought to transform the political body of the nation into a political structure of empire. At the time the process had two dimensions. On the one hand, its goal was to assimilate the colonies into the national body by treating conquered peoples as both "subjects" and, eventually, "brothers."

On the other hand, the project progressively put into place a series of mechanisms through which ordinary French people were brought to constitute themselves, sometimes without realizing it, as racist subjects, as much through the way they looked at the world as through their gestures, behaviors, and language. The process stretched across a relatively long period. It was founded in particular on a psycho-anthropology whose function was the racial classification of human species. Theories of inequality among races laid the foundation for a system of classification that would also receive validation through practices of eugenics. Racial classification reached its peak use during the wars of conquest and under colonial brutality, and later in the 1930s within anti-Semitism.[38] At the turn of the nineteenth century, the formation of a racist consciousness, the fact of getting used to racism, was one of the cornerstones of the socialization of French citizens. It functioned as a form of overcompensation for the sense of national humiliation provoked by the Prussian victory over France in 1870 and was part of the fabric, if not the raw material, of national pride and patriotic culture. Known as "the colonial education of the French," this enterprise presented colonization as a pathway to a new age of virility.[39] The role of the colony was to be the location for the exaltation of power and the renewal of national energy. Such an undertaking required a colossal effort on the part of the state and the business community. Its goal was not just to legitimate and promote the imperial project. It also sought to cultivate and disseminate the reflexes and ethos of racialism, along with the nationalism and militarism that were its constitutive elements.

As early as 1892, a vast movement of what we might call *national colonialism* began in France. The national colonialist movement brought together all of the political families of the period, from centrist Republicans to Radicals, from Boulangistes and Monarchists to Progressives. It involved lawyers, businessmen, clergy, journalists, and soldiers and a complex web of organizations, associations, and committees. Working in both the political and cultural realms, they sought to give an expressive voice to the colonial idea through a network of newspapers, periodicals, bulletins, and so-called scientific societies.[40] The great rib of the imperial project was racial difference. It took shape in a number of disciplines: ethnology, geography, missiology. The thematic of racial difference, in turn, was normalized within mass culture through the establishment of institutions such as museums and human zoos; through advertisements, literature, art, the creation of archives, and the dissemination of fantastical stories relayed in the popular press (in magazines such as the *Journal Illustré, L'Illustration,* and *Tour du Monde* and the illustrated supplements of the *Petit Journal* and the *Petit Parisien*); and in international expositions.

Generations of French people were exposed to pedagogy aimed specifically at habituating them to racism. It was founded essentially on the principle that the relationship to Blacks must be a relationship of nonreciprocity. Nonreciprocity was justified by the *qualitative difference between the races,* a thematic that was inseparable from older ideas of blood that had been used to justify the privileges of the nobility and that were now redeployed by the colonial project. People became convinced that the civilization of the future could be created only with White blood. The peoples who accepted racial intermixing fell into abjection. Salvation depended on the absolute separation of races. The Black and Yellow multitude was prolific, a burdensome herd that had to be deported elsewhere and whose males at the very least had to be sterilized, as some would later insist upon and even try to accomplish.[41] Some dreamed of a time in the future when it would be possible to fabricate life, to obtain what one was set on obtaining, as a being who could choose. The colonial project nourished a new form of raciology, one of whose cornerstones was the dream of upending the rules of life to pave the way for the creation of a race of giants.

The thematic of the qualitative difference between the races is an old one.[42] It infected and traversed culture over the course of the last quarter of the nineteenth century. But it was during the 1930s that it became banal to the point of representing a kind of common sense.[43] It nourished fears about depopulation, immigration, and "racial grafting," and even phantasms about the possibility of Asian imperialism.[44] The colonial idea and the racist ethos that was its corollary traveled along many byroads, one of which was education. Pierre Nora, for instance, ranks the *Petit Lavisse* among the "French sites of memory" on the same level as *Le tour de France par deux enfants* (1887) by "G. Bruno" (a pseudonym for Augustine Fouillée) and *In Search of Lost Time* by Marcel Proust. In the *Petit Lavisse* in particular, Republican discourse was steeped in nationalist and militaristic values.[45] The educational system and the military system were already in dialogue long before the adoption of the Jules Ferry laws of 1881–1882, which made school obligatory. Students were educated to become citizen-soldiers. Civic pedagogy and colonial pedagogy were deployed in the context of a crisis of masculinity and an apparent moral disarmament. Beginning in the 1880s, all twelve-year-old students studied the colonial expansion of their country in their history textbooks (notably those by Augé and Petit in 1890, Cazes in 1895, Aulard and Debidour in 1900, Calvet in 1903, Rogie and Despiques in 1905, Delagrave in 1909, and Lavisse in 1920).[46] In addition to a prescriptive and normalizing presentation of history, there was also a children's literature (the works of Jules Verne and illustrated magazines such as *Le Petit Français Illustré*, *Le Petit Écolier*, *Le Saint-Nicolas*, *Le Journal de la Jeunesse*, *L'Alliance Française Illustrée*, and so forth).

In all of these publications, the African is presented not only as a child but as a stupid child, prey to a handful of petty kings who are cruel and fierce potentates. This idiocy is the result of the congenital vice of the Black race, and colonization is a form of assistance, the education and moral treatment for such idiocy. It is an antidote to the spirit of cruelty and the anarchic functioning of "indigenous peoples." From this point of view, it is a gift of civilization. Colonization was viewed as a form of general treatment for the idiocy of races predisposed to degeneration. Such a belief led Léon Blum himself to say in 1925: "We admit the right and even the duty of superior races to attract to themselves those which have not reached the same degree of culture, and to call them to the progress realized thanks to the efforts of Science and Industry."[47] Colonists are not cruel and avid masters but guides and protectors. French troops are heroic and intrepid. They remove the iron yokes from slaves and unshackle their legs. The newly emancipated poor are so happy that they sing and dance, which proves inarguably that France is good and generous to the people that it subjugates. Jean Jaurès affirmed as much in 1884: "We can say to these people confidently that . . . wherever France is established, she is beloved; that wherever she has only passed through, she is missed; that wherever her light shines, it is benevolent; that where it does not shine, it leaves behind a long and soft twilight in which eyes and hearts remained chained."[48]

At first glance, the reasons put forth to justify colonialism were of an economic, political, military, ideological, or humanitarian order: conquering new lands in order to settle the excess population of France; finding new outlets for the nation's products, factories and mines; accessing raw materials for French industries; planting the flag of "civilization" among inferior races and savages and piercing the shadows that surrounded them; using colonial domination to assure peace, security, and riches for those who had never before experienced such benefits; establishing, in infidel lands, a hardworking, moral, and Christian population and thus spreading the gospel among pagans; and destroying the isolation created by paganism through the introduction of commerce. But all of these justifications mobilized the racial signifier, which was never considered a subsidiary factor. Race always appears in the argument for colonialism, operating simultaneously as a material matrix, a symbolic institution, and a psychic component of the consciousness of empire. In the defense and illustration of colonization, no justification escapes a priori from the general discourse on what were considered at the time to be the *qualities of the race.*

Such was the case, particularly near the end of the nineteenth century and the beginning of the twentieth, because there prevailed in the West an interpretive system about the world that viewed history as a struggle to the death for existence. Numerous writings published in the 1920s, for example, by more or less well-known essayists are infused with a radical racial pessimism. The heart of culture at the time was haunted by the idea of degeneration, the opposite of social Darwinism.[49] These ideas were certainly contested and attacked. But many firmly believed that the struggle for life was one that opposed fundamentally different human groups, peoples, or races. Each was believed to have stable characteristics, and to be endowed with a biological inheritance that had to be defended, protected, and preserved. Not only individuals held this belief. It was also a cardinal dimension of the colonial policies of the European states and of the ways in which each conceived of the right of war against non-European peoples and entities.

As Paul Leroy-Beaulieu explained at the time, the colonial order was a way of ratifying the relations of power that resulted from such struggle. Colonization, he argued, "was the expansion power of a people, its power of reproduction, its expansion and multiplication across space; it is the submission of the universe or a vast portion of it to its language, its customs, its ideas and its laws."[50] The colonial order was founded on the idea that humanity was divided into species and subspecies that could be differentiated, separated, and classed hierarchically. Both from the point of view of the law and in terms of spatial arrangements, species and subspecies had to be kept at a distance from one another. The *Précis de législation et d'économie coloniales* by Alexandre Mérignhac (published in 1912 and reissued in 1925) is explicit on this point. To colonize, he writes, "is to put oneself in relation to new countries in order to profit from the resources of all kinds in them. . . . Colonization is therefore an establishment founded in a new country by a race of advanced civilization, in order to realize the . . . goal we have just mentioned."[51] It is no exaggeration to say that the colonial state functioned only through the nationalization of the biological.

Frivolity and Exoticism

The French logic of racial assignation had three distinct traits. The first—and probably the most important—was the refusal to see, the practice of occultation and denial. The second was the practice of restoration and disguise. The third was a tendency toward frivolity and exoticism. There exists in France a very long tradition of erasure, of the relegation of the violence of race to the realm of what is not worth showing, knowing, or allowing to be seen. The tradition of dissimulation, denial, and camouflage, whose reactualization we see in the contemporary context, dates from the sixteenth and seventeenth centuries. It emerged in the founding context, at a time when France was seeking to codify its relationship to its slaves.

An edict of 1570 limited both the entrance of Blacks into metropolitan territory and the exhibition or loading of Black slaves in the ports of the country.[52] With this inaugural gesture, France announced its will not to know anything about the victims of its racial logic—a logic for which the Black slave represented the most accomplished witness at the time. That the slave was the object of such a ban can perhaps be explained by the fact that there is nothing to see in the Black slave other than a "nothing being." But the exclusion of all that Black slaves would make apparent from the realm of what could be represented probably had another goal: the veiling of the economic and commercial mechanisms through which they came to be produced as slaves.

This slow process dates to the beginnings of the slave trade, which itself peaked during the eighteenth century, in the middle of the Enlightenment period. New ideas about the relationship between subjects and authority developed while France was deeply implicated in the "triangle machine" that produced slavery and servitude overseas. In their philosophical work, Jean-Jacques Rousseau and Voltaire in particular recognized the vile character of the trade in slaves. But they pretended ignorance of the traffic that was under way at the time, and of the chains that made it possible. In the process they inaugurated a tradition that would later become one of the central characteristics of the consciousness of empire: making slavery a metaphor for the condition of human beings in modern European society. Tragic events concerning savages, in which Europeans were partly implicated as responsible parties, were turned into metaphors. This gesture of ignorance, this dialectic of distance and indifference, dominated the French Enlightenment.[53]

The second distinctive trait of the French logic of racial assignation was the practice of cleansing, disfiguration, and disguise. The relegation of the Black slave to the realm of the unrepresentable, to *that about which we do not want to know anything*, was not the same as the pure and simple ban on the figuration or representation of Blacks. On the contrary, the French logic of race from the beginning has operated on the basis of the annexation of the racial Other and its cleansing through the triple wash of exoticism, frivolity, and entertainment. From the start, people were willing to see the Black Man only as the object of disguise, through costume, color, or scenery. In painting or theater it was necessary until relatively recently to dress him up in an oriental costume, in turbans and feathers, in puffy pants or little green clothes.[54] Paradoxically, in order to emerge into the realm of the visible, his face could not show traces of the fundamental violence that from the beginning had stolen his humanity and reconstituted him as Black.

Most preferable were little ebony Black girls, little Black boys, and colored pages playing the role of the lady's companion, treated as parrots, dolls, or some other kind of pet. There were laughing Blacks, carefree, good dancers, good Blacks with their good masters, free slaves who were grateful and loyal, whose role was to foreground the magnanimity of Whites. None of this is a recent invention. As a habitus, it sedimented progressively over a long period. These were the types of Blacks who, in the nineteenth century, were tolerated at court, in the salons, in painting, and in the theater. As Sylvie Chalaye writes, "they amused the gatherings of high society, brought a touch of exoticism and color to balls, as the painters of the period show: Hogarth, Raynolds, Watteau, Lancret, Pater, Fragonard, Carmontelle."[55] To a large extent, French racism was a willfully carefree, libertine, and frivolous racism.[56] Historically, it was always deeply linked to a society that was itself carefree and libertine and never wanted to open its eyes to "the terrible dunghill hidden under the gilding and the crimson."[57]

It is important to pause a moment on the figure of the Black Woman, a figure that played a key role in the articulation of racism, frivolity, and libertinage in France. The three privileged loci of this articulation were literature, painting, and dance. Here, too, the tradition is an old one. The figure of the Black Woman haunts Charles Baudelaire's entire corpus, and it is possible that the "flowers of evil" directly refer to it. Whether it is Dorothée l'Africaine (encountered on the Île de Bourbon in 1841) or Jeanne Duval (who was born in Haiti and was Baudelaire's lover for twenty years), the evocation of "Black beauties" was always connected to descriptions of their svelte voluptuousness, their naked breasts, their feathered belts, and their hindquarters, with or without satin underwear.[58] The figure of the Black Woman constituted one of the most fertile sources for artistic creation for the poet. More broadly, it was a central, though ambivalent, feature of French exoticism. On the one hand, it called up the sense of a physical world, of rhythm and color. On the other hand, it was associated with the ideal of the hermaphrodite. "Black beauties" were seen as indolent, available, and submissive. They were living examples of the triumph of lust, activating the phantasmagoric impulses of the French male, who, in turn, could imagine himself as a White explorer at the borders of civilization. Discovering savages, he mixed with them by making love to one or more of their women, in a landscape of boats in harbors, a tropical paradise of gleaming palm trees and the scent of tropical flowers.

Similarly evocative scenes were interspersed in the writings of François-René de Chateaubriand, alongside those of lions procreating. Free under the banana trees, with pipes full of incense, drinking coconut milk under the arcade of fig trees and in forests of clove and *acajou* trees, one of the heroes proclaims that he wants to "devour the leaves of your bed, for where you sleep is as divine as the nest of African swallows, like the nest served at the table of our kings, made of the debris of flowers and the most precious of spices."[59] In his poem "Reine noire" ("Black Queen"), Guillaume Apollinaire drew on the same poetic-exotic fiber, bringing together beauty, nakedness, and sensuality. His Black Woman is characterized by her white teeth, her dark mane, her blue body, and her firm breasts. As for others, we know of Henri Matisse's *Haïtienne* (1943) and her whispering lace, the symbol of happy sensuality and the light of desire; of Pablo Picasso's *Les Demoiselles d'Avignon* (1907), *Femme nue* (1910), and *Femme au bord de la mer* (*Baigneuse*) (1909), which offer a glimpse of the phantasm of a devouring Black female sexuality; and of Georges Braque's *Femme assise* (1911).

It is probably the figure of Josephine Baker that cemented this form of casual, insouciant, and libertine racism within France's popular culture and exotic imaginary. The following account of scenes performed by Baker's troupe during a rehearsal in Paris in the 1920s aptly summarizes this mode of racism: "We don't understand their language, we can't find a way to tie the scenes together, but everything we've ever read flashes across our enchanted minds: adventure novels, glimpses of enormous steamboats swallowing up clusters of Negroes who carry rich burdens, a caterwauling woman in an unknown port, . . . stories of missionaries and travelers,

Stanley, the Tharaud brothers, Batouala, sacred dances, nurses, the Negro soul with its animal energy, its childish joys, the sad bygone time of slavery, we had all that listening to the singer with the jungle voice."[60]

Blinding Oneself

The other foundation for the consciousness of empire has always been the tremendous will to ignorance that, in every case, seeks to pass itself off as knowledge. The ignorance in question here is of a particular kind: a casual and frivolous ignorance that destroys in advance any possibility of an encounter and a relationship other than one based on violence. In his "Lettre sur l'Algérie," Tocqueville highlights precisely this policy of ignorance. He suggests that, in the context of the policy of empire (which is just another name for a policy of war), the will to ignorance is based on the principle according to which "on the field of battle, victory goes . . . to the strongest, and not the most knowledgeable."[61] The fact that colonizers knew almost nothing, and were not worried about learning much of anything, can be explained by their conviction that, when it came to relations with Africans, violence would always compensate for the absence of truth or the lack of law.

For a long time, in the Western imagination, Africa was an unknown land. But that hardly prevented philosophers, naturalists, geographers, missionaries, writers, or really anyone at all from making pronouncements about one or another aspect of its geography, or about the lives, habits, and customs of its inhabitants. Despite the flood of information to which we now have access and the number of academic studies at our disposal, it remains unclear whether the will to ignorance has disappeared, not to mention the age-old disposition that consists in making pronouncements on subjects about which one knows little or nothing. In 1728 Jean-Baptiste Labat concisely summarized the idea that truth did not matter at all when it came to Africa: "I have seen Africa, but I have never set foot there."[62] In France and in much of Europe from the eighteenth century on, narratives of all kinds flourished, in encyclopedia entries; works of geography; treatises of natural history, ethics, or aesthetics; and novels, plays, and collections of poetry. The majority of such legends, ethnographic reveries, and occasional travel narratives dealt with Africa. From the beginning of the Atlantic trade, the continent became an inexhaustible well of phantasms, the raw material for a massive labor of imagination whose political and economic dimensions we can never underscore enough. Nor can we emphasize enough how much it continues to inform, up to the present, our representations of Africans, their lives, their work, and their languages.

As we have noted, such false knowledge of Africa is above all misunderstanding and fantasy. But here one fantasizes only in order to exclude, to close in on oneself. One fantasizes only to veil the kind of sovereign disdain that always accompanies claims that the Other is our "friend," whether the "friendship" is real or imaginary, reciprocal or not. The French variant of the violence of race always takes the form of a face that, as soon as it is born and gazed on, must be immediately rendered invisible. It is as if it convokes a voice only to muffle it as soon as it is audible, thus reducing it to silence, preventing it from expressing itself in the first person singular form. The imaginary object that erupted into the psychic life of the West at the dawn of the slave trade has two faces that have remained connected to one another, like a mask and its double in a tragic play of mirrors.

The first is a diurnal face—a geographic location and a region of the world about which almost nothing is known but which is described with an apparent authority, the authority of fiction. Description oscillates constantly between two extremes. Africa is sometimes a strange land, marvelous and blinding, and at other times a torrid and uninhabitable zone. It appears sometimes as a region afflicted with an irreparable sterility; at others, as a country blessed with spontaneous fertility. It is also, often, the name of something else, something colossal and impenetrable, whose enormity is mixed up with figures of the monstrous and of absolute license, a license that is at times poetic, sometimes carnivalesque, too often cynical and shadowy—a horrible mix of fetishism and cannibalism. But whatever the beauty or ugliness of its face, the destiny of Africa is to be possessed.

Victor Hugo explained as much in phallic terms during a banquet commemorating the abolition of the slave trade in 1879:

> It is there, in front of us, that block of sand and ash, that inert and passive mound which for six thousand years has been an obstacle to the march of universal progress, this monstrous Ham that stops Sem with its enormity: Africa. Oh what a land is Africa! Asia has its history, America has its history, even Australia has its history, dating back to its beginnings in human memory. Africa has no history. There is a kind of vast and obscure legend enveloping it. Rome touched it in order to get

rid of it, and when Rome thought it had been delivered from Africa it cast upon this immense death one of those untranslatable epithets: *Africa portensa*, it is both more and less than a marvel, it is what is absolute within horror; Africa, in effect, is the tropical blaze, and it seems as if to see Africa is to be blinded: an excess of sun and an excess of night.[63]

He added this command:

Africa imposes on the universal such a suppression of movement and circulation that it limits universal life, and the march of human progress can no longer accept that a fifth of the globe remains paralyzed.... To make old Africa fit for civilization, that is the problem. Europe will resolve it. Go, peoples, take this land! Who owns it? No one! Take this land that is God's land. God gives land to men. God offers Africa to Europe. Take it!... Pour your surplus into Africa and, at the same time, solve your social problems. Transform your proletarians into property-owners.... Go, build roads, build ports, build cities, expand, cultivate, multiply, and may the divine spirit affirm itself through peace in this land, more and more free from the influence of priests and princes.[64]

At the time the knowledge of the continent was full of lacunae. It was founded essentially on rumors, on erroneous and unverifiable phantasms and suppositions. Perhaps they functioned as metonymies for the moral deficiencies of the time, or as mechanisms through which Europe at the time sought to reassure itself by compensating for its own sense of insufficiency. But no matter. As Jonathan Swift remarked in "On Poetry" (1733), wise geographers engaged in making maps of Africa "with savage pictures fill their gaps." "And o'er unhabitable downs / Place elephants for want of towns."[65]

Then there is the nocturnal face. Europe does not simply conjure an imaginary object. It offers itself an imaginary human being, the Black Man. He was first called "Nègre" (a kind of human thing, or quantifiable merchandise) and then "Black Man" (*l'homme noir*), in which they located an imperishable substance called the "Black soul." At its origin, the term "Black Man" served first and foremost to describe and imagine African difference. It mattered little that "Nègre" designated the slave while "Black Man" designated the African who had not yet been subjected to slavery.

Particularly during the period of the slave trade, it was the presumed absence of humanity that characterized the difference. Color was, from this perspective, only the exterior sign of a basic indignity, a foundational form of degradation. Over the course of the eighteenth and nineteenth centuries, the epithet or attribute "Black" referred to this inaugural absence. At the time, the term "Black Man" was the name given to a species of human who, although human, barely deserved the name of human. It was not known whether this species really was human; it was sometimes described as "the most atrocious creature of the human race," at others as a dark mass of undifferentiated matter of flesh and bone—as a "natural" man, in the words of François Le Vaillant in his 1790 travel account.[66]

The term "Black Man" is also the name given to the polygamist whose temperament and misery predispose him to vice, indolence, luxury, and dishonesty. Indeed, in a later description of the sexuality of this kind of man, the writer Michel Cournot said that he had a "sword": "When the [sword of the Black Man] has pierced your wife, she will have felt something" in the order of a "revelation." But this kind of sword also leaves behind a sort of abyss in which "your charm is lost."[67] The penis of the Black Man is compared to a palm or a breadfruit tree that will never grow limp, even for an empire. He is a man whose wives, usually numerous, are slaves to lascivious dances and sensual pleasures, as Olfert Dapper wrote as early as 1686.[68] To hypersexuality was added idolatry, primitivism, and paganism, all of which were henceforth interconnected. Finally, the Black Man's difference could be recognized distinctly in the black membrane that was his wooly hair, in his smell, and in his limited intellectual capacities.

In the lexicon of the nineteenth century, the term "Black" was a major component of the taxonomy of segregation that dominated the discourse on human diversity. The term served to designate "that man" about which Europe kept asking questions as it encountered him: "Is this another man? Is this other than a man? Is he an example of the same or other than the same?" Suddenly, to call someone a "Black Man" was to define him as a being that was biologically, intellectually, and culturally predetermined by his irreducible difference. He belonged to a distinct species. And it was as a distinct species that he must be described and catalogued. For the same reason, he was the object of a distinct moral classification. In the proto-racist European discourse in question here, to say "Black Man" was to evoke the disparities of the human species and refer to the inferior status to which he was consigned. It was to call up a historical period during which all Africans carried the status of potential merchandise, or, in the terminology of the time, of a *pièce d'Inde*.[69]

On the Limits of Friendship

Let us now turn to another aspect of the vocabulary of the period—that which deals with friendship toward Africans. Here, too, we find an old and deeply ambiguous French tradition.[70] Its goal was to end the racial hostility that was characteristic of the consciousness of slavery and empire. The tradition has two facets. The more visible side of friendship was shaped by the logic of universalization and directly influenced by concerns about ethics and law. There was a search for, if not full equality, at least a sense of equity and justice. But friendship in this sense did not come from links of kinship or even of familiarity with or proximity to Blacks. It aimed rather to be callout, a friendship of quotation that cited the very slave about which French society wanted to know nothing. It was meant as a cry or protest with a political dimension. This new politics demanded a way of behaving toward Blacks that was just, based on the recognition that between them and us there existed a degree of mutuality. There was an obligation to respond to them. The friendship was founded on the idea that, in the end, the difference between them and us was not irreducible.

On its less visible side, friendship was fundamentally a friendship of compassion, of empathy and sympathy shaped by encounters with Black suffering. Beginning in the eighteenth century, and influenced by authors such as Jean-Baptiste Du Tertre and Labat, and the works of the Abbé Raynal (*Histoire des deux Indes*, 1770), Louis-Sébastien Mercier (*L'an 2440*, 1771), and the Marquis de Condorcet (*Réflexion sur l'esclavage des Nègres*, 1781), the French public was made aware of the cruel and inhuman character of the slave trade. Although several of these works argued for the equality of the races, most pushed only for an enlightened application of colonial policy and of the Code Noir promulgated by Louis XIV in 1685. The dominant idea of the period was that Blacks were made to be slaves because of their inferiority. Only in the service of a good master could they attain happiness. In many ways the activities of the abolitionist Société des Amis des Noirs was rooted in this politics of kindness.

The politics of kindness also shaped the fiction and novels of the period, such as Aphra Behn's *Oroonoko*, translated into French in 1745. The book opened the way for a "negrophile" current in French literature evident in the works of Jean-François Saint-Lambert (*Ziméo*, 1769), Joseph Lavallée (*Le Nègre comme il y a peu de Blancs*, 1789), and Germaine de Staël (*Mirza*, 1795). Olympe de Gouges's play *L'esclavage des noirs* was performed at the Comédie-Française in 1789. But this sympathy largely decreased after the insurrection of the slaves in Saint-Domingue and the massacres of planters in Guadeloupe during the 1790s. These events made it possible to suppress abolitionism in the following decades, notably under Napoleon, whose politics were profoundly racist.[71] Only starting in the 1820s was there a rebirth of currents of sympathy toward Blacks, in works by Prosper Mérimée (*Vivre*, 1829), Claire Duras (*Limites*, 1823), George Sand (*Indiana*, 1832), and Alphonse de Lamartine (*Louverture*, 1850). There was a vein of this kind of friendship, founded on the politics of kindness, that did not fundamentally contest the prejudice of inferiority directed toward Blacks. It subscribed to the idea that the Black Man lived in a miserable and sordid condition, and it accepted that there were physical, anatomical, and mental disparities between Europeans and Africans. It did acknowledge, however, that, despite their inferior status, Africans were still endowed with speech. They merited the same compassion accorded to other human beings. And their inferiority did not give us the right to abuse their weaknesses. On the contrary, it imposed on us the duty to save them and elevate them to our level.

During the period of the slave trade, most of the "Friends of the Blacks" were convinced that Africans were inferior but did not believe that they deserved to be reduced to slavery because of it.[72] They attributed to the Black Man an allegorical role within a largely speculative history of humanity. In their eyes, the Black Man was the living symbol of an ancient humanity, happy and simple. During the colonial period, the idea passed on to the "African peasant," held as the prototype of child-humanity and of the simple life, joyous and without artifice. In his noble savagery, the child-human, draped in the innocent night of primitive times, lived in harmony with nature and with the spirits who lived in the forest or sang in the springs. The "Friends of the Blacks" could challenge the institution of slavery and condemn its effects. Voltaire, for instance, confronted the cruelty and cupidity of the slave-owning planters, in the process demonstrating his sense of universalism and pity. But even as he denounced the evil system of slavery, his discourse remained inscribed within the paradigm of condescendence.

In his *Essai sur les moeurs et l'esprit des nations* (1789), for instance, he could affirm:

> Their round eyes, squat noses, and invariable thick lips, the different configuration of their ears, their woolly heads and the measure of their intellects, make a prodigious difference between them and other species of men; and what demonstrates, that they are not indebted for this difference to their climates, is that Negro men and women, being transported into the coldest countries, constantly produce animals of their own species; and that mulattoes are only a bastard race of black men and white women, or white men and black women, as asses, specifically different from horses, produce mules by copulating with mares.[73]

Hugo, meanwhile, swore by one detail, "which is but a detail, but is immense: . . . Whites made Blacks into men; . . . Europe will make Africa into a world."[74] This same detail was evoked by Jules Ferry in 1885 when he defended a colonial policy that disregarded the rights of man—a doctrine that successive French governments have been committed to applying to Africa ever since then. "We must speak louder and more truthfully!" Ferry exclaimed. "We must say openly that in effect the superior races have a right with regards to inferior races." The Declaration of the Rights of Man had not been "written for the Blacks of Equatorial Africa." "I repeat that superior races have a right because they have a duty. They have the duty to civilize the inferior races."[75]

The dogma of the "civilizing mission" infused most of the attempts at solidarity with Blacks, even during the anticolonial struggles. French anticolonialism was never monolithic.[76] There were those, on the one hand, who still wanted a colonial empire but believed that it should be founded on humanism and efficiency. On the other hand, there were those who refused to recognize the right of France to impose its will on foreign peoples in the name of civilization. Between the 1890s and the beginning of the twentieth century, Jaurès, for example, accepted the concept of the civilizing mission, which he defined in terms of volunteer work. But his position changed in 1905 when Gustave Rouanet of the newspaper *L'Humanité* exposed scandals in the Congo.[77] Before his conversion to nationalism,

Charles Péguy published exposés on the conditions in the two Congos in his *Cahiers de la Quinzaine*.[78] But he called for reform, not for the abandonment of the civilizing mission. The socialist Paul Louis and the Anarchists, however, offered an uncompromising critique of colonialism.[79] Louis in particular considered colonialism an organic manifestation of capitalism in an era that saw the expansion of mechanization, the ruin of small industry, and the continual growth of the proletarian army. His anticolonial critique was part of a position that saw the working class as the privileged institution for the unification of future humanity. Colonialism, for such critics, had the capacity to universalize class conflict. This critique was deployed during a period when the struggles of workers were beginning to impose limitations on forms of overexploitation in countries at the center of capitalism. The result of such successes was the appearance of a salaried class that was more or less integrated in the expanded circuits of accumulation. For this fragile equilibrium to hold, the most brutal methods of overexploitation were delocalized into the colonies. Capital depended heavily on its racial subsidies to mitigate the crises of accumulation.

THREE
DIFFERENCE AND
SELF-DETERMINATION

Whether in literature, philosophy, the arts, or politics, Black discourse has been dominated by three events: slavery, colonization, and apartheid. Still today, they imprison the ways in which Black discourse expresses itself. These events have acquired certain canonical meanings, three of which are worth highlighting. First, as we have suggested in the previous chapters, there is *separation from oneself*. Separation leads to a loss of familiarity with the self to the point that the subject, estranged, is relegated to an alienated, almost lifeless identity. In place of the being-connected-to-itself (another name for tradition) that might have shaped experience, one is constituted out of an alterity in which the self becomes unrecognizable to itself: this is the spectacle of separation and quartering.[1] Second is the idea of *disappropriation*.[2] This process refers, on the one hand, to the juridical and economic procedures that lead to material expropriation and dispossession, and, on the other, to a singular experience of subjection characterized by the falsification of oneself by the other. What flows from this is a state of maximal exteriority and ontological impoverishment.[3] These two gestures (material expropriation and ontological impoverishment) constitute the singular elements of the Black experience and the drama that is its corollary. Finally, there is the idea of *degradation*. Not only did the servile condition plunge the Black subject into humiliation, abjection, and nameless suffering. It also incited a process of "social death" characterized by the denial of dignity, dispersion, and the torment of exile.[4]

In all three cases, the foundational events that were slavery, colonialism, and apartheid played a key role: they condensed and unified the desire of the Black Man to *know himself* (the moment of sovereignty) and *hold himself* in the world (the moment of autonomy).

Liberalism and Racial Pessimism

From a historical perspective, the emergence of the plantation and the colony as institutions coincides with the very long period in the West during which a new form of governmental reason emerged and was affirmed: that of mercantile reason. It considered the market as the ultimate mechanism for exchange and the privileged locus of the veridiction both of the political and of the value and utility of things in general. The expansion of liberalism as an economic doctrine and a particular art of governance took place at a time when European states, in tight competition with one another and against the backdrop of the slave trade, were working to expand their power and saw the rest of the world as their economic domain and within their possession.

The plantation specifically and later the colony were in gestation from the second half of the fifteenth century. They constituted an essential machinery within a new form of calculation and planetary consciousness. It considered merchandise to be the elemental form of wealth and saw the capitalist mode of production as being fundamentally about the immense accumulation of merchandise. Merchandise had value only to the extent that it contributed to the formation of wealth, which constituted the reason for its use and exchange. From the perspective of mercantilist reason, the Black slave is at once object, body, and merchandise. It has form as a body-object or an object-body. It is also a potential substance. Its substance, which creates its value, flows from its physical energy. It is work-substance. In this view the Black Man is material energy. This is the first door through which he enters into the process of exchange.

As an object of value to be sold, bought, and used, the Black Man also has access to a second door. The planter who purchases a Black slave does so neither to destroy nor to kill him but rather to use him in order to produce and augment the planter's own power. Not all Black slaves cost the same. The variability in price corresponds to the formal quality attributed to each of them. But any use of the slave diminishes the attributed formal quality. Once subjected to use, consumed and exhausted by their owner, the object returns to nature, static and henceforth unusable. In the mercantilist system, the Black Man is therefore the body-object, the merchandise, that passes from one form to another and—once in its terminal phase, exhausted, destroyed—is the object of a universal devalorization. The death of the slave signals the end of the object and escape from the status of merchandise.

Mercantilist reason thinks of the world as an unlimited market, a space of free competition and free circulation. The two approaches to the world that developed during the period were linked: the idea of the globe as a surface connected by commercial relations that cross state borders and thus threaten sovereignty, and the birth of international law, civil law, and cosmopolitan law, whose combined goal was to guarantee "perpetual peace." The modern idea of democracy, like liberalism itself, was inseparable from the project of commercial globalization. The plantation and the colony were nodal chains holding the project together. From their beginnings, as we well know, the plantation and the colony were racial dispositions whose calculus revolved around an exchange relationship based on property and profit. Part of liberalism, and racism, is therefore based on naturalism.

In his study *The Birth of Biopolitics*, Michel Foucault highlights the fact that, at its origin, liberalism "entails at its heart a productive/destructive relationship [with] freedom." He forgot to specify that the high point, historically, of the destruction of liberty was the enslavement of Blacks. According to Foucault, the paradox of liberalism is that it "must produce freedom, but this very act entails the establishment of limitations, controls, forms of coercion, and obligations relying on threats, etc." The production of liberty therefore has a cost whose calculating principle is, adds Foucault, security and protection. In other words, the economy of power that defines liberalism, and the democracy of the same name, depends on a tight link between liberty, security, and protection against omnipresent threat, risk, and danger. Danger can result from the poor adjustment of the mechanisms balancing the diverse interests that make up the political community. But it can also come from outside. In both cases "liberalism turns into a mechanism continually having to arbitrate between the freedom and security of individuals by reference to this notion of danger." The Black slave represents the danger.[5]

One of the motors of liberalism is the permanent animation, or the re-actualization and placement into circulation, of the topic of danger and

[margin, handwritten vertically: There is no balance.]

threat—and the resulting stimulation of a culture of fear. If the stimulation of a culture of fear is the condition, the "internal psychological and cultural correlative of liberalism," then, historically, the Black slave is its primary conduit.[6] From the beginning, racial danger has been one of the pillars of the culture of fear intrinsic to racial democracy. The consequence of fear, as Foucault reminds us, has always been the broad expansion of procedures of control, constraint, and coercion that, far from being aberrations, constitute the counterpart to liberty. Race, and in particular the existence of the Black slave, played a driving role in the historical formation of this counterpart.

The plantation regime and, later, the colonial regime presented a problem by making race a principle of the exercise of power, a rule of sociability, and a mechanism for training people in behaviors aimed at the growth of economic profitability. Modern ideas of liberty, equality, and democracy are, from this point of view, historically inseparable from the reality of slavery. It was in the Caribbean, specifically on the small island of Barbados, that the reality took shape for the first time before spreading to the English colonies of North America. There, racial domination would survive almost all historical moments: the revolution in the eighteenth century, the Civil War and Reconstruction in the nineteenth, and even the great struggles for civil rights a century later. Revolution carried out in the name of liberty and equality accommodated itself quite well to the practice of slavery and racial segregation.

These two scourges were, however, at the heart of the debates surrounding independence. Seeking to enlist slaves in the fight against the revolution, the English offered them sparkling promises of liberty. From then on, the specter of a generalized insurrection of the slaves—an old fear, part of the American system from its beginnings—shadowed the War of Independence. In fact, during the hostilities tens of thousands of slaves proclaimed their own freedom. There were important defections in Virginia. But there was a gap between the way Blacks conceived of their liberty (as something to conquer) and the ideas of the revolutionaries, who saw it as something that should be gradually granted. At the end of the conflict, the slave system was not dismantled. The Declaration of Independence and the Constitution were clearly texts of liberation, except when it came to race and slavery. A new kind of tyranny was consolidated at the very moment of liberation from tyranny. The idea of formal equality between

White citizens emerged in a roundabout way from the revolution. It was the consequence of a conscious effort to put social distance between Whites on the one hand and African and Native American slaves on the other. The dispossession of the latter was justified through references to their laziness and lust. And if later, during the Civil War, there was a relatively equal amount of blood spilled by Whites and Blacks, the abolition of slavery did not lead to compensation for ex-slaves.

In this regard the chapter in Alexis de Tocqueville's portrait of American democracy devoted to "the Present State and Probable Future of the Three Races that Inhabit the Territory of the United States" is particularly interesting. He writes both of the race of men "par excellence," the Whites, the "first in enlightenment, in power, in happiness," and of the "unfortunate races": Blacks and Native Americans. These three racial formations are not part of the same family. They are not just distinct from one another. Everything, or almost everything, separates them: education, law, origins, and external appearance. And the barrier that divides them is, from his point of view, almost insurmountable. What unites them is their potential enmity, since "the European is to the men of other races what man himself is to the animals" to the extent that he "makes them serve his purposes, and when he cannot make them bend, he destroys them." Blacks have been the privileged subjects of this process of destruction, since their oppression has taken from them "nearly all the privileges of humanity." "The Negro of the United States has lost even the memory of his country; he no longer hears the language spoken by his fathers; he has renounced their religion and forgotten their mores. While thus ceasing to belong to Africa, however, he has acquired no right to the good things of Europe; but he has stopped between the two societies; he has remained isolated between the two peoples; sold by the one and repudiated by the other; finding in the whole world only the home of his master to offer him the incomplete picture of a native land."[7]

For Tocqueville, the Black slave embodies all the traits of debasement and abjection. He arouses aversion, repulsion, and disgust. A herd animal, he is the symbol of castrated and atrophied humanity from which emanates poisoned exhalations: he is a kind of constitutive horror. To encounter the slave is to experience an emptiness that is as spectacular as it is tragic. What characterizes him is the impossibility of finding a path that does not always return to servitude as its point of departure. It is the slave's taste for subjection. He "admires his tyrants even more than he hates them, and finds his joy and his pride in servile imitation of those who oppress him." As the property of another he is useless to himself. Since he does not dispose of the property of himself, "the care for his own fate has not devolved upon him. The very use of thought seems to him a useless gift from Providence, and he peacefully enjoys all the privileges of his servility." The enjoyment of the privileges of servility is an almost innate disposition. Here is a slave who is not in a struggle with his master. He risks nothing, not even his life. He does not struggle for his animal needs, much less to express sovereignty. He prefers his servitude and recoils when faced with death: "Servitude brutalizes him and liberty destroys him." The master, by contrast, lives in a constant fear of menace. The terror that envelops him is the possibility of being killed by his slave, a mere figure of a man that he does not even recognize as fully human.[8]

The fact that there is not a single Black person who has come freely to the shores of the New World is, for Tocqueville, one of the great dilemmas of American democracy. For him, there is no solution to the problem of the relationship between race and democracy, even though the central fact of race constitutes one of the future dangers for democracy. "The most formidable of all the evils that threaten the future of the United States arises from the presence of Blacks on their soil." "You can make the Negro free, but he remains in the position of a stranger vis-à-vis the European." In other words, the emancipation of the slaves cannot erase the stain of ignominy on them because of their race—the ignominy that means that Black necessarily rhymes with servitude. "The memory of slavery dishonors the race, and race perpetuates the memory of slavery," claims Tocqueville. "In this man who is born in lowliness," furthermore, "in this stranger that slavery introduced among us, we scarcely acknowledge the general features of humanity. His face appears hideous to us, his intelligence seems limited to us, his tastes are base; we very nearly take him for an intermediate being between brute and man."[9]

In liberal democracy, formal equality can therefore be paired with the natural prejudice that leads the oppressor to disdain those who were once his inferior even long after they have been emancipated. Without the destruction of prejudice, equality can only be imaginary. Even if the law makes of the Black Man an equal, he will never be like us. Tocqueville insists that there is an "insurmountable distance" separating the Blacks of

America from the Europeans. The difference is unchangeable. It has its roots in nature itself, and the prejudice that surrounds it is indestructible. For this reason, the relationship between the two races can only oscillate between the degradation of the Blacks and their enslavement by Whites, on the one hand, and the fear of the destruction of Whites by the Blacks, on the other. The antagonism is unsurpassable.[10]

The second kind of fear experienced by the White master is that he will be confused for the debased race and end up resembling his former slave. It is important, therefore, to keep his slaves at the margins, as far away from himself as possible—thus the ideology of separation. Even if the Black Man has obtained formal liberty, "he is not able to share either the rights or the pleasures or the labors or the pains or even the tomb of the one whose equal he has been declared to be; he cannot meet him anywhere, either in life or in death." As Tocqueville specifies, "the gates of heaven are not closed to him: but inequality scarcely stops at the edge of the other world. When the Negro is no more, his bones are thrown aside, and the difference in conditions is found again even in the equality of death." In fact, racial prejudice "seems to increase proportionately as Negroes cease to be slaves," and "inequality becomes imprinted in the mores as it fades in the laws." The abolition of the principle of servitude does not necessarily signify the liberation of the slaves and equal access. It only contributes to transforming them into "unfortunate remnants" doomed to destruction.[11]

Tocqueville believes that the question of the relationship between race and democracy can be resolved only in one of two ways: "Negroes and Whites must either blend entirely or separate." But he conclusively sets aside the first solution. "I do not think that the white race and the black race will come to live on an equal footing anywhere." This kind of mixing would only be possible, he argues, under a despotic regime. In a democracy the liberty of Whites can only be viable if accompanied by the segregation of Blacks and the isolation of the Whites among themselves. Since democracy is fundamentally incapable of resolving the racial question, the question that remains is how America can free itself of Blacks. To avoid a race war, Blacks must disappear from the New World and return home, to their countries of origin. This will allow an escape from slavery "without [Whites] having anything to fear from free Negroes." Any other option would result only in the "the ruin of one of the two races."[12]

Human like All Others?

In Tocqueville's period the terms of the question were therefore clear: could Blacks govern themselves? The doubt regarding the aptitude of Blacks for self-governance led to another, more fundamental doubt, one deeply embedded in the modern approach to the complex problem of alterity—and to the status of the *African sign* in the midst of the economy of alterity. To understand the political implications of these debates, we must remember that, despite the romantic revolution, Western metaphysics has traditionally defined the human in terms of the possession of language and reason. In effect, there is no humanity without language. Reason in particular confers on the human being a generic identity, a universal essence, from which flows a collection of rights and values. It unites all humans. It is identical in each of them. The exercise of this faculty generates liberty and autonomy, as well as the capacity to live an individual life according to moral principles and an idea of what is good. That being the case, the question at the time was whether Blacks were human beings like all others. Could one find among them the same humanity, albeit hidden under different designations and forms? Could one detect in their bodies, their language, their work, or their lives the product of human activity and the manifestation of subjectivity—in short, the presence of a conscience like ours—a presence that would authorize us to consider each of them, individually, as an alter ego?

These questions gave rise to three different kinds of answers with relatively distinct political implications. The first response was that the human experience of Blacks should be understood as fundamental difference. The humanity of Blacks had no history as such. Humanity without history understood neither work nor rules, much less law. Because they had not liberated themselves from animal needs, Blacks did not see either giving or receiving death as a form of violence. One animal can always eat another. The *African sign* therefore had something distinct, singular, even indelible that separated it from all other human signs. The best testament to this was the Black body, its forms and colors.[13] The body had no consciousness or any of the characteristics of reason or beauty. It could not therefore be considered a body composed of flesh like one's own, because it belonged solely to the realm of material extension as an object doomed to peril and destruction. The centrality of the body—and especially of its color—in the calculus of political subjection explains the importance assumed by theories of the physical, moral, and political regeneration of Blacks over the course of the nineteenth century. These theories developed conceptions of society and the world—and of the good—that claimed an absence among Blacks. They lacked the power of invention and the possibility of universalism that comes with reason. The representations, lives, works, languages, and actions of Blacks—or even their deaths—obeyed no rule or law whose meaning they themselves could, on their own authority, conceive or justify. Because of this radical difference, this *being-apart*, it was deemed legitimate to exclude them in practice and in law from the sphere of full and complete human citizenship: they had nothing to contribute to the work of the universal.[14]

A significant shift occurred at the moment of abolitionism and the end of the slave trade. The thesis of Blacks as "humans apart" certainly persisted. But there was a slight slippage within the old economy of alterity that permitted a second kind of response. The thesis of *nonsimilarity* was not repudiated, but it was no longer based on the emptiness of the sign as such. Now the sign was filled with content. If Blacks were beings *apart*, it was because they had things of their own, customs that should not be abolished or destroyed but rather modified. The goal was to inscribe difference within a distinct institutional system in a way that forced it to operate within a fundamentally inegalitarian and hierarchical order. The subject of this order was the native, and the mode of governance that befitted him was indirect administration—an inexpensive form of domination that, in the British colonies especially, made it possible to command natives in a regularized manner, with few soldiers, and to pit them against one another by bringing their own passions and customs into play.[15] Difference was therefore relativized, but it continued to justify a relationship of inequality and the right to command. Understood as natural, the inequality was nevertheless justified by difference.[16] Later, the colonial state used custom, or the principle of difference and inequality, in pursuit of the goal of segregation. Specific forms of knowledge (colonial science) were produced with the goal of documenting difference, purifying it of plurality and ambivalence, and fixing it in a canon. The paradox of the process of abstraction and reification was that it presented the appearance of recognition. But it also constituted a moral judgment since, in the end, custom was singularized only to emphasize the extent to which the world of the native, in its naturalness, did not coincide in any way with our own. It was not part of our world and could not, therefore, serve as the basis for a common experience of citizenship.

The third response had to do with the policy called assimilation. In principle, the idea of assimilation was based on the possibility of an experience of the world common to all human beings, or rather on the possibility of such an experience as premised on an essential similarity among all human beings. But this world common to all human beings, this similarity, was not granted outright to natives. They had to be converted to it. Education would be the condition under which they could be perceived and recognized as fellow human beings. Through it, their humanity would cease to be indefinable and incomprehensible. Once the condition was met, the *assimilated* became full individuals, no longer subject to custom. They could receive and enjoy rights, not by virtue of belonging to a particular ethnic group, but because of their status as autonomous subjects capable of thinking for themselves and exercising that particular human faculty that is reason. The *assimilated* signaled the possibility that the Black Man could, under certain conditions, become—if not equal or similar to us—at least our alter ego. Difference could be abolished, erased, or reabsorbed. Thus, the essence of the politics of assimilation consisted in desubstantializing and aestheticizing difference, at least for the subset of natives co-opted into the space of modernity by being "converted" or "cultivated," made apt for citizenship and the enjoyment of civil rights.

The Universal and the Particular

When Black criticism first took up the question of self-governance at the end of the Atlantic slave trade, and then during the struggles for decolonization, it inherited these three responses and the contradictions they had engendered. Criticism essentially accepted the basic categories then used in Western discourse to account for universal history. The notion of civilization was one of the categories.[17] It authorized the distinction between the human and the nonhuman—or the not-yet-sufficiently human that might become human if given appropriate training.[18] The three vectors of the process of domestication were thought to be conversion to Christianity, the introduction of a market economy through labor practices, and the adoption of rational, enlightened forms of government.[19] Among the first modern African thinkers, liberation from servitude meant above all the acquisition of the formal power to decide autonomously for oneself. Postwar African nationalism followed the tendencies of the moment by replacing the concept of civilization with that of progress. But this was simply a way to embrace the teleologies of the period.[20] The possibility of an alternative modernity was not excluded a priori, which explains why debates about "African socialism," for example, were so intense. But the problematic of the conquest of power dominated anticolonial national- ist thought and practices, notably in cases involving armed struggle. Two central categories were mobilized in the struggle to gain power and to jus- tify the right to sovereignty and self-determination: on the one hand, the figure of the Black Man as a "suffering will," a victimized and hurt subject, and, on the other, the recovery and redeployment by Blacks themselves of the thematic of cultural difference, which, as we have seen, was at the heart of colonial theories of inferiority and inequality.

Defining oneself in this way depended on a reading of the world that later ideological currents would amplify, one that laid claim as much to progressivism and radicalism as to nativism. At the heart of the paradigm of victimization was a vision of history as a series of inevitabilities. History was seen as essentially governed by forces that escape us, following a linear cycle in which there are no accidents, one that is always the same, spasmodic, infinitely repeating itself in a pattern of conspiracy. The con- spiracy is carried out by an external enemy that remains more or less hid- den and that gains strength from private complicities. Such a conspiratorial reading of history was presented as the radical discourse of emancipation and autonomy, the foundation for a so-called politics of Africanity. But behind the neurosis of victimization lurks in reality a negative and circular way of thinking that relies on superstition to function. It creates its own fables, which subsequently pass for reality. It makes masks that are con- served and remodeled in different epochs. So it is with the couple formed by the executioner (enemy) and his victim (the innocent). The enemy—the executioner—incarnates the absolute form of cruelty. The victim, full of vir- tue, is incapable of violence, terror, or corruption. In this closed universe, where "making history" becomes nothing more than flushing out one's en- emies or destroying them, any form of dissent is seen as extremism. There exists a Black subject only within a violent struggle for power—above all, the power to spill blood. The Black Man is a castrated subject, a passive instrument for the enjoyment of the Other, and becomes himself only through the act of taking the power to spill blood from the colonizer and using it himself. In the end, history moves within a vast economy of sorcery.

As we have underscored, Black discourse consists in part in appropriating the ideology of cultural difference for one's own purposes, in internalizing it and using it to one's own benefit. The ideology leans on the three crutches that are race, geography, and tradition. In fact, most political theories of the nineteenth century established a tight link between the human subject and the racial subject. To a large extent, they read the human subject first through the prism of race. Race itself was understood as a set of visible physiological properties with discernible moral characteristics. It was thought that these properties and characteristics were what distinguished human species from one another.[21] Physiological properties and moral characteristics made it possible to classify races according to a hierarchy whose violent effects were both political and cultural.[22] As we have already noted, the dominant classification during the nineteenth century excluded Blacks from the circle of humanity or at least assigned them an inferior status in the hierarchy of races. It is this denial of humanity (or inferior status) that forces such discourse to inscribe itself, from the beginning, in a tautology: "We are also human beings."[23] Or better yet: "We have a glorious past that proves our humanity."[24] That is also the reason that, at its origins, the discourse on Black identity is infused with a tension from which it still has difficulty escaping: are Blacks part of a generic humanity?[25] Or, in the name of difference and singularity, do Blacks insist on the possibility of diverse cultural forms within a single humanity—cultural forms whose vocation is not simply to reproduce themselves but also to seek a final, universal destination?[26]

In this sense, the reaffirmation of a human identity denied by others is part of a discourse of refutation and rehabilitation. But if the discourse of rehabilitation seeks to confirm the *cobelonging* of Blacks to humanity in general, it does not—except in a few rare cases—set aside the fiction of a racial subject or of *race in general*.[27] In fact, it embraces the fiction. This is true as much of Negritude as of the various versions of Pan-Africanism. In fact, in these propositions—all of them imbued with an imagined culture and an imagined politics—race is the foundation not only of difference in general but also of the very idea of nation and community, since racial determinants are seen as the necessary moral basis for political solidarity. Race serves as proof of (or sometimes justification for) the existence of the nation. It defines the moral subject as well as the immanent fact of consciousness. Within much of Black discourse, the fundamental foundations of nineteenth-century anthropology—the prejudice of evolutionary thinking and the belief in progress—remain intact. And the racialization of the nation and the nationalization of race go hand in hand.

The latent tension that has always broadly shaped reflection on Black identity disappears in the gap of race. The tension opposes a universalizing approach, one that proclaims a *cobelonging* to the human condition, with a particularizing approach that insists on difference and the dissimilar by emphasizing not originality as such but the principle of repetition (custom) and the values of autonomy. In the history of Black thought during the last two centuries, race has been the point of reconciliation between the two politico-cultural approaches. The defense of the humanity of Blacks almost always exists in tandem with claims about the specific character of their race, traditions, customs, and history. All language is deployed along this fault line, from which flow representations of what is "Black." We rebel not against the idea that Blacks constitute a distinct race but against the prejudice of inferiority attached to the race. The specificity of so-called African culture is not placed in doubt: what is proclaimed is the relativity of cultures in general. In this context the "work for the universal" consists in expanding the Western *ratio* of the contributions brought by Black "values of civilization," the "specific genius" of the Black race, for which "emotion" in particular is considered the cornerstone. It is what Senghor calls the "encounter of giving and receiving," one of whose results should be the mixing of cultures.[28]

The discourse of cultural difference was developed on the basis of these common beliefs. In the nineteenth century, there emerged attempts to settle on a general denomination and locate a place in which to anchor the prose of Black difference and the idea of African autonomy. Its geographic locus was tropical Africa, a place of fictions if ever there was one. The goal was to abolish the fantastic anatomy of the place that Europeans had invented and that Hegel and others echoed.[29] Somehow, the scattered limbs of Africa were gathered up and reattached, its fragmented body reconstructed in the imaginary zenith of race and in the radiance of myth.[30] The project was to locate Africanness in a collection of specific cultural traits that ethnographic research would furnish. Finally, nationalist historiography sought out what was lacking in ancient African empires—even in pharaonic Egypt.[31] This approach, taken up by ideological currents linked to progressivism and radicalism, consisted first in establishing a quasi-equivalence between race and geography, and then in creating a cultural identity that flowed from the relationship between the two terms. Geography became the ideal terrain in which the power of race and institutions could take form.[32] Pan-Africanism effectively defined the native and the citizen by identifying them as Black. Blacks became citizens because they were human beings endowed, like all others, with reason. But added to this was the double fact of their color and the privilege of indigeneity. Racial authenticity and territoriality were combined, and in such conditions Africa became the land of the Blacks. As a result, everything that was not Black had no place and consequently could not claim any sort of Africanity. The spatial body, racial body, and civic body all became one. The spatial body served as a witness to the common indigeneity by virtue of which all of those born there or sharing the same color and the same ancestors were brothers and sisters. The racial referent became the basis for civic kinship. In the process of determining who was Black and who was not, there was no way to imagine identity without racial consciousness. The Black Man would henceforth no longer be someone who simply participated in the human condition but *the person who, born in Africa, lives in Africa and is of the Black race*. The idea of an Africanity that is not Black simply became unthinkable. In this logic of identity assignation, non-Blacks were not from Africa (they were not natives) since they came from elsewhere (they were settlers). As a result, it was impossible to conceive of Africans of European origin.

But, because of the slave trade, it so happened that Blacks inhabited faraway lands. How was their inscription in a racially defined nation to be conceived when geography had separated them from their place of birth, which was far from the place where they lived and worked? Some proposed that the best way for them to consecrate their Africanity was purely and simply to return to Africa. Since the African geographic space constituted the natural homeland for Blacks, those who through slavery were taken far from the bosom of Africa lived in a condition of exile.[33] To a large extent, the horizon of the ultimate return (the back-to-Africa movement) infused the Pan-Africanist movement. More fundamentally, Pan-Africanism developed within a racist paradigm that triumphed in Europe during the nineteenth century.[34] It was a discourse of inversion, drawing its fundamental categories from the myths that it claimed to oppose and reproducing their dichotomies: the racial difference between Black and White, the cultural confrontation between the civilized and the savage, the religious opposition between Christians and pagans, the conviction that race founded nation and vice versa. It inscribed itself within an intellectual genealogy founded on *the territorialization of identity on the one hand and the racialization of geography on the other*, or the myth of a racial polis. And it forgot a key fact: that if exile was certainly the result of the rapacity of capitalism, its origins also lay in a family murder. There were fratricides.[35]

Tradition, Memory, Creation

We have just shown that, behind a particular rhetoric of cultural difference, a certain kind of political work was in fact being done, one that made choices within a form of memory that sought to order itself around the double desire for sovereignty and autonomy. Paradoxically, such work only reinforced the sense of resentment and the neurosis of victimization among Blacks. How might one take up the interrogation of Black difference in a new way, as a gesture not of resentment and nostalgia but of self-determination? Was it possible to take up this new line of questioning without critiquing memory and tradition, and with conscious effort to determine what, within difference itself, offered possibilities for creation and re-creation?

That was the question posed in 1885 by Alexander Crummell and framed in terms of a possible politics of the future, of "the time to come." He had in mind a category that was at once political and existential. For Crummell, the starting point for thinking about "the time to come" was the recognition that one cannot live in the past. The past can serve as inspiration. One can learn from the past. But the moral concepts of duty and responsibility, of obligation, flow directly from our understanding of the future. The time of the future is that of hope. The present is the time of duty. Crummell reproached Blacks for modeling their behavior excessively on that of the "children of Israel." "Long after the exodus from bondage, long after the destruction of Pharaoh and his host, they kept turning back, in memory and longings, after Egypt, when they should have kept both eye and aspiration bent toward the land of promise and of freedom." He saw this as a sign of "morbidity," the development of an economy of memory that turned "repulsive things" into residence, "to hang upon that which is dark, direful, and saddening," all of which led to degeneration. Such an attachment signaled an appetite for death. Against memory deployed as an irrepressible appetite for death, he opposed two kinds of capacities and practices: hope and imagination. Crummell distinguished between the memory of slavery and permanent reference to a history of misery and degradation. The passage from slavery to liberty required not only a subtle treatment of memory but also a reworking of dispositions and tastes. The reconstruction of oneself at the end of slavery consequently involved a tremendous amount of work on the self. The work consisted of inventing a new interiority.[36]

Fabien Eboussi Boulaga suggests that we read difference anew, as a vigilant form of memory, a critical model of identification, and a utopian project, all at once.[37] The assertion of Black difference in itself does not enable a gesture of either innocence or self-determination. It is a form of memory rooted in a vanquished and humiliated difference, parts of which have suffered an irredeemable loss and can never be recovered—they can only ever be evoked. The function of evocation can also be a function of deliverance, on the condition that evocation never lose itself in nostalgia and melancholia. There are internal aspects to any form of difference that expose it to violation and that "call for attack," as Boulaga puts it. And there are ways of summoning difference that seem like consent to subjection, just as there are forms of alienation in which one succumbs to constraint as well as seduction. Certain forms of difference carry within them the germs of their own destruction, their finitude. They represent a negative paradigm of difference, one that opens the door to the forces of dehumanization. And there is no reason a priori to remain in blind attachment to them.

Examining "tradition," Boulaga shows how the function of vigilance makes it possible to avoid repetition. "Vigilant memory seeks liberation from the repetition of the alienation of slavery and colonization," that is to say, "the domestication of man, his reduction to the condition of an object," the stripping of his world to the point that he "renounces or destroys himself, a stranger to his land, language, body, an excess within existence and history."[38] Other modalities of difference translate into either rejection or the fetishization of the foreign, and in some cases even the retranslation of everything new into old terms—which serves only to deny or neutralize. In other cases, negative difference takes form as the abandonment of responsibility, the culpabilization of everyone but oneself, or the permanent imputation that initial servitude was the result of external forces, which means throwing away one's own power. That said, Boulaga does not reject difference in itself. For him, recognizing the existence of what is not oneself, and what does not bring one back to oneself, goes hand in hand with the gesture of separation from others and identification with oneself. This moment of autonomy in relation to other humans is not, in principle, a negative moment. Because of the vicissitudes of history, such a moment, if experienced well, allows the Black Man to rediscover himself as an autonomous source of creation, to attest that he is human, to rediscover direction and a foundation for what he is and what he does. Positive difference is also an opening onto the future. It points not to an apologia but to the recognition of what each person, as a human, contributes to the work of the constitution of the world. In any case the attempt to destroy difference and the dream of imposing a single language on all are both doomed to failure. Unity is always just another name for multiplicity, and positive difference can only be a difference that is lively and interpenetrating. It is fundamentally an orientation toward the future.[39]

What remains is the deconstruction of tradition itself, which often serves as the counterpoint to the discourse of difference and reveals its invented character. In this view Africa as such—and we should add the Black Man—exists only on the basis of a text that constructs it as the fiction of the Other.[40] The text subsequently acquires such structuring power that the self, seeking to speak in its own authentic voice, runs the risk of speaking only in accordance with a preconstituted discourse that masks, censures, or requires imitation. In other words, Africa exists only because of a colonial library that intervenes in and interferes with everything—including the discourse that seeks to refute the library—to the extent that, in terms of identity, tradition, and authenticity, it is impossible, or at least very difficult, to distinguish the original from the copy, from its simulacrum. All one can do, therefore, is to problematize Black identity as an identity in the process of becoming. From this perspective, the world no longer constitutes a threat in itself but appears instead as a vast reservoir of affinities.[41] No Black identity exists in the form of a book of Revelation. There exists instead an identity in the process of becoming, nourished by the ethnic, geographic, and linguistic differences among Blacks and by the traditions inherited through the encounter with what Édouard Glissant calls the *Tout-Monde*, the *All-World*.

The Circulation of Worlds

Within the history of cultural practices, difference is constituted through a triple process of entanglement, mobility, and circulation. Let us take as an example the disciplines of Islam and Christianity. As one of the oldest containers for Black identity, at least in certain regions of the continent, Islam long preceded the Atlantic trade and the colonial period. It consisted of different traditions organized within brotherhoods in which the religious elites reinterpreted and taught the Koran, seeking to translate its protocols into a legal order that could be imposed on both believers and nonbelievers. From this point of view, Islam functioned as a formal system of governance, as a producer of subjects and a figure of sovereignty.

Despite their diversity, one element united the different traditions: the privilege that they accorded to faith in determining the relationship between identity, politics, and history. In many ways the authority carried by these traditions was a conquering identity that was sure of itself. The ways of governing, believing, and trading were linked according to the principle of communicating vessels. And if there is something that separated Islam from other religions in Africa, it was probably the way in which the act of piety responded, like an echo, to the act of war. In effect, in order to impose itself, the Islamic faith used both power and a certain aesthetic of violence. So-called holy wars and forced conversions were legitimized and authorized through invocations of the necessity of rectitude and salvation. When forced conversion overtook voluntary adhesion, a master–slave relationship superimposed itself on the ties linking believer to nonbeliever.

With laws of religion defining the modes of belonging and exclusion, the observance of religious precepts (how to live morally in the eyes of God) became the condition of admission into an imagined nation whose physical and symbolic borders encompassed a wide-ranging community of believers. Outside of the domain of believers, outside of its towns, caravans, merchants, and scholars, there existed nothing but impiety. Everything situated outside the limits of the world of revelation (the *dar al-Islam*, or the empire of Islam) was destined to be raided and reduced to slavery. The new lands sought out for Islam constituted the *dar al-harb*, the land of war. As Islam penetrated Africa, it carried this bellicose intent, along with the appetite for luxury and brutality that was its corollary. Yet warring hardly prevented Islam from offering the proposition of a fully ethical life to the converted.

The second discipline is Christianity. In the beginning the Judeo-Christian relationship with Africa was dominated by the motif of darkness, of a primordial tragedy that consisted in masking what was true beneath all kinds of superstition. In the Judeo-Christian narrative Africa serves as the metaphor par excellence of the Fall. Inhabited by humans chained in a night of shadows, Africa lived away from God. This in fact was the essence of paganism: disguise everywhere, distraction, the absence of discernment, the refusal to look toward the light—in short, the corruption of what is. But Judeo-Christianity replaced the bellicose relationship of Islam with another form of violence: that of mercy and pity. The project, in effect, aimed to remove the chains, to separate the world of appearances and the regime of falsehood from truth. It was a theology of foreshadowing: appearances simulate presence, and it was this presence that had to be awakened.

Christianity offered itself as a replacement for a life lived purely as an object, stripped of all moral and aesthetic content, in a static and unchanging world peopled with masks and fetishes and a multitude of profane objects and brute human material. It offered the natives initiation into a process of seizing the truth, a project of deliverance and healing, in short, the promise of a new life. In the process Christianity did not simply abolish the world of allegory. Rather, it established a new relationship between it and the world of the event. The event was the promise of being chosen for salvation—itself a collection of ideas that could be qualified as magico-poetic, given their bewitching power. Such was the case with the resurrection of the dead, a sublime dream driven by the desire for an absolute time, the infinite horizon of the time and space of immortality. The price of admission to promised salvation was the abandonment of a dissipated existence in exchange for redemption. Conversion and the truth that it revealed required, in turn, true work on oneself, the erasure of any distinct and separate identity, the abolition of difference, and a process of rallying to a humanity that was henceforth considered universal.

We find the same project of universalization in colonization. It presented itself, at least rhetorically, as the daughter of the Enlightenment and as such proclaimed a form of governance that flowed from universal reason. Universal reason assumed the existence of subjects of the same name, whose universality was founded on their humanity. The recognition of a common humanity made it possible to consider each individual as a juridical person within civil society. It was possible to speak of a universal subject only because a certain notion of rights in which all were considered identical, and all had value, was generally recognized. Colonial discipline formalized two mechanisms of social and political organization that were justified by the invocation of reason: the state and the market. The state appeared first in its primitive form, that of "commandment," before mutating into a system for the civilization of habits. In its primitive form, the market was inscribed in the native imaginary in its most abject form: the traffic in human beings. As the appetite for merchandise intensified, only gradually did the market transform itself into a vast machine for the production of desire. After World War II, colonial discipline offered the colonized a glimpse of three other kinds of goods: citizenship, nation, and civil society. But it outlawed their access to them until its final phase. As with Islam and Christianity, colonization was a project of universalization. Its purpose was to inscribe the colonized in the space of modernity. But its vulgarity, its often casual brutality, and its bad faith all made it a perfect example of antiliberalism.

Contemporary African identities were not formed in relation to a past experienced like a spell cast once and for all. Rather, they often depended on a general capacity to bracket the past. This was the condition for being open to both the present and life under way. A historical reading of the local reappropriations of the three disciplines evoked above indicates as much. Africans countered the Islamic project with what we might call a response of creative assimilation. Cultures shaped by oral communication relativized the hegemony of the book. The doctrinal core was reinterpreted in a way that largely left open the question of what truly constituted an Islamic society or government. From this openness—which at the same time was a refusal to foreclose on new encounters—there emerged popular practices of observance of the faith and the law that gave ample space to the arts of healing and divination, for example, or to the interpretation of dreams—in sum, to the resources of mysticism and the great orphic knowledge of local traditions.

Islamic Africa also produced scholars and reformers, most of whom were also warriors. Others were great merchants involved in long-distance trade. Scribes, scholars, jurists, and interpreters of the Koran, along with simple slaves and griots, built the terrestrial community and reinterpreted the inherited stories of the Prophet, their eyes fixed on merchandise. Some heeded the call of luxury. Attentive to the details of the location and the situation, and in bold commerce with the world, they rewrote Islam itself and African identity, often in unexpected ways. Out of this process emerged several varieties of Islam and a plurality of politico-religious cultures. At the heart of certain traditions, the state itself became just one possible variant of social organization, one that could not solely contain the imaginary of the community. In others, political authority itself was marked with suspicion. Did it not threaten to corrupt religion? From this emerged the argument for "retreat" put forth by many scholars. Elsewhere, an Islamic form of public life depended not on inherited status but on spiritual submission to the sheikh (in the case of the Sufis). For others, voluntary membership in a brotherhood became more important than religious conscription.

In all of these cases, the diversity of doctrinal responses was expressed as much from a theological point of view as through popular faith practices. The three categories of rational judgment (the necessary, the impossible, and the contingent) significantly softened the dogma of absolute divinity. And a pedagogy based on memorization gave birth to a religious and profane culture in which it was not necessary to master the Arabic language, and where esoteric signs took on a weight equal to, or even greater than, objective reality. Among all of the encounters between Africa and the monotheistic religions, it is probably with respect to Islam that the metaphor of the "marriage of the tree and language" evoked by Walter Benjamin is most apt. Limbs grow and the peak gains in height, but the branches conceal neither their form nor their inaccessibility. A gentle breeze sways and scatters leaves, which curl inward to protect themselves, while the trunk remains forever seated on the roots.

Many factors explain the diversity of responses to religion. The first is linked to the capacity for extension and spatial dispersion, and therefore to the negotiation of distance. In West Africa several channels connect the Arabic/Berber and Black/African worlds. Brotherhoods disperse from certain geographic poles in organized migration and long-distance trade.

No matter how far they travel, migrants maintain tight links with their places of departure. Something of the nature of an image attaches them to their places of origin and compels them to return. Identity, then, is created at the interface between the ritual of rootedness and the rhythm of distancing, in a constant passage from the spatial to the temporal, from the imaginary to the orphic.

The second factor has to do with a border practice that privileges *itinerant identities* and circulation. Historically, attachment to Africa—to the territory, to its soil—was always contextual. In some cases political entities were delimited not so much by borders in the classic sense but by an imbrication of multiple spaces, constantly produced, unmade, and remade as much through wars and conquests as by the movement of goods and people. Productive correspondences between people and things were established through the deployment of extremely complex scales of measurement. People could be converted into things, as was the case during the slave trade. One might say that precolonial territoriality, by operating through thrusts, detachments, and splits, was an *itinerant territoriality*, a fact that shaped the constitution of identities.

In other cases the mastery of space depended on the control of human beings. And in still others it depended on the control of localities. Sometimes it was a combination of the two. There could exist vast distances between distinct political entities, true buffers without direct control, exclusive domination, or close supervision. Occasionally, spatial dynamics seeking to make the border a true physical and social limit went hand in hand with the principle of dispersion and the deterritorialization of allegiances. Strangers, slaves, and subjects could in effect rely on several different sovereignties at one time. The multiplicity of allegiances and jurisdictions itself responded to the plurality of the forms of territoriality. The result was often an extraordinary superposition of rights and an entanglement of social links that were not based on kinship, religion, or castes understood in isolation. Such rights and links combined with the signs of local belonging. Yet they simultaneously transcended them. Diverse centers of power could exert control in a place that itself depended on another that was close by, far away, or even imaginary.

Borders, whether of a state or not, acquired meaning only through their relationships to other forms of difference and social, jurisdictional, and cultural distinctions, or through the forms of contact and interpenetration at work in a given space. They were not borders in the legal sense of the term but rather the outlines of imbricated countries and spaces. They could be expanded through conquest and acquisition. Borders were often characterized by their extensibility and incompleteness. It is therefore likely that, in the past, the processes of identity formation were shaped by the same logic that governed the institution of borders and the social struggles linked to their constitution. It was a logic of networks that operated according to the principle of entanglement. The institutions tasked with negotiating the border were the same as those charged with negotiating identities, regulating the caravan trade, cementing vertical and lateral alliances, and sometimes carrying out war. In fact, war, mobility, and commerce were combined in most cases, notably where war and commerce went together with the propagation of Islam. There is indeed no trade that does not have the capacity to create transversal alliances, to extend and invest nodal points within a space that is constantly in motion. And war is always a war of movement. True identity, in this context, is not necessarily what fixes a location. It is what makes it possible to negotiate the crossing of spaces that are themselves in circulation because they are of variable geometry.

Finally, there was mimetic genius. From end to end, the cultural history of Islam in Africa is marked less by critical exactitude than by an extraordinary power of imitation and an unparalleled talent for producing resemblances on the basis of different signs and languages. Many African Islamic traditions resolve the problem of the foreignness of Islam in complex ways. Their religious identity is constructed by gathering together words that signify different things in different languages and ordering them around a central signifier that functions at once as image and mirage, parable and allegory. Because it manages to weave onomatopoeic relationships between writing and language, Islam constitutes the most perfect archive of resemblance in the history of identity formation in Africa.

Compared with the very old presence of Islam on the continent, the process of osmosis between Christianity and indigenous cultural forms is a recent one. But African responses to the universalist Judeo-Christian project have been equally complex. African Christian theology followed nativist discourse and, from the beginning, crystallized around the notion that the encounter between Christian dogma and the indigenous universe of signification was one of loss and splitting that led to the erasure of identity.[42] But recent anthropology and historiography have revealed that the practices of the actors have been very different. While theologians of enculturation worried that conversion would involve the abolition of the self, Christianity in practice was turned upside down, undone, and then outfitted in masks and ancestral bric-a-brac, all without ever being stripped of its core concept. It appeared to Blacks as, first of all, an immense field of signs that, once decrypted, opened the way for an array of practices that moved constantly away from orthodoxy.[43] Africans used Christianity as a mirror through which to represent their own society and history to themselves.

To a large extent, this explains the apparent facility with which Christianity was domesticated and translated into local systems of intelligibility. It offered itself to Africans as a form of allegory and aesthetics as well, becoming the object of a great deal of work on forms and languages. Among these was the language of the Spirit and its absolute power, which offers simultaneously an entry into utopia and a spectacle that repeatedly authorizes the doubling of time and an upside-down approach to the world and to things. And we cannot underestimate Christianity's power of enchantment. Like colonialism, it was received as a kind of magic: a combination of terror and seduction that perfectly translated the categories of salvation and redemption. From this point of view, the desire for sovereignty so well condensed in the idea of the resurrection of the dead played a crucial role in the reception of Christianity among Blacks. The power of the metaphor resided in its tragico-poetic depth, its dreamlike violence, and its capacity to produce symbols. On the one hand, it was a manifestation—in all its splendor and misery—of the limits of the principle of divinity itself: the history of a God whose existence ends on a cross. On the other hand, there resides within the dream a power to create enchantment in human life precisely where it is most difficult to capture: it is the triumph of a man clothed in the finery of divine sovereignty, a man whose omnipotence disappears abruptly on the evening of his death, at his exit from his tomb.

Most Pentecostalist movements in Africa use the power of enchantment and symbol creation as a resource. Both allow believers to envision their existence not in a purely political or instrumentalist way but rather as a site for artistic gestures, an aesthetic project that opens up space as much for action toward oneself and the world as for meditation and contemplation. It is impossible to understand the contemporary forms of African identity without taking into consideration the heretical genius at the root

FOUR
THE LITTLE
SECRET

This chapter diverges, in several ways, from the preoccupations that usually surround debates on memory, history, and forgetting. My concern is not to specify the status of memory within historiography or within processes of knowledge more generally, much less to untangle the relations between collective memory and individual memory, or between living memory and dead memory. The differences (but also the similarities) between memory as a sociocultural phenomenon and history as epistemology are clearly complex, and the interferences between historical discourse and the discourse of memory are obvious. The goal here is rather to say a few words about how we might think through the modes of inscription of the colony within the Black text.

Defining the problem presents obvious difficulties. The Black forms of mobilizing the memory of the colony vary depending on the period, the stakes, and the context. As for the modes of representation of the colonial experience as such, they extend from active commemoration to forgetting, passing through nostalgia, fiction, repression, amnesia, and reappropriation as well as diverse forms of instrumentalization of the past in the service of ongoing social struggles. Countering instrumentalist readings of the colonial past, I will stress that memory, like remembrance, nostalgia, or forgetting, comprises first and foremost interlaced psychic images. It is in this form that they appear in the symbolic and political fields, and in the field of representation. Their content consists of primary, original experiences that took place in the past, to which one was not necessarily a witness. The significance of memory, remembrance, and forgetting lies less in truth than in the play of symbols and their circulation, in the gaps, lies, difficulties of articulation, and many small failures and slips—in sum, in the resistance to confession. Memory, remembrance, and forgetting are powerful systems of representation and, strictly speaking, also symptomatic acts. They have meaning only in relation to a secret that in reality is not a secret but that one nonetheless refuses to admit. They are thus the products of psychic work and of a critique of time.

I am especially interested in those aspects of Black memory of the colony that transform memory into a site of loss, on the one hand, and into the place where debts are settled, on the other. In certain canonical Black texts the colony appears foremost as a site of loss, which in turn makes it possible to demand that the ex-colonizer pay a debt to the ex-colonized. This is connected to the very nature of the colonial potentate and the manner in which it implements the two means of control that are terror (the accursed share) and fantasia (its little secret). The fact remains, nonetheless, that to remember the colony is not simply to begin the process of psychic work. It is also to undertake a critique of both time and the artifacts that ultimately serve as substitutes for the substance of time itself (statues, steles, monuments, effigies).

Histories of the Potentate

In African writings of the self, the colony appears as a primal scene. But it occupies more than just the space of memory, functioning in the manner of a mirror. The colony is also represented as one of the signifying matrices of the language on past and present, identity and death. The colony is the body that gives substance and weight to subjectivity, something one not only remembers but continues to experience viscerally long after its formal disappearance. Blacks bestow on the colony the attributes of a founding power in possession of a psyche, that which doubles the living body, "a copy that one substitutes for the body, that shares its same appearance, manner of dress, gestures and voice," while at the same time participating in a shadow whose essence is evanescence—a fact that only adds to its morphogenous power.[1]

Through literature, music, religions, and cultural artifacts, Blacks have therefore developed a phenomenology of the colony that in various ways resembles what is referred to in psychoanalysis as "the experience of the mirror." It is not only the confrontation between the colonized and his mirror image that is acted out on this stage but also the relation of capture that bound his descendants to the terrifying image and demon of the Other—to its totem, reflected in the mirror. More radically, in canonical Black texts the colony always appears as the scene where the self was robbed of its content and replaced by a voice, one that, in the form of a sign, always turns away, revokes, inhibits, suspends, and obstructs the will for authenticity. For this reason, in African discourse, to remember the colony is almost always to recall the primordial displacement between the self and the subject.

One may generally deduce from the original diffraction that the *authentic self has become another*. An (alienated) foreign self has been substituted for the real self, turning the Black into a carrier, despite himself, of secret significations, of obscure intentions, of something uncanny that determines his existence unbeknownst to him and that confers a nocturnal, even demonic character on certain aspects of his psychic and political life. The West, subsequently, is allegedly entirely guilty of this internal fracture. The process of healing, then, depends on putting an end to the psychic split. To escape *this* (the colony as a figure of intrusion and discord) requires that an original symbolic matrix (tradition)—capable of preventing the division of the Black body—be restored to the subject. The ex-colonized will henceforth be able to be born into themselves, and into a world entirely their own in all ways, and the madness to which the mirror leads will finally be conjured away. It is hardly surprising that such a central place has been ascribed to the colony in the discourse on the formation of the Black "self," and that the colony has been accepted as an experience so crucial to the advent of subjectivity. This relates, on the one hand, to the nature of the colonial potentate and, on the other, to the manner in which the potentate produced its subjects, and to the way they welcomed the power that presided over their placement in the world.

In his time Frantz Fanon, who experienced all of this directly, demonstrated that the colony was the result of a "continuous military conflict, reenforced by a civil and police administration." In other words, the principal matrix of the technique of domination that is colonialism is war, that maximal form of *struggle to the death*.[2] We could add, paraphrasing Michel Foucault, that struggle to the death in the colony is, at its most basic level, a racial war.[3] The civil administration and police attempted to transform this original relationship of violence, this first relationship of confrontation, into a permanent social relationship and an inescapable foundation for all colonial institutions of power. That is why Fanon writes that violence is not just consubstantial with colonial oppression. In such a system established through violence, time itself is a "function of the maintenance of violence."[4]

This violence has three dimensions. It is violence in the "daily behavior" of the colonizer toward the colonized; "violence in regards to the past" of the colonized, which is "emptied of all substance"; and violence and insult in relation to the future, "for the colonial regime offers itself as having to be eternal." But in reality colonial violence is a network, "a node of encounter between multiple, diverse, re-iterated and cumulative forms of violence," experienced as much on the level of the spirit as in "muscles, and blood."[5] For Fanon, the muscular dimension of colonial violence is such that the dreams of the native are profoundly affected. The muscular tension of the colonized is liberated periodically either in sanguinary explosions (notably in tribal conflicts) or in dance and possession. Moreover, practices such as dance and possession constitute, in Fanon's eyes, forms of relaxation for the colonized, which tend to take the form of a "muscular orgy in which the most acute aggressivity and the most impelling violence are canalized, transformed, and conjured away."[6]

Fanon went on to show that the colony had to be thought as a formation of power endowed with a characteristic sensory life. In order to function, this power structure depended on a phantasmagoric mechanism without which each repetition of the founding colonial gesture was bound to fail. Before him, Aimé Césaire stressed that colonization in principle was driven by two maleficent shadows: on one hand, what he designated as its "appetite" or "cupidities" and, on the other, violence (notably the fact of killing, pillaging, brainwashing). To this he added "sadistic pleasures, the nameless delights, that send voluptuous shivers and quivers through Loti's carcass when he focuses his field glasses on a good massacre of the Annamese." Césaire—and later Fanon—explained that this archaic gesture (to kill, pillage, brainwash) constituted the *accursed share* of the colony and originated in the principle of sacrifice. The colonizer insists on "seeing the other man as *an animal*, accustoms himself to treating him like an animal, and tends objectively to transform *himself* into an animal."[7] In other words, the deep roots of the colony must be sought in the unlimited experience of death or in the expenditure of life. That experience, as we know, has been a major feature of European history, of its social operations of production and accumulation, of its statism, its wars, and even its religious and artistic production. But its most incandescent point was race, because it was there that the desire for sacrifice manifested itself.[8]

Fanon stressed that life in the colony was constituted by impulses and conflicts, by psychosomatic and mental disturbances—an agitated existence, a quasi-permanent state of alarm. He also stressed that underlying the colonial potentate were two contradictory logics that, together, operated to annul the possibility for the emergence of an autonomous subject within the colonial context. The first logic consisted in not accepting difference, and the second in refusing similarities. The colonial potentate was thus a narcissistic potentate.[9] By hoping that the colonized would imitate it, while also prohibiting such imitation, the potentate transformed the colony into the very figure of the "anticommunity," a place where, paradoxically, division and separation (what Fanon calls the "principle of reciprocal exclusivity") constituted the very forms of being together and where the principal form of communication between colonial subjects and their masters (namely, violence and profits) constantly reiterated the sacrificial relation and ratified the generalized exchange of death.[10] If there is a domain in which all of these paradoxes become evident, it is, according to Fanon, in the relation between medicine (*to heal*) and colonialism (*to harm*).[11] The body that at times is locked up, "stripped down, chained, forced to labor, beat, deported, and killed" is the same one that, elsewhere, is "cared for, educated, dressed, nourished, and compensated."[12] In the colony the subject that receives care is the same one that, elsewhere, is the object of mutilation.[13] It is as human waste, reject, and residue that the subject appears at the site of therapy. Wretched and constantly exposed to injury, he will previously have been totally disgraced, like a slave under the plantation regime.[14] Defined by indignity and vulnerability, filled here and there with pieces of an ill-assorted and pathetic humanity, he responds only to abjection and to the very forms of the misery to which he has been reduced.[15]

As a result, instead of inspiring empathy, his suffering and his cries arouse only more disgust. It is in this relationship between healing and injuring that the paradox of "commandment" appears in all its violence. It is a grotesque and brutal power that in theory brings together the attributes of logic (reason), fantasy (the arbitrary), and cruelty.[16] Whether in acts of destruction (for example, wars, torture, massacres, and even genocides), in rage directed against the native, or in expressions of power directed against the native-as-object within purely sexual or sadistic activities, the lived impulses of commandment are inseparable from the ways in which the colonial potentate perceives itself as a racial potentate, or in conflict with "inferior races."[17] Regarding torture in particular, Fanon says that it is "not an accident, or an error, or a fault. Colonialism cannot be understood without the possibility of torturing, of violating, or of massacring. Torture is an expression and a means of the occupant-occupied relationship."[18] It starts with an action carried out in public: "a father taken into custody in the street in the company of his children, stripped along with them, tortured before their eyes."[19] It continues when the colonized finds himself with the "electrode at his genitals" and soon takes shape at the very heart of practices aimed at human health, those that heal wounds and silence pain—in the collusion between medical personnel, the police, and the military.[20] But one of the effects of torture is also to pervert those who are its instruments. Such was notably the case with certain police torturers who were haunted by their victims and pushed to the edge of madness during the Algerian war: "They hit their children hard, for they think they are still with Algerians. They threaten their wives, for 'I threaten and execute all day long.' They do not sleep, because they hear the cries and the moans of their victims."[21]

The colonial potentate, then, reproduces itself in several ways. First, it invents the colonized: "it is the settler who has brought the native into existence and who perpetuates his existence."[22] Then it crushes this inessential invention, making it sometimes a thing, sometimes an animal, sometimes a human being in perpetual becoming. And, finally, it constantly injures the humanity of the subjected, multiplies the wounds on his body, and assails his mind in the hope of leaving scars: "Because it is a systematic negation of the other person and a furious determination to deny the other person all attributes of humanity, colonialism forces the people it dominates to ask themselves, constantly, the question: 'In reality, who am I?'" To grasp the magnitude of the mental pathologies produced by oppression, writes Fanon, one has only "to study" and be "alive to" the "number and the depth of the injuries inflicted upon a native during a single day spent amidst the colonial regime."[23] "To command," moreover, requires above all the capacity to silence the native. In various respects the colony is a place where the colonized are not permitted to speak for themselves. The prohibition on speech is linked to the process that confines the colonized to appearing naked: either as a castoff or residue or as something emptied of content, whose life, bereft of any significance except that granted by the master, is only worth something based on its ability to generate profit. The body of the colonized becomes his tomb. Not only does commandment attempt to create prejudice in the name of civilization. It goes hand in hand with the resolve to humiliate and injure the native, to make him suffer, while at the same time taking satisfaction in his suffering and the sense of pity and disgust that it ultimately generates. And if in the end one must take his life, the native's death must take place as close to the mud as possible.[24] Henceforth a wandering shadow, he must go through his own demise without crossing through it.

The colonial potentate also strives to create its own world out of the debris of the one that it found when it arrived. It intends to arrange the world that it has discovered according to its own logic. "In order to better erase the vestiges of enemy domination, we previously took care to tear up or burn all the written documents, administrative registers, authentic or other records, that could have perpetuated the traces of what was done before us," writes Alexis de Tocqueville on the subject of the French occupation of Algeria. "The conquest," he continues, "was a new era, and out of fear of mixing the past and the present in an irrational fashion, we even destroyed a great many of the streets of Algiers, in order to rebuild them according to our own method, and we gave French names to all those that we consented to have remain."[25] The potentate wants to arrange the world it has found according to a logic of its own liking. It puts a great deal of affect and energy into the project. As it modifies agricultural systems, deals with money and value, transforms housing patterns, dresses the colonized, and cures the natives, transforming them into new "moral subjects," commandment is ashamed of its fantasies and barely conceals them.[26] There is thus something Dionysian about the act of colonization. It is a grand, narcissistic outpouring. The mix of voluptuousness, frenzy, cruelty, drunkenness, and dreaming that is one of the structural dimensions of the colonial enterprise can be understood only in relation to that form of enchantment that is both unrest and turmoil. The colonial world, after all, includes many of the characteristics that Friedrich Nietzsche recognized in Greek tragedy: "the phenomenon that pain arouses pleasure, that exultation tears cries of agony from the breast," while "out of the most extreme moment of joy the scream of terror or the yearning lament for an irreplaceable loss sounds forth."[27]

The Enigmatic Mirror

Race is at the center of this tragedy. To a large extent, race is an iconic currency. It appears at the edges of a commerce—of the gaze. It is a currency whose function is to convert what one sees (or what one chooses not to see) into a specie or symbol at the heart of a generalized economy of signs and images that one exchanges, circulates, attributes value to or not, and that authorizes a series of judgments and practical attitudes. It can be said of race that it is at once image, body, and enigmatic mirror within an economy of shadows whose purpose is to make life itself a spectral reality. Fanon understood this and showed how, alongside the structures of coercion that presided over the arrangement of the colonial world, what first constitutes race is a certain power of the gaze that accompanies a form of voice and, ultimately, touch. If the gaze of the colonist "shrivels me" or "freezes me," if his voice "turns me into stone," it is because he believes that my life does not have the same weight as his does.[28] Describing what he called the "lived experience of the Negro," Fanon analyzes how a certain manner of distributing the gaze ends up creating its object, fixing it, or destroying it, or returns it to the world but under the sign of disfiguration or at least of "another me," a me that is an object, a marginal being. A certain form of the gaze has, in effect, the power to block the appearance of the "third-being" and his inclusion in the sphere of the human: "I simply wanted to be a man among other men."[29] "And here I am an object in the midst of other objects." How, starting from the desire to be a human being like others, does one arrive at the realization that we are what the Other has made of us—its object? "And then we were given the occasion to confront the white man's gaze. An usual weight descended on us. The real world robbed us of our share," he continues.[30]

The final recourse of colonial racism is to dispute the humanity of this "triple person." The struggle fixates first on the body. For Fanon, the appearance of the third-being within the field of racism happens first in the form of a body. "All around the body reigns an atmosphere of certain uncertainty." Very quickly the body becomes a weight—the weight of a "malediction," which makes it into the simulacrum of the void and fragility. Even before it appeared, this body was already put on trial: "I thought I was being asked to construct a physiological self," but "the white man" had "woven me out of a thousand details, anecdotes, and stories." The body from then on is an apparently formless form that incites surprise, dread, and terror: "Look, a Negro! Mama, look, a Negro, I'm scared!" He exists only through his inspection and assignation within a skein of significations that are beyond him: "I was responsible not only for my body but also for my race and my ancestors."[31] For the Black Man to be seen and for him to be identified as such, a veil must have already been placed over his face, making it a face "bereft of all humanity."[32] Without this veil there is no Black Man. The Black Man is a shadow at the heart of a commerce of the gaze. Such commerce has a gloomy dimension, almost funereal, for in order to function it demands elision and blindness.

To see is not the same as to look. You can look without seeing. And it is not clear that what one sees is in fact what is. But looking and seeing have in common the fact that they solicit judgment, enclosing what is seen or the person who is not seen in inextricable networks of meaning—the beams of history. In the colonial distribution of seeing, the desire for either objectification or erasure, or an incestuous desire, a desire for possession or rape, is always there.[33] But the colonial gaze also serves as the very veil that hides this truth. Power in the colony therefore consists fundamentally in the power to see or not to see, to remain indifferent, to render invisible what one wishes not to see. And if it is true that "the world is that which we see," then we can say that in the colony those who decide what is visible and what must remain invisible are sovereign.[34]

Race, then, exists only by way of "what we do not see." Beyond "what we do not see," there is no race. The pou(voir), or seeing power, of race is expressed first in the fact that the persons we choose not to see or hear cannot exist or speak for themselves. When necessary, they must be silenced. But their speech is always indecipherable, or at least inarticulate. Someone else must speak in their name and in their place so that what they say makes complete sense in our language. As Fanon, and before him W. E. B. Du Bois, has shown, the person dispossessed of the faculty to speak is constrained always to think of himself, if not as an "intruder," then at least as someone who can only ever appear in the social world as a "problem."

Race is also the expression of a desire for simplicity and transparence—the desire for a world without surprises, without drapery, without complex shapes. It is the expression of resistance to multiplicity. It is, in the end, an act of imagination as much as an act of misunderstanding. All of this is then deployed in the calculation of power and domination to the extent that race not only excites the passions but heats the blood and leads to monstrous acts. But considering race as a simple "appearance" is not enough. Race is not only a regulating fiction, nor merely a more or less coherent group of falsifications and nontruths. The power of race derives precisely from the fact that, in racist conscience, appearance is taken as the true reality of things. In other words, appearance is not the opposite of reality. As Nietzsche would say, "appearance is reality."[35]

Finally, colonial racism also originates in what Fanon sometimes calls "sexual anxiety" or "sexual inferiority." He argues that if we want to understand psychoanalytically how the racial situation is experienced by certain consciences, "considerable importance must be given to sexual phenomena." More specifically, the archaic origin of racism—and its vacillating object negrophobia—is fear of the hallucinatory sexual power attributed to the Black Man. For the majority of Whites, he affirms, the Black Man represents the uneducated sexual instinct. "Isn't the white man who hates Blacks prompted by a feeling of impotence or sexual inferiority? Since virility is taken to be the absolute ideal, doesn't he have a feeling of inadequacy in relation to the black man, who is viewed a penis symbol? Isn't lynching the black man sexual revenge?"[36] This phenomenon is not specifically colonial. The lynching of Black men in the U.S. South during the time of slavery and after the Emancipation Proclamation (1862–1863) was based in part on a desire to castrate them. Overcome by anxiety about their own sexual potential, the racist poor Whites and the planters were seized with terror when they thought about the "black sword," which they feared not only for its supposed size but also for its penetrative and assailing essence. In the obscene gesture of lynching, the goal was to protect the supposed purity of the White woman by holding the Black Man up to the level of his death. He was meant to contemplate the obscuring and extinction of what, in the racist fantasy, was seen as his "sublime sun," his phallus. The rending of his masculinity was achieved by transforming his virile attributes into a field of ruins—their separation from the powers of life. All this occurs because, as Fanon puts it, the Black Man does not exist in this configuration. Or, rather, the Black Man is above all only a member.

For Fanon, granting the Black Man a sexual power that he does not have is the expression of a double logic: the logic of neurosis and that of perversity, such as in a sadomasochistic act. In reality, the specular hallucination revolving around the Black phallus manifests the incest problem that inhabits all racist consciousness. It is also the manifestation of nostalgia for "extraordinary times of sexual licentiousness, orgies, unpunished rapes, and unrepressed incest." Projecting his fantasies onto the Black Man, the racist acts as if the Black Man whose imago he has constructed actually exists. The alienation begins in earnest once the Black Man, in response, reproduces this imago, not only as if it were true, but as if he himself were its author. But racism aims symbolically above all for castration, or the annihilation of the penis, the symbol of virility. "But the black man is attacked in his corporeality," Fanon points out. The paradox of the gesture is that "no longer do we see the black man, we see a penis; the black man has been occulted. . . . He *is* a penis."[37]

The Erotics of Merchandise

In parallel with this accursed share, whose origins are located in terror, colonization presents two other characteristics to which Fanon attends. The first is the *violence of ignorance*—that "profound ignorance" that Tocqueville had identified in 1837 in his "Letter on Algeria." In it he mentions, naturally, the ignorance of languages, of the "different races" that inhabit the colony, of the division of "tribes" and their customs, of the "country itself, its resources, its rivers, its towns, its climate." The French, he writes, "didn't know what the military aristocracy of the *spahis* was, and as for the *marabouts*, it took them a long time to figure out, when they talked about them, people were referring to a tomb or a man." He concludes, "The French didn't know about any of these things and, in truth, they didn't worry about learning them."[38] The colony was instead conceived of as a battlefield. And on a battlefield, victory goes to the strongest—not to the most knowledgeable.

Second, Fanon characterizes colonization as a prodigious machine for the production of desires and fantasies. It puts into circulation an ensemble of material goods and symbolic resources that are all the more coveted by the colonized because they are rare, because they have become objects of desire and act as operators of differentiation (in terms of prestige, status, hierarchy, or class). Corruption, terror, enchantment, and stupefaction all constitute resources managed and administered by the potentate. The administration of terror and the management of corruption work through a certain modulation of the true and the false, through a certain rationing of profits and bonuses, through the production of things that are sometimes moving, sometimes captivating, and always spectacular and that the colonized, because they are stupefied, have difficulty forgetting.[39] From this point of view, colonial domination requires an enormous investment in affect and ceremony and a significant emotional expenditure that few have analyzed until now.

This emotional economy must include everything that bears the mark of life and death, abundance and plenitude—in short, wealth. The desire for wealth insinuates its way into the body of the colonized and infuses every corner of his psyche. "The land of the Kabyles is closed to us, but the spirit of the Kabyles is open to us and it is not impossible for us to penetrate into it," Tocqueville observed in this regard. He reasoned that "the great passion of the Kabyles is the love of material pleasures, and it is through this that we can and must capture them." He said of Arabs that personal ambition and cupidity occupied a greater place in their hearts than among other groups. In his eyes there were two ways of taming them. The colonized could flatter their ambition and make use of their passions by turning them against one another while keeping them in a dependent relation to colonial power through the distribution of money and gifts. Alternatively, they could be disgusted and exhausted through war.[40] The potentate therefore attempts to drive the native subject to renounce the choices and desires to which he is attached, or at least to replace them with new idols, the law of new commodities, the price of new values, a new order of truth.

The potentate's mechanism of fantasy pivots on the regulation of needs and the flow of desire. The latter is determined by the fluxes of desire. Between the two is merchandise, notably the type of merchandise that the colonized admire and seek to access. In both cases merchandise is subjected to a triple use—symbolic, psychic, and instrumental. In the colony especially, it acquires the characteristics of an imaginary place. Merchandise is the absolute essential core of every colonial operation, a dazzling mirror on whose surface life, work, and the language of the colonized are reflected. Depending on the context, merchandise serves either a sedative or an epileptic function. The potentate dazzles the colonized with the possibility of an unlimited abundance of objects and goods. The cornerstone of the potentate's fantasy mechanism is the idea that *wealth and property, and therefore desire, know no limit.* The "little secret of the colony," the idea of an *imaginary without symbolism*, explains the colonial potentate's power of enchantment. Moreover, the success of this "imaginary without the symbolic" may be explained by the fact that it echoes and is anchored in both history and the symbolic categories of the indigenous themselves.

We know, for instance, that, at the first moment of contact between European merchants and Atlantic societies, the power of European goods to define and produce flows of desire was much more important—at least in Africa—than the idea of profit as such. The mystery that generally surrounds the value of objects was revealed in the ways in which Africans exchanged gold and ivory for apparently useless products, those with very little real economic value. But once they were integrated into local networks of meaning, once their bearers invested them with extensive powers, cheap objects of *pacotille* apparently devoid of economic value suddenly acquired a considerable social and symbolic—and indeed aesthetic—value. We also know of the sense of wonder that European weapons produced in Africa, of the fascination that Western technology exercised on African minds (beginning with ships, masts, sails, portholes, compasses, and maps), as well as of the terror produced by instruments of surveillance. The material world and the world of objects that Africans encountered were considered vehicles of causality, in the way that ancient fetishes were. That these imported objects exerted such an influence on the indigenous imaginary can be partly explained by the fact that the cult of "fetishes" was, strictly speaking, a materialistic cult. Religious and sacred objects, erotic and aesthetic objects, objects of commercial value, technical objects, and talismans—all could find a place within the economy of enchantment and charms. The existence of a cult of fetishes of a specifically materialistic and ceremonial nature (amulets, necklaces, pendants, finery, charms, ornaments) offered a cultural substrate on which a mercantile ideology developed as a *power over life* (necromancy, the invocation of spirits, witchcraft) and as a figure of abundance. In fact, many travelers of the period affirmed that the religion of the fetish and the African social order depended entirely on utilitarian principles.[41]

The same is true of the categories of excess and doubling, or of the existence of monstrous figures and ambivalent creatures that assimilate the fetishes and turn into terrifying masters of the forces of shadow and night, capable of upending the world. Such is the case of chiefs who one day drink beer from the skulls of their ancestors or enemies, and the next are symbolically put to death as substitute human sacrifices. Freed from their ties to the clan, they affirm their virility by sleeping with a sister, or by marrying a great-niece from their own matrilineal group, or by simply transforming themselves into leopards. The great diversity of the categories of spirits—each corresponding to the logic of juxtaposition, permutation, and multiplicity—explains the fact that there is no limit to desire. "All these characteristics," explains Luc de Heusch, "more or less developed in each particular case (royal incest, anthropophagy, the assimilation of the king with a sorcerer, the prohibitions surrounding him, and finally regicide), must be brought together under the same symbolic structure." Taken together, they "define the formidable magic force which abolishes the border between culture—from which the chief is separated when he is sacralised—and nature, of which he becomes the sovereign master."[42] This is also the case for those enchanted objects that are invested with dangerous power and that as a result operate on the same level as royalty's accursed share. Their secret is to take part in the "resurrection of things."

Furthermore, an accursed share is constitutive of the history of the relationship between African and European commodities, which took shape during the period of the slave trade. As a result of the Atlantic trade, the relationship of Africans to European goods was rapidly structured around a triptych composed of the desire to consume, death, and genitalia. In various respects the political economy of the slave trade was a fundamentally libidinal economy. It had the particularity of possessing a center of gravity, a driving force, which was partly a desire for consumption and partly a desire for absolute and unconditional expenditure. In turn, this desire maintained a close relationship with the procedures of sexual reproduction. Early on, it acquired the characteristics of a kind of corruption that even the possibility of self-destruction (the sale of close relatives and the dissolution of social connections) was unable to limit. In fact, one can say of this economy that it made self-destruction and waste the ultimate signs of productivity. African slave traders consumed European commodities in exchange for the expenditure of their own people, and as a means by which to sublimate their own desire for death, which is a part of all power. Those in power during the period maintained a relationship with commodities that viewed the latter as sources of the erotic, not just as objects. In this context enjoyment became the equivalent of absolute license, while everything incarnated in a practice of transgression was considered a form of power. But this form of practice also saw itself, at the same time, as a kind of aesthetic.

Domination, meanwhile, consisted less in the exploitation of the labor of those who had been subjugated than in the transformation of the latter into objects within a general economy of expenditure and sensation, which were both mediated by commodities. To consume was, as a result, the symbol of a power that never renounced any of its desires, even if these led to a collision with the ultimate master: death. Human beings, subjects of the potentate or prisoners of war, could be converted into objects and commodities sold to the slavers. Their value was measured against the value of the commodities that the potentate obtained in return for the sale of human beings. The conversion of human beings into commodities could even affect members of the potentate's immediate or extended family. The objects received in exchange were subsequently incorporated into a double calculus: the calculus of domination (to the extent that the commerce of slaves helped establish centers of political power) and the calculus of sensual pleasures (smoking tobacco, seeing oneself in a mirror, drinking rum and other kinds of alcohol, dressing oneself, copulating, and accumulating women, children, and dependents). In African history there is, then, a figure of the commodity that has as its main signifier the "family member who was sold or handed over to be killed" in return for goods. We should understand the term "desire" as a description of this gap in the structure of the subject.

The instinct for enjoyment to which African elites were subjugated during this period depended on a collection of symbolic repertoires deeply rooted in the thought, behavior, and life of the societies they dominated. One of the fundamental pillars of the metaphysics of life was the communion between human beings, on one hand, and objects, nature, and invisible forces on the other. Another pillar was the belief in the division of the world between the visible and the occult. The division granted supremacy to the invisible world, the secret origin of all sovereignty. It turned human beings into the puppets of forces beyond their comprehension. The absence of individual autonomy was expressed through an economy of subordination whose forms varied endlessly. But subordination also existed in the form of a debt owed in return for protection. During the time of the slave trade, however, subordination existed first and foremost as subjection to the present. In the majority of cases, time and value were perceived as being contained within, and exhausted in, the present moment. Nothing was certain, and everything was possible. And so risks were taken with commodities just as much as with the body, power, and life. Time as well as death was reduced to the terrifying game of chance.

On the one hand, then, there was a forced awareness of the volatility and frivolity of money and fortune. On the other, there was the perception that time and value existed only in the present moment. From this followed the subjugation of people to fetishes, as well as that of women to men, of children to parents, and, more significantly, of everyone to their ancestors and therefore to the power of death over life. The latter was carried out as a fusion that affected relationships to both objects and the family. All of this (more so than people have tended to think) accounts for the form taken by despotic African regimes across the period, along with the forms through which social violence was expressed—tangibility, tactility, palpability. On another level the relationship between goods for consumption and prestige goods (including women, children, and even allies) was henceforth manifested as the penetration of commodities into the core of the subject. Relationships to people were reduced to a conglomeration of debts, as was the case in the system of "ancestors." Everything, including social violence, was structured according to the creditor–debtor relationship.

To a large extent, colonization only reinforced these systems. The subjugation of Africans under colonization was also largely mediated through goods. The more goods and objects radiated in their rarity, the more intense became the libidinal investment in them. But as had been the case during the era of the slave trade, the desire for goods was spurred on by death, or at least by the figure of servitude. Like the Atlantic trade, colonization marked the entry of Africans into a new era characterized by the frantic pursuit of desire and enjoyment—a desire free from responsibility, and the pursuit of enjoyment as a mentality.[43] Here the raw material of enjoyment was the pleasure of the senses. The slave trade in particular constituted a moment of extreme exuberance during which the equivalence between objects and humans was almost total. Both were reduced to the state of signs. The relation to objects was one of immediate consumption, of raw pleasure. The colonized, like the slave driver before him, was fascinated and captivated by the idol behind the mirror, by the specular image that was fabric and loincloth, rum, guns and hardware, roads, monuments, railroads, bridges, and hospitals.

To obtain new goods, however, the colonized had to put himself in a position of complete servitude to the potentate. He had to inscribe himself in a relation of debt—the debt of dependence on the master. He had to commit himself to a pedagogy aimed at inculcating the vices of venality, vanity, and cupidity. As both natural instincts and deliberately cultivated impulses, vanity, venality, and cupidity constituted the three privileged expressions of servitude with regard to the master and the cult of the potentate. The colonized thus set off on a long and winding path toward the enjoyment of new possessions and the promise of citizenship, but the possibility of any real fulfillment of the newly born desires was constantly deferred. For this reason there was always a neurotic and playful dimension to the colony, one of chance, a radical ambivalence that recent criticism has brought to the fore. Does not the colony produce in the colonized a dreamworld that turns rapidly into a nightmare? The dialectic of the dream that is always on the verge of becoming a nightmare is one of the driving forces behind the potentate. But it is also its Achilles' heel. In many ways African nationalisms are the product of the conflict between dreams and the frustration born of the impossibility of truly satisfying them.

If there is a secret to the colony, it is clearly this: *the subjection of the native by way of desire.* In the colonial context it is subjection to desire that ultimately draws the colonized "outside themselves," deceived as they are by the vain chimera of the image and of the spell. Allowing himself to be pulled in, the colonized penetrates another being and subsequently experiences their work, language, and life as processes of bewitchment and disguise. It is because of this experience of bewitchment and "estrangement" that the colonial encounter incited a proliferation of phantasms. It awakened desires that both colonizers and colonized had to hide from themselves and that were, precisely for this reason, repressed and buried in the unconscious. In the Black text, the memory of the colony necessarily takes two forms. The first consists in inscribing the colony within a mythology of indebtedness by emphasizing what Africa lost through the encounter. The debt itself has two dimensions. On the one hand is the debt of procreation (development), and on the other, the debt of hospitality (immigration). In both instances the goal of the discourse of loss and debt is to incite guilt. The African world, born of the colony, is a world of loss—a loss occasioned by crime. The perpetrator of the crime is not only guilty but also indebted to those whose natural rights were violated.

In addition, the memory of the colony becomes a kind of *psychic work* that seeks to cure. Let us accept that, generally speaking, the cure consists in bringing into consciousness two types of secrets evoked by Sigmund Freud in *The Uncanny*: those of which one is aware and which one attempts to hide, and those of which one is not aware because they do not appear directly in one's consciousness.[44] In the Black (con)text, these two types of secrets are in reality but one. The African text refuses to confess that the enigma of absence at the heart of desire is the principal cause for the loss of the proper name. The enigma explains the "yawning gap" (in Jacques Lacan's terms) that is addressed in African literature and that announces and confirms the loss. Under such conditions an authentic form of healing consists in liberating oneself from the secret even as one recognizes, once and for all, "the other within" and accepts the "detour through alterity" as the foundation for a new understanding of the self. Such knowledge is necessarily divided; it is a *knowledge of the gap and its representation*. That such a great psychic weight continues to be attributed to the colony is, strictly speaking, due to a resistance to confession: a resistance to confess the subjugation of Africans to desire, a resistance to confess that they had allowed themselves to be had, a resistance to admit that they had been seduced and fooled by the "great threat of the machinery of the imaginary" that was the commodity.[45]

Black Time

I have stressed that Blacks remember the colonial potentate as a founding trauma, yet at the same time refuse to admit their unconscious investment in the colony as a desire-producing machine. This can be explained by focusing on the ways in which they offer a criticism of time. But what is time, and what should we understand by it? Maurice Merleau-Ponty describes time as that which one inevitably encounters on the path to subjectivity. He also says of time that it is the "most general characteristic of psychic events."[46] By this we must understand two things: first, that there is an intimate relationship between time and subjectivity, made up of a series of psychic events; and, second, that time and the subject communicate from within, so that to analyze time is to gain access to the concrete and intimate structure of subjectivity. What Merleau-Ponty says about time can easily be extended to memory and even remembrance, given that each fundamentally constitutes a form of the presence of the past (and of its traces, remains, and fragments) within consciousness, whether such consciousness is rational or dreamlike and imaginative. The remarks that follow therefore aim, first, to show how the literary archive provides a way of explaining the reasons for the refusal to confess about which we spoke earlier. Second, the goal is to identify the cognitive and expressive parameters that have shaped the Black critique of time and, more generally, the elaboration of memories of the colony and of the potentate.

Literary texts highlight how languages of remembrance among Blacks depend to a large extent on the critique of time. Everything in the Black novel seems to indicate that time is not a process that one can simply register as what we might call a "succession of the present." In other words, there is no time in itself. Time is born out of the contingent, ambiguous, and contradictory relationship that we maintain with things, with the world, or with the body and its doubles. As Merleau-Ponty notes, time (and we can easily say as much about remembrance) is born in the gaze directed toward oneself and toward the Other, the gaze that one casts on the world and the invisible. It emerges out of a certain *presence* of all these realities taken together. The African novel also clearly demonstrates that time always exists in relation to its doubles. To experience time is in part to know no longer where one stands in relation to oneself. It is to experience the self as "duplicated, divided, and interchanged."[47] In the works of Amos Tutuola, Sony Labou Tansi, Dambudzo Marechera, Yvonne Vera, and Yambo Ouologuem, time is experienced by attending to the senses (seeing, hearing, touching, feeling, tasting).

Memory and remembrance put into play a structure of organs, a nervous system, an economy of emotions centered necessarily on the body and everything that exceeds it. The novel also demonstrates how remembrance is activated through dance and music, or disguise, trance, and possession.[48] All forms of memory therefore find consistent expression in the universe of the senses, imagination, and multiplicity. For this reason, in African countries confronted with the tragedy of war, the memory of death is directly written on the injured or mutilated bodies of survivors, and the remembrance of the event is based on the body and its disabilities. The coupling of imagination and memory enriches our knowledge of both the semantics and the pragmatics of remembrance.

But the critique of time as it is unfolds in contemporary Black fiction also teaches us that time is always unpredictable and provisional. It changes endlessly, and its forms are always uncertain. It therefore always represents a heterogeneous, irregular, and fragmented region of human experience. The relation of the subject to time, then, is one that always aims to evade the past and the future, or at least to redeem and subsume them.[49] This does not mean, however, that there is no distinction between before and after, or past and future. The present, as present, draws on both the sense of the past and that of the future or, more radically, seeks to abolish both, hence, in novelistic writing, the predominance of a time that might be called paradoxical, since it is never fully anchored in the present, nor is it ever completely cut off from the past or the future.[50] It is a time of differential duration whose two laws are those of disjuncture and simultaneity (co-occurrence). The Black novel therefore always speaks of time and its flow in the plural. Novelistic writing is preoccupied with describing the processes of the transmutation of time, or the accumulation of time.[51]

Memory and remembrance, furthermore, acquire meaning only in relation to the notion that time is in reality a sort of *antechamber of the real and of death*.[52] In the antechamber lie novel and unexpected things, or—more radically still—"hidden possibilities," all sorts of creative and destructive potentialities, an invisible and hidden world that constitutes the true face of the real, without which there can be no redemption of the real.[53] It is along this surface that the transition from the real to the phantasmagoric, from inside to outside—the conversion from one to another—takes place.[54] In these conditions, to remember is above all to distribute difference and produce a doubling precisely because there always exists an essential *disjuncture* between the different units of time in their relation to the event.[55]

And the event never simply takes place. One must be able to decipher and express it—hence the importance of divinatory practices.[56] But how can one express an "event" except, in a general sense, through an association of words and images, with certain words clearly serving as empty forms that one fills with images, and others existing solely to serve as vehicles for signs, to which they remain nevertheless irreducible? Remembrance exists only at the intersection between an event, words, signs, and images. This encounter may lead to rituals. The quasi-indissolubility of words, signs, and images disallows not only the representation of the event but also, and more radically, its manifestation in the form of an epiphany.[57] Within these processes of remembrance as practices of healing, images may vary and substitute for one another. An extremely complex relationship is established between meaning/signification and designation, or what I have just termed "manifestation." The subject who remembers, meanwhile, is inherently a contested subject as a result of the inaugural event: the apparent loss of their proper name. Such a loss is all the more traumatic because it is accompanied by the profound instability of knowledge, the destruction of common meaning, and radical uncertainty with regard to the self, time, the world, and language. This state of radical uncertainty constitutes the objective structure of the event itself, but also of the story that one tells of it, its narration. It makes any attempt to assign fixed identities impossible. This partly explains the very close relation established in the Black novel between the loss of the proper name (the destruction of moderation) and the process of going mad, or of opening oneself up to a convulsive life, or even suicide.[58]

To remember, in this context, means repeatedly overcoming the limits of what can be expressed through language.[59] Thus, writers use several simultaneous languages of time and the body. In the works of Tutuola, for example, each body penetrates another and coexists with it, not always completely, but at least in its essential parts.[60] When one is asked who one is, or what happened, remembrance takes the form of stuttering. The same process takes place in relation to the memory of the postcolonial potentate, that magnificent manifestation of time with no past or future tense, or of a fallen past that one ceaselessly tries to revive but whose meaning appears only as fracture and dissipation.[61]

Let us take, for example, the first chapter of Kossi Efoui's novel *La Polka*. As the novel opens, the narrator is seated, looking out on an empty street. Before we know the name of the subject telling the story, his senses are called up: in this case, sight. But what is seen? A pile of rubble, "sections of walls fallen down, with doors and windows and their frames denuded by fire." Behind these objects is ruin: the time of ruin and of destruction. As a result, time presents itself first in its capacity to leave traces of a primordial event—a destructive event for which fire is one of the major signifiers. Time lives in the landscape. It can be seen there, read there. Before memory there is the view. To remember is literally to see the physical traces left on the *body of a place* by the events of the past. But there is no body of a place that is not on some level linked to a human body. Life itself has to be "embodied" so it can be recognized as real. The novelist pays particular attention to the face and its traits, which he specifies have been redrawn "by something that brutally forced its way into the gaze." He takes care to mention, together, the bodies and faces of women, men, and animals, all similarly rendered immobile by something whose irruption into life takes the form of brutality. Distinctions between species and genders are therefore attenuated. From then on, they are linked in an apparent community by resemblance. The face itself maintains a tight link with the mask: "Men and animals shared the same face, the same mask of astonishment."[62]

We said earlier that sight comes before the name. In fact, sight and the name echo one another. The name revives sight and vice versa. One cannot exist without the other, and both lead to the voice, to gesture, and finally to life itself. So the time of ruin, according to the novelist, is when "the gestures of life are no longer followed by the gaze." It is when the body stiffens and the timbre and rhythm of the voice become agitated. It quivers, or becomes gravelly. It may at other moments become "asthmatic." It becomes clear "soon enough that every word [emitted by the voice] is a false escape," since from then on the voice, cut in two, "goes nowhere." Speech no longer knows "how to catch up to or grasp the present moment." Time can no longer be mastered. And so speech escapes "into a see-saw between before and after the return," finding itself "outside life's words." We could add that the event itself is the placement of time outside of life's words.[63]

One might say that *La Polka* is a novel that turns the body into the ultimate site of memory. At times it seems as if the body belongs to no one in particular. It belongs to what we might call the *numerous*. So it is in the bar, late at night, with those seeking anonymous debauchery in alcohol and prostitutes: "The girls come and go and turn about chummily asking: 'Who's turn is it? How much for this ass?'" In the suffocating heat of bodies, "there are those who touch, . . . those who pinch, . . . the sailors who slap and those who content themselves with watching." There is, above all, the body of the woman: "They know how to ration the energy of their bodies. The smile first, then the bobbing of the bust.... And then it starts again with the smile, a look lights up—how much for this ass? As soon as he is aroused, he looks down towards the thighs. The girl snuffs out her smile and moves her legs around." And, as if everything has to pass through it, there is generalized copulation.[64]

In *La Polka* the body is destined for disguise and finery, which is partly what makes it shine: crowns of flowers, giant hats trimmed with ribbons, decorations of all kinds—rows of pearls around the naked necks of the girls, golden bells around the ankles of the dancing musicians. But this ceremonial performance is never too far from the evocation of death. Above the hearse whose ribs are made of braided palm there stands, "immobile, a living corpse all dressed in white." It is the mascot for a carnival. But the multitude is always at risk of being reduced to a crush of bodies that are "emaciated, stumbling, upon which no clothes can hang any longer." More seriously still, they risk expulsion from time, and from themselves: "We spend the night fighting these organs scattered in our bodies: the exhausted stomach that leaves an emptiness where we were once hungry or thirsty, the tongue turning back into the throat, dangling arms, shoulders that truly fall, and eyes in our backs. The mouth opens suddenly, stays open, without shouting, awaiting a belch, a sudden uprising of viscera or a brutal escape, bone after bone, along the entire frame of the body. Bone after bone, the long ones, the short ones, the flat ones, those that falsely seem round and rough, a rosary of vertebrae rushing out of this open mouth until the flabby skin sags and turns inside out and becomes distended. A body suspended, falling, the warning signs of epilepsy." In *La Polka* the enormous trembling of the body is linked to death and disappearance, or the sepulcher. The problem, according to the novelist, is that death does not necessarily produce remembrance. Moreover, "these seemingly dead people that we have, how could they serve to help us remember? With each disappearance, the memory of names shrinks, as if all these lives were classified affairs." Henceforth, "the mask of astonishment comes when everything shrinks and all that is left is the rumination of a final image seeking its place between the before and the after." It is equally possible that time is rebellious: it refuses to tire and sets out to trap people.[65]

personification

Bodies, Statues, and Effigies

Statues, effigies, and colonial monuments clearly perform this function of entrapment. Although diverse, they share three characteristics. In the first instance, they are objects, strictly speaking, made from all sorts of materials: marble, granite, bronze, steel, and so forth. As objects, they constitute inert blocks standing in place, apparently mute. Second, they are objects in the form of a human body or an animal (for example, a horse carrying a conqueror). They represent the dead, who, in them, become finely crafted things. Third, the dead were all subjects at a given moment in their lives. The statues that represent them attempt to preserve the quality of the subject. There can be no statue without a fusion of objectness, subjectivity, and mortality. And there are no colonial statues that do not refer us back in time. Almost without exception, colonial statues and effigies testify to this mute genealogy. At its heart lies the subject who outruns death, just as death in turn outruns the object—which itself is assumed to occupy simultaneously the place of the subject and the place of death.

Alongside statues exist other objects, monuments, and infrastructures: train stations, the palaces of colonial governors, bridges, military camps, and fortresses. In the French colonial empire, the majority of these were built in the nineteenth and twentieth centuries. This was a period in which the aesthetic mission of art, despite the appearance of secularization, was still conceived of in a religious mode. Art, it was thought, should heal the West of its unhappy memories and new fears.[66] It would, in its way, contribute to a heroic narrative. To this end, it was to awaken dormant powers while also renewing practices of celebration and the spectacle. In the colony, celebration took a primitive turn. The public works and other kinds of infrastructure (palaces, museums, bridges, monuments, etc.) were not just part of a collection of new fetishes. Tombs had to be desecrated so that they could be built. Skulls of dead kings had to be brought out into the daylight, their coffins dismantled. The corpse was stripped of all the objects that adorned it (jewels, coins, chains, and so forth) before museums would accept the funerary objects taken from the tombs as part of their collections. The function of the unearthing of the dead is to put the colonized into a trance, to force them henceforth to celebrate a "sacrifice without gods or ancestors."[67] In this context the symbolic economy of the colony becomes a vast economy of gifts that cannot be reciprocated. The exchange that develops around public works and infrastructural projects is one of sumptuary loss. Objects that cannot be returned (bridges, museums, palaces, infrastructures) are ceded to the indigenous subjects by a cruel authority during a savage festival that entangles body and matter.

Those colonial statues and monuments that continue to occupy the entrances of African public squares long after proclamations of independence have multiple meanings. But it is important to relate them to a style of power and domination. The *remains* of the potentate are the signs of the physical and symbolic struggle directed against the colonized. We know that, to endure, a form of domination must not only inscribe itself on the bodies of its subjects but also leave its imprint on the spaces that they inhabit as indelible traces on the imaginary. Domination must envelop the subjugated and maintain them in a more or less permanent state of trance, intoxication, and convulsion so that they are incapable of thinking lucidly for themselves. This is the only way that the potentate can lead them to think, act, and behave as if they were irrevocably caught in an unimaginable spell. Subjection must also be inscribed into the routine of daily life and the structures of the unconscious. The potentate must inhabit its subjects in such a manner that the latter can no longer see, hear, smell, touch, stir, speak, move, imagine, or even dream except in reference to the master signifier that weighs over them, forcing them to stutter and falter.[68]

The colonial potentate scarcely deviated from this rule. In all phases of daily life, the colonized was constrained to a series of rituals of submission, each more prosaic than the next. He might be commanded to shake, cry, and tremble, to prostrate himself while shivering in the dirt, to go from place to place singing, dancing, and living his subjection as if it were a providential necessity. Such was the case during the inauguration of different monuments, the unveiling of commemorative plaques, or the anniversaries and other celebrations shared by both colonizers and colonized.[69] All the moments of their lives had to be governed by a negative consciousness that emptied them of free will (the negative awareness of being nothing without one's master, of owing everything to one's master, who at times is even thought of as a relative).[70] In this context, then, colonial statues and monuments did not serve primarily as aesthetic artifacts destined for the embellishment of towns or the living environment. From start to finish, they served as manifestations of the absolute arbitrariness of colonial power, whose foundations were already visible in the ways in which the wars of conquest and "pacification" were carried out, and armed uprisings quelled.[71] They were expressions of the power of disguise, sculptural extensions of a form of racial terror. At the same time, they were the spectacular expression of the power of destruction and theft that animated the entire colonial project.[72]

But, above all, there is no domination without a *cult of spirits*—in this case, the dog-spirit, pig-spirit, the spirit of the riffraff that is so characteristic of all imperialism, past and present. The cult of spirits always requires a means of conjuring up the dead—a necromancy and a geomancy. The colonial statues and monuments clearly belong to the double universe of necromancy and geomancy. They constitute in effect a caricatural exaggeration of that dog-spirit, pig-spirit, and riffraff spirit that animated colonial racism and the power that shares its name—and, moreover, everything that came after in the time of the *postcolony*. Necromancy and geomancy constitute the shadow or the pen that carved the postcolony's profile into a space (the African space) that was ceaselessly violated and spurned.

To see these faces of "death without resurrection," it is easy to understand what the colonial potentate was—a typically *funerary* power that tended to reify the death of the colonized and deny that their life had any kind of value.[73] In reality, the majority of the statues represent the ancient dead of the wars of conquest, occupation, and "pacification"—the lugubrious dead, raised to the status of tutelary divinities by vain pagan beliefs. The presence of the lugubrious dead in the public arena is meant to ensure that both murder and cruelty, which the dead personify, continue to haunt the memories of the ex-colonized, to saturate their imaginary and the spaces of their lives. The result is a strange failure of consciousness that prevents them ipso facto from thinking clearly. The role of colonial statues and monuments is to resurrect, in the present, those who during their own lifetimes had threatened Blacks with the sword and with death. The statues function as rituals that conjure dead men in whose eyes Black humanity counted for nothing, which was reason enough for their lack of scruples at spilling Black blood over a trifle.

FIVE
REQUIEM FOR
THE SLAVE

In the previous chapters we saw how, throughout the modern period, the two notions of Africa and Blackness were mobilized in the process of the fabrication of racial subjects. Their major signature was degradation, and their role was to belong to a humanity pushed to the side, held in contempt as the waste of mankind. Still, as mythic resources, Africa and Blackness were also meant to sustain an untenable limit—both the shattering of meaning and joyous hysteria.

Even at the zenith of the logic of race, these two categories were always marked by ambivalence—the ambivalence of repulsion, of atrocious charm and perverse enjoyment. In Africa and in all things Black, many saw two blinding forces—at times only clay barely touched by sculpture, at others a fantastical animal, a metamorphic, heterogeneous, and menacing figure, capable of exploding into shards. In this chapter we seek to evoke this order, which was always in the process of ebullition, half solar and half lunar, and of which the slave was the cornerstone. This chapter, then, constitutes the foundation of the entire book, its ground zero. But to understand the status of the Black slave in the first era of capitalism, we must return to the figure of the ghost. A plastic subject who suffered a process of transformation through destruction, the Black Man is in effect the ghost of modernity. It is by escaping the slave-form, engaging in new investments, and assuming the condition of the ghost that he managed to endow such transformation by destruction with a significance for the future.

The phenomenon of the slave trade must, then, be analyzed as an emblematic manifestation of the nocturnal face of capitalism and of the negative labor of destruction, without which it has no proper name. Only through a *figural writing* can we provide an account of the nocturnal face and of the status of the ghost at the heart of its nocturnal economy. It is, in truth, a maze of interlocking loops, constantly oscillating between the vertiginous, dissolution, and scattering, and whose ridges and lines meet up on the horizon. This scriptural style, the reality that it evokes, and the categories and concepts necessary for its elucidation can be found in three works of fiction: Sony Labou Tansi's *Life and a Half* and Amos Tutuola's *The Palm-Wine Drinkard* and *My Life in the Bush of Ghosts*.

Multiplicity and Surplus

The phenomenon of *multiplicity* and surplus is one of the central dimensions of the nocturnal economy. What is called real at the heart of this economy is by definition dispersed and elliptical, fleeting and on the move and essentially ambiguous. The real is composed of several layers or sheets, several envelopes. It is an uncomfortable thing, one that can only be seized in bits, provisionally, through a multiplicity of approaches. And even if seized, it can never be reproduced or represented either fully or accurately. In the end there is always a *surplus* of the real that only those endowed with extra capacities can access.

On the other hand, the real rarely lends itself to precise measurement or exact calculation. Calculation is, on principle, a game of probabilities. It is, to a large extent, the calculation of chance. We add, subtract, multiply, divide. But above all we evoke, convoke, draw everything along a fugitive and elliptical line in zigzags, interpenetrating, sometimes curved, sometimes sharp, as a form of divination. The encounter with the real can only ever be fragmentary and chopped up, ephemeral, made up of dissonance, always provisional, always starting anew. And there is no real—and therefore no life—that is not at the same time a spectacle or theater, the product of dramaturgy. The event par excellence is always floating. The image, or the shadow, is not illusion but fact. Its content always exceeds its form. A regime of exchange exists between the imaginary and the real—if such a distinction even means anything. For, in the end, one serves to produce the other. One is articulated to the other, can be converted into the other, and vice versa.

The true core of the real is a kind of reserve, a surplus situated in an elsewhere, a future. There is always an excess, the possibility of an ellipse and of separation, and it is these factors that make it possible to enter into orphic states reached through dance or music, possession or ecstasy. The truth is to be found in this reserve and surplus, in this oversaturation and ellipse. But they can be accessed only through the deployment of a function of clairvoyance, which is not the same thing as the function of the visual.

Clairvoyance consists in deciphering the glimmers of the real and interpreting them according to whether they take form on the surface of things or beneath them, and whether they refer to their quantity or quality. All of this can be explained only in relation to the fundamental mystery that life ultimately represents. Life is a mystery because, in the end, it is made up of knots. It is the result of a montage of things both secret and manifest, of an ensemble of accidents that only death punctuates and perfects, in a gesture at once of recapitulation and of appearance—or emergence. This explains death's foundational status. As an operation of recapitulation, it is not situated only at the end of life. At its core, the mystery of life is that of "death in life," of "life in death," a braiding that is the very name for power, knowledge, and force. The two bodies (the power of life and the power procured from the knowledge of death) are not separate. One works the other, is worked by the other, and the function of clairvoyance consists in making such work reciprocal in the clarity of the day, with a lucidity of spirit. These are the conditions required for any confrontation with the threat of the dissipation of life and the desiccation of the living. Life springs, then, from the split, from the doubling and disjunction. Death does as well, in its ineluctable clarity, which itself is also like the beginning of a world—a gushing emergence, a sudden appearance.

Faced with a real that is characterized by multiplicity and an almost unlimited capacity for polymorphism, what is power? How can it be acquired and conserved? What are its relationships to violence and trickery? Power is acquired and conserved owing to its capacity to create changing relations with the half-world of silhouettes, or with the world of doubles. Power comes to those who can dance with the shadows, weave tight links between their own vital strength and other chains of power always situated in an elsewhere, an outside beyond the surface of the visible. Power cannot be enclosed within the limits of a single, stable form because, in its very nature, it participates in the surplus. All power, on principle, is power thanks only to its capacity for metamorphosis: today a lion, tomorrow a buffalo or warthog, and the day after tomorrow an elephant, panther, leopard, or turtle. That said, the true masters of power, those who hold the truth, are those who can travel the path of shadows that calls to them, a path that one must embrace and go down precisely with the goal of becoming another, of multiplying, of being in constant movement. To have power is therefore to know how to give and receive forms. But it is also to know how to escape existing forms, how to change everything while remaining the same, to marry new forms of life and constantly enter into new relationships with destruction, loss, and death.

Power is also body and substance. First and foremost, it is a fetish-body and, as such, a medicine-body. As a fetish-body, it demands to be venerated as well as fed. The body of power is a fetish only because it participates in someone else's body, preferably someone dead who was once endowed with power and whose double it aspires to become. From this point of view, it is a body-corpse, at least on its nocturnal side. It is also a body-jewel, a body-ornament, a body-decoration. Relics, colors, concoctions, and other "medicines" give it its power to seed (fragments of skin, a piece of a skull or forearm, fingernails and locks of hair, precious fragments of the bodies of old sovereigns or fierce enemies). Power is the pharmacy, thanks to its capacity to transform the sources of death into a seeding strength, or to convert the resources of death into the capacity for healing. And it is because of its dual ability to be the force of life and the principle of death that power is at once revered and feared. But the relationship between the principles of life and death is fundamentally unstable. The dispenser of fertility and abundance, power must be in full possession of its virile strength.

This is one of the reasons why power resides at the center of a vast network for the exchange of women and clients. But above all it must be capable of killing. Power is recognized as much by its capacity to engender as by its equivalent capacity to transgress—whether in the realm of symbolic or in real practices of incest and rape, the ritual absorption of human flesh, or the capacity to spend without limits. In certain cases the killing of a human victim by its own hand is the primary condition for any ritual of regeneration. In order to sustain itself, power must be capable of breaking a fundamental law, whether it is the law of the family or the law of all that has to do with death and profanation, including the disposal of human lives, even the lives of kin. There is therefore no power that is free of an accursed share, that is not part scoundrel or part pig. Power is that which is made possible by splitting, that which is paid for in human lives, whether those of the enemy or, if necessary—as is often the case—that of a brother or parent.

In these conditions effective action consists in creating montages and combinations, of advancing masked, always ready to begin again, to improvise, to install oneself in the provisional before seeking to cross boundaries, to do what one does not say and say what one does not do; to say several things at once and marry the opposite; and, above all, to proceed by metamorphosis. Metamorphosis is possible only because the human person can only ever refer back to himself by relating to another power, another self—the capacity to escape oneself, to double, to become a stranger to oneself. Power is being simultaneously present in different worlds, under different modalities. It is, in this sense, like life itself. And power is what was able to escape death and return from among the dead. For it is only in escaping death and returning from the dead that one acquires the capacity to make oneself into the other side of the absolute. There is, therefore, in power as in life itself, a share that depends on the ghost—a spectral share.

The human figure is by definition plastic. The human subject par excellence is the one who is capable of becoming another, someone other than himself, a new person. It is the one who, constrained to loss, destruction, even annihilation, gives birth to a new identity out of the event. What gives the human subject its symbolic structure is the animal figure for which it is, in several ways, the vague silhouette. The human figure carries within it not only the structure of the animal but also its spirit.[1] The nocturnal power is that which knows, when necessary, how to take on an animal existence, give shelter to an animal, preferably a carnivore. The complete form or figure is always the emblem of a paradox. The same is true of the body—that privileged instance of aberration. All bodies are fundamentally committed to disorder and discord. The body is also, in itself, a power that willingly wears a mask. Before it is domesticated, the face of nocturnal power must be covered up, even disfigured, returned to its status as a kind of horror. One has to be unable to recognize anything human, to see a petrified object of death, but one that includes still pulsing organs of life. The face of the mask doubles as the face of the flesh and transforms itself into a living, figurative surface. That is the ultimate definition of the body—a network of images and heterogeneous reflections, a compact density, liquid, osseous, shadowy, the concrete form of the disproportion and dislocation that is always on the verge of exceeding the real.

The Rag-Humans

The body, flesh, and meat all create an inseparable totality. The body is a body only because it is potentially a kind of meat that can be eaten: "The soldier stood stock-still like a rod of khaki-colored meat," writes Sony Labou Tansi. He describes a scene during which the meal and the sacrifice become one: "The Providential Guide withdrew the knife"—which he had just plunged into the throat of one of the "rag-humans"—and turned back to the meat he is eating, "which he cut and ate with the same bloody knife."[2] This constant movement—between the body and blood of the torture victim and the meat of the meal—is presented almost as a simple dinner party. The point is to spill blood, to open wounds and inflict pain. Isn't it necessary, after all, for power to "kill from time to time"?[3] The enemy is brought naked in front of the Providential Guide: "You better tell me, or I'll devour you raw." To eat him raw requires a systematic destruction of the body:

> The Providential Guide got really angry now, slashing the rag-father's upper body in all directions with his gold-sparking saber. He tore apart the thorax, then the shoulders, the neck, the head. Soon there was nothing left but a crazy tuft of hair floating in the bitter emptiness. The lopped off pieces formed a kind of termite nest on the ground. The Providential Guide kicked it all over the place and then ripped the tuft of hair from its invisible suspension. He tugged with all his strength, first with one hand, then with two. The turf released, but carried by the force of his own effort, the Providential Guide fell over backwards and bashed his neck on the tiles.[4]

The body takes on a new shape through the destruction of its previous shapes: "Several of his toes were left in the torture chamber, saucy scraps of flesh hung in place of lips, and he had two wide parentheses of dried blood in place of ears. His eyes had vanished in his hugely swollen face, leaving just two glints of black light from two large shadowy holes. One wondered how a life could persist at the bottom of this human wreck that even human shape had fled. The others have stubborn lives." The Providential Guide eats bloody meat to which oil, vinegar, and three doses of local alcohol have carefully been added. He roars out his questions. His privileged instruments are tableware. "The fork struck bone; the doctor felt the pain turn on and off, turn on and off. The fork sunk deeper into his ribs, registering that same wave of pain."[5]

But what is a rag, if not what has been but no longer is, except in the form of a degraded shape, damaged, unrecognizable, ruined, an entity that has lost its authenticity, its integrity? The rag-human is that which presents human characteristics but is so disfigured that it is at once outside and within the human. It is infrahuman. You recognize the rag from what is left of its organs—the throat, the blood, lungs, the stomach from the plexus to the groin, intestines, eyes and eyelids. But the rag-human still has a will. There is more than organs left within it. Speech remains, the last breath of a pillaged humanity, which all the way to the doorway of death refuses to be reduced to a pile of meat, to die a death it does not want: "I don't want to die this death."[6]

Having held on to speech, the rag is dissected: "The rag-father was quickly cut in half at the height of his navel." After having been cut into pieces, the body opens up its cavernous mysteries. The intestines appear. Then the organ of speech, the mouth, is literally "mangled." There is no longer a body as such, as an intrinsic unity. There is just an "upper body" and a "lower body." But even cut in half, the torture victim continues to refuse. He repeats, over and over, the same phrase: "I don't want to die this death."[7]

It requires energy to transform a body into meat. The autocrat must wipe sweat off his brow and rest. Meting out death is tiring, even when it is interrupted by various pleasures, like smoking a cigar. What enrages the murderer is the obstinacy of the victim, who refuses to accept the death offered to him, who wants, at any price, a different death—that which he would have given himself. The victim refuses to grant to power the power to give him the death of its choice, enraging the Guide: "He bit down hard on his lower lip, his chest puffed up in a violent rage, causing his little eyes haphazardly tossed on his face to spin. A moment later he appeared calmer and slowly walked around the upper body suspended in space and looked with a twinge of sympathy at the blood-black mud that covered the trunk like tar." Power can mete out death. But the victim must accept it. For to die truly he has to accept not only the offer of death but the form that death takes. He who offers death, in opposition to he who receives it, is confronted with the limits of his own will. He has to experiment with different tools of death: guns, swords, poison (a "death by champagne"), which is the equalization of death and pleasure, moving from the world of meat to the world of liquor—death as a moment of drunkenness.[8]

The nocturnal world is dominated by antagonistic forces engaged in unrelenting conflict. Against each power is opposed another capable of undoing what the first has created. You can recognize power by its capacity to introduce itself among its subjects, to "mount" them, take possession of them, including of their body and above all of their "double." It is this taking of possession that makes of power a true force. The principle of its force is to dislodge the self from the one subjected, to take the place of that self. Power acts as if it is the mistress of its body and its double. From this point of view, force is shadow, above all the shadow of death domesticated and subjected. Power is the spirit of death, the shadow of the dead. As the spirit of the dead, it seeks to steal the heads of its subjects—preferably in such a way that they will not know what is happening to them, that they will be oblivious to everything they see and hear, everything they say and do.

A priori, there is no difference between the nocturnal will to power and the will of the dead. Nocturnal power owes its existence and its survival to a series of transactions with the dead of which it makes itself the vessel and which, in return, are transformed into vessels of its will. This will consists, above all, in knowing who the enemy is. Its slogan is this: "You will know your enemy and vanquish your brother, parent, or rival by exciting against them terrible evil powers." Nocturnal power, to do this, must constantly feed the spirits of the dead, who, as true wandering dogs, are not content with just any bit of food but demand pieces of meat and bone. Nocturnal power, then, is a force inhabited by the spirit of the dead. But it attempts at the same time to make itself mistress to the spirit of the dead that possesses it and with which it enters into a pact.

The question of the pact with the dead, of the appropriation of a dead person or else of the spirit of another world, is, to a large extent, the question at the heart of the history of slavery, race, and capitalism. The world of the slave trade is the world of the hunt, of capturing and gathering, selling and buying. It is the world of raw extraction. Racial capitalism is the equivalent of a giant necropolis. It rests on the traffic of the dead and human bones. To evoke and summon death demands that we know how to dispose of the remains or relics of the bodies of those who were killed so that their spirits can be captured. The labor of nocturnal power is the process by which the spirits and shadows of those who have been killed are captured and subjected. For there is no nocturnal power that does not subject the object and the spirit of the dead trapped within it to appropriation in due form. The object can be a piece of skull, the phalanx of a pinky finger, or a bone from the skeleton. But in a general sense the bones of the dead must be combined with pieces of wood, bark, plants, stones, and the remains of animals. The spirit of the dead has to invest this mix of objects, in short, to live within these objects, in order to consummate the pact and activate the invisible powers.

Of the Slave and the Ghost

Let us turn now to Amos Tutuola, to his *The Palm-Wine Drinkard* and *My Life in the Bush of Ghosts,* two primordial texts that deal with the figure of the ghost and the theme of shadows, of the real and of the subject.[9] We can say that it is in the nature of the shadow or the reflection to link the subject of the human person to its own image or double. The person who has identified with their shadow and accepted their reflection enters into a process of constant transformation. They project themselves along an irreducible, fugitive line. The *I* unites itself to its image as if to a silhouette, in a purely ambiguous relationship between the subject and the world of reflections. Situated in the twilight of symbolic efficiency, the part that is shadow constitutes the domain at the threshold of the visible world. Among the various properties that constitute what we have called the part that is shadow, there are two that deserve particular mention. The first is the power—which those-who-see-the-night dispose of—to summon, to call back, to make visible the spirit of the dead or their shadow. The second is the power—which the *initiated subject* disposes of—to escape oneself and become a spectator to oneself, to the struggle that is life, including the events that constitute one's own death and funeral. The initiated subject watches the spectacle of his own doubling, acquiring along the way the capacity to separate from the self, and to objectivize even as he subjectivizes. There is sharp awareness of the fact that the one seen beyond matter and the curtain of the day is truly his own self—but a self doubled by its reflection.

The autonomous power of the reflection depends on two things: first, on the possibility that the reflection can escape the constraints that structure sensed reality. The reflection is a fleeting double, never immobile. It cannot be touched. One can only *touch oneself*. This divorce between seeing and touching, this flirtation between what can be touched and what is untouchable, this duality between that which reflects and that which is reflected, forms the foundation for the autonomous power of the reflection, an intangible but visible entity—the negative that is the hollow between the *I* and its shadow. What remains is the explosion. There is, in effect, no reflection without a certain way of playing light against shadow and vice versa. Without this game there can be neither appearance nor apparition. To a large extent, it is the explosion that makes it possible to open up the rectangle of life. Once this rectangle is open, the initiated can finally see, as if upside down, the back of the world, the other face of life. They can, finally, go to meet the solar face of the shadow—the true and final power.

The second property of the shadow is its power to *horrify*. Such power is born of the worrisome reality that this entity, the reflection, constitutes a reality that seems not to rest on firm ground. For what ground, what geography, carries it? In her treatment of the mirror in Western tradition, Sabine Melchior-Bonnet offers this response: "The subject is at once here and elsewhere, perceived in a troubling ubiquity and depth, at an uncertain distance: we see in a mirror, or rather the image seems to appear behind the material screen, so that the person looking at himself can ask whether he is seeing the surface itself or through it." "The reflection," she adds, "creates, beyond the mirror, the sensation of an immaterial back-of-the-world, and invites the eye to cross through appearances."[10] But, strictly speaking, to cross through appearances is not only to surpass the gap between what can be seen and what can be touched. It is also to risk an autonomy of the psyche in relation to corporality, an expropriation of the body accompanied by the worrying possibility of the emancipation of the fictive double that acquires a life of its own along the way—a life devoted to the gloomy work of the shadow: magic, dreams, divination, desire, envy, and the risk of madness that is part of any relationship with oneself. There is, finally, the power of fantasy and imagination. As we have just noted, the play of shadows always depends on the constitution of a gap between the subject and its representation, a space of theft and dissonance between the subject and its fictive double, reflected by the shadow. The subject and its reflection can be superimposed, but the duplication can never be smooth. Dissemblance and duplicity are therefore an integral part of the essential qualities of nocturnal power and of the way it relates to life and the living.

Let us break the mirror on Tutuola's writing. What do we see? The spectacle of a world in motion, ever reborn, made up of fold upon fold, of landscapes, figures, histories, colors, of an abundance of the visual, of sounds and noises. A world of images, one could say. It is, above all, a world inhabited by beings and things that pass for what they are not and that, sometimes, are effectively taken for what they pretend to be even though they are not. More than geographic space, the ghostly realm belongs simultaneously to the orphic field and the visual field, to visions and images, strange creatures, frenzied fantasies, and surprising masks forming a permanent commerce with familiar signs that intersect, contradict, and nullify one another, launch themselves again, and go astray within their own boundaries. Perhaps for this reason, the ghostly realm escapes synthesis and geometry: "There were many images and our own too were in the centre of the hall. But our own images that we saw there resembled us too much and were also white colour, but we were very surprised to meet our images there. . . . So we asked from Faithful-Mother what she was doing with all of the images. She replied that they were for remembrance and to know those she was helping from their difficulties and punishments."[11]

It is also a world that one experiences and creates, in instability, in evanescence, in excess, in that inexhaustible depth that is generalized theatralization. We penetrate into the ghostly realm through its border, across the edges. The ghostly sphere is a stage where events unfold constantly but never congeal to the point of becoming history. Life unfolds in the manner of a spectacle where the past is in the future and the future is in an undefined present. There is only life that is fractured and mutilated—a reign of heads without bodies, bodies without heads, dead soldiers awakened once more, their decapitated heads replaced with those of others. The vast operation of substitution is not without its dangers, especially when the head of a ghost is mistakenly put in the place of someone else's head, one that "was always making various noises both day and night and also smelling badly." "Whether I was talking or not it would be talking out the words which I did not mean in my mind and was telling out all my secret aims which I was planning in mind whether to escape from there to another town or to start to find the way to my home town as usual."[12] Onto the trunk of the body, which remains unchanging, is added someone else's organ, a talking prosthesis, but in a way that makes the body spiral about in a void, so creating disorder and abolishing all notion of secrecy and intimacy. The conjunction of one's own body with someone else's head makes of the subject an emitter of speech over which he has no control.

Sent back across the edge, the self is projected at a moving horizon, the core of a reality whose center is everywhere and nowhere, and where each event engenders another. Events do not necessarily have recognizable origins. Some are pure memory-screens. Others crop up unexpectedly without apparent cause, or have a beginning but not necessarily an end. Still others are stopped, to be taken up again at a later time, in other places and other circumstances, perhaps in different guises or sequences or by different actors, in an indefinite declension of profiles and figures that are as ungraspable as they are unrepresentable, and within complex designs ever liable to modification.

Nocturnal power surrounds its prey from all sides, invests and encloses it to the point of cracking and suffocating it. Its violence is primarily of a physico-anatomical order: half bodies cut in all directions, made incomplete through mutilation and the resulting absence of symmetry, maimed bodies, lost pieces, scattered fragments, folds and wounds, totality abolished—in short, a generalized dismemberment. There is another face of ghostly terror that ensues from the ghost's ugliness. The ghost's body teems with a multiplicity of living species: bees, mosquitoes, snakes, centipedes, scorpions, and flies. From it emanates a pestilential odor fed by never-ending feces, urine, blood—the waste of the victims that ghostly power endlessly crushes.[13] Ghostly terror also operates through capture, the most ordinary form of which is physical capture. It consists simply in binding the subject hand and foot and gagging him like a convict until he is reduced to immobility. From then on, he is paralyzed and becomes a spectator of his own powerlessness. Other forms of capture occur through the projection of a light whose starkness, harshness, and brutality invests objects, erases them, re-creates them, and then plunges them into quasi-hallucinatory drama:

> So as he lighted the flood of golden light on my body and when I looked at myself I thought that I became gold as it was shining on my body, so

at this time I preferred most to go to him because of his golden light. But as I moved forward a little bit to go to him then the copperish-ghost lighted the flood of his own copperish light on my body too ... and my body was then so bright that I was unable to touch it. And again as I preferred this copperish light more than the golden-light then I started to go to him, but at this stage I was prevented again to go to him by the silverfish-light which shone onto my body at the moment unexpectedly. This silverfish-light was as bright as snow so that it transparented every part of my body and it was this day I knew the number of bones of my body. But immediately I started to count them these three ghosts shone the three kinds of light on my body at the same time in such a way that I could not move to and fro because of these lights. But as these three old ghosts shone their lights on me at the same time so I began to move round as a wheel at this junction, as I appreciated these lights as the same.[14]

The light reflects its brilliance and its total power on the body that has become, under the circumstances, luminous dust, porous and translucent matter. The fluidification of the body results in the suspension of its prehensile and motor functions. Its component parts become legible. The light also causes new forms to emerge from the shadows. The startling combination of colors and splendor institutes a different order of reality, one that not only transfigures the subject but plunges him into an infernal whirlwind. He becomes a whirligig, the plaything of antagonistic powers that tear at him until he cries out in horror. Still other forms of capture are tied to hypnotism and bewitching. Such is the case of the song that accompanies the drum. There is a type of drum that resonates as if several are being beaten at once. The same is true for certain voices and songs. Dancers are capable of drawing in all who witness their prowess, even the spirits of the dead. Drum, song, and dance are truly living beings. They have a seductive, even irresistible, power. All three together produce a concatenation of sounds, rhythms, and gestures that gives rise to a half-world of specters and reveals the return of the dead. Sounds, rhythms, and gestures can themselves be infinitely multiplied according to the principle of dissemination—sounds especially, owing to the unique ways in which they can be unleashed and wrapped up within other sounds, one upon another, one into the other. Their power to take flight links them to winged matter. Rhythms and sounds have the power to arouse and indeed to revive, to raise up. The act of rising up is then taken over by the rhythm, with which gesture itself is associated. Rhythms and gestures appear equally in great numbers. Lives are suddenly seized from the dungeon of death, from the grave, and are healed, in an instant, by sound, rhythm, and dance. In the act of dancing, the dead momentarily lose the memory of their chains. They discard their habitual gestures and liberate themselves from their bodies in order to erase away figures that are barely sketched, thus prolonging the creation of the world in a multiplicity of crisscrossing lines:

> When "Drum" started to beat himself, all the people who had been dead for hundreds of years, rose up and came to witness "Drum" when beating; and when "Song" began to sing all domestic animals of that new town, Bush animals with snakes, etc., came out to see "Song" personally, but when "Dance" (that lady) started to dance the whole bush creatures, spirits, mountain creatures and also all the river creatures came to the town to see who was dancing. When these three fellows started at the same time, the whole people that rose up from the grave, animals, snakes, and spirits and other nameless creatures were dancing together with these three fellows and it was that day that I saw that snakes were dancing more than human-beings or other creatures.[15]

All of the energy imprisoned in bodies, beneath the earth, in streams, on mountains, in the animal and vegetable worlds, is suddenly liberated. And none of these entities retains an identifiable equivalent or referent. In fact, they are no longer referents to anything. They are nothing more than their own inherent reality. The dead, the spur of dance, the whip of the drum, and the ritual of resurrection dissolve into an ambivalence and general dispersion of all things imaginable as if they have been suddenly let loose at random: a telluric sequence through which all that was buried has been jolted out of sleep.

There is also noise. Ghostly violence consists equally in an art of making noise. Such noise is almost always linked to specific operations of control and surveillance. One noise almost always calls forth another, which in turn sets the crowd in motion. Too much noise can lead to deafness. Ghostly violence is also capricious by nature. But the caprice here is not just an exercise in arbitrariness. It involves two distinct possibilities, the first of which consists in laughing at the subject's misfortune, and the second in overturning everything, associating every single thing with many others that do not necessarily resemble it. Caprice dissolves the identity of each thing within an infinity of identities not directly linked to the original. Ghostly terror, from this perspective, is based on the negation of all essential singularity. This is how the master, in the presence of his hosts, seeks to transform his captive into various kinds of creatures. First, he changes him into a monkey. He climbs into fruit trees to pick fruit for them. Soon afterward, he becomes a lion, then a horse, then a camel, then a bull with horns. Then he reverts to his original form.[16]

Of Life and Work

In Tutuola's universe the slave appears not as an entity made once and for all but as a subject *at work*. Work itself is a permanent activity. Life unfolds in constant flux. The subject of life is a subject at work. Several levels of activity are mobilized in this *work for life*, one of which consists in trapping those who carry danger or death. *Work for life* consists in capturing death and exchanging it for something else. Capture requires subterfuge. The effective actor is he who, unable to kill with the first blow, shows himself to be cleverer than the other. Having prepared the trap, he must draw the other in through intelligence and ruse. The goal each time is to immobilize the other by enticing his body into a snare. Central to the *work for life* is the body, that fact of being to which are attached properties, a number, or a figure.

The body, as such, is not endowed with intrinsic meaning. Strictly speaking, within the drama of life, the body itself signifies nothing in itself. It is an interlacing, a bundle of processes that in and of themselves have no immanent or primordial meaning. Vision, movement, sexuality, and touch have no primordial meaning. There is an element of thingness in every form of corporeality. The *work for life* consists in sparing the body from degenerating into absolute thingness, in preventing the body from becoming a simple object. There is only one mode of existence that makes this possible: an ambiguous mode of existence, a manner of groping along the back of things and playing out the comedy before oneself and others. The body, here, is an anatomical reality, an assemblage of organs, each with a specific function. As such, it is not the basis of any kind of singularity that would enable one to declare once and for all, absolutely: "I possess my body." True, it belongs to me. But this belonging is not absolute; I can, in fact, hire out parts of my body to others.

The ability to dissociate oneself from one's own body is therefore a prerequisite for all *work for life*. Through this operation the subject can, if necessary, protect his life from a burst of borrowing. He can feign his existence, get rid of the signs of servitude, participate in the masquerade of the gods, or even, under the mask of the bull, abscond with virgins. Indeed, he can dissociate himself from parts of his own body one moment and then recover them once the exchange is completed. This does not mean that parts of the body can be considered excess baggage and squandered. It simply means that one does not need all of the parts of one's own body at the same time. The primary virtue of the body does not reside in the rays of symbolism it sends out, or in its constitution as a privileged zone for the expression of the senses. It resides in the potential of organs taken as a whole or separately, in the reversibility of its fragments, their mortgaging and restitution for a price. More than symbolic ambivalence, then, it is instrumentalization that we must bear in mind. The body is alive to the extent that its organs function and express themselves. It is the deployment of the organs, their malleability and their more or less autonomous power, that makes the body forever phantasmagoric. The meaning of the body, then, is tightly linked to its functioning in the world and to the power of fantasy.

But the body must be able to move. The body is made first and foremost to move, to walk, which is why every subject is a wandering subject. The wandering subject goes from one place to another. The journey itself need not have a precise destination: the wanderer can come and go as he pleases. Destinations may be the predetermined stages of a journey, and yet paths do not always lead to the desired destinations. What is important is where one ends up, the road traveled to get there, the series of experiences in which one is an actor and to which one is a witness, and, above all, the role played by the unexpected and the unforeseen. We therefore need to pay more attention to the path itself, to itineraries, than to destinations. Hence the importance of the road.

The other ability required for the *work for life* is the ability to metamorphose. The subject can morph under any circumstances. This is notably the case in situations of conflict and adversity. The ultimate act of metamorphosis consists in constantly escaping oneself, getting ahead of oneself, in placing oneself ahead of others in an agonizing, centripetal movement that is all the more terrifying because the possibility of return is never guaranteed. When existence is tethered to very few things, identity lives its life fleetingly, for one risks being killed by never getting ahead of oneself. The time spent as a particular being can only ever be provisional. One must be ready to desert at any moment, to dissimulate, repeat, fissure, or recover, to live within a form of existence where the whirlwind brings vertigo and circularity. There are also circumstances in life in which, despite an insatiable desire to exist, the living being is condemned to assume the identity of a dead person, rather than an individual or singular shape:

> He was exceedingly glad as he discovered me as the dead body of his father, then he took me on his head and kept going to the town at once with joy. . . . When he carried me and appeared in the town all his town's ghosts asked him what sort of heavy load he was carrying and sweating as if he bathed in water like this, so he replied that it was the dead body of his father. . . . But when the town's ghosts and ghostesses heard so, they were shouting with joy and following him to his house. Having reached his house and when his family saw me . . . they thought that it was true I was the dead body of their father, so they performed the ceremony which is to be performed for deads at once. . . . Then they told a ghost who is a carpenter among them to make a solid coffin. Within an hour he brought it, but when I heard about the coffin it was at that time I believed that they wanted to bury me alive, then I was trying my best to tell them that I am not his dead father, but I was unable to talk at all. . . . So after the carpenter brought the coffin, then they put me inside it and also put more spiders inside it before they sealed it at once. . . . After that they dug a deep hole as a grave in the back yard and buried me there as a dead man.[17]

The father thus dies without leaving behind an exact replica of himself. The void created by the absence of the essential trace that is the cadaver of the deceased is experienced as an immense breach in the real. For in the trace of the cadaver is an essential component of the signifier that is his death. Without the trace the dead person and his death are inscribed in a fictional structure. For the reality of death gains its shadowy authority from the cadaver. The absence of the trace opens up the possibility that the living subject will stand witness to his own burial. To reach this stage, he must be ripped from his own rhythm and captured in the imagination of another. Protest as he might, there is nothing to be done. He is taken for someone else, and, despite himself, he has to carry that person's story, notably its ending, even as he protests that he is unique. This inexorable process continues to its conclusion in the tomb. The subject is truly there, for himself, in his own right. He is not perceived in any kind of ubiquity. The dead person nevertheless hangs over him as a kind of material screen that abolishes the identity of the victim who is being prepared for burial, and melts it into an identity that is not his own. By a perverse genius, the dead man is activated at the surface of a living being, in a form that is not spectral but palpable. Even if opaque, it is truly material.

The dead person accedes to the status of the sign through the mediation of the body of another, in a theatrically tragic scene that forces each of the protagonists into the unreality of an appearance that is endlessly renewed, and into an emblematic mirroring and shimmering of identities. From then on, the object (the cadaver) and its reflection (the living subject) are superimposed. The living subject insists in vain that he is not the dead person, for he no longer possesses himself. Henceforth his signature has become *taking the place of*. With its vertiginous speed and power of abstraction, the impassable demon of death has taken possession of him. The body of the dead person is not, strictly speaking, the same as the body of the person who despite himself is being passed off as him. But the disappeared henceforth finds himself in two places at once, even though he is not the same in both places. The living being destined for the tomb becomes another while remaining the same. It is not that he is divided, nor that the dead person that he must mimic possesses any of his essential attributes. Everything is played out in the somnolence of appearances. To a large degree, both the dead person and the living one have lost possession of their own death and their own life. They are now joined in spite of themselves to spectral entities that transform both of them into primitive and undifferentiated forms. Through a strange process of designation, the signifier is destroyed and consumed by the signified, and vice versa. Neither can be extricated from the other.

There is, finally, the load that is borne—here again, often against one's wishes.

> He begged us to help him carry his load which was on his front. . . . We did not know what was inside the bag, but the bag was full, and he told

us that we should not put the load down from head until we should reach the said town. Again he did not allow us to test the weight of it, whether it was heavier than we could carry. . . . I told my wife to put the load on my head and she helped me. When I put it on my head it was just like a dead body of the man, it was very heavy, but I could carry it easily. . . . We did not know that the load was the dead body of the Prince of the town that we entered. That man had mistakenly killed him in the farm and was looking for somebody who would represent him as the killer of the prince. . . . Early in the morning the king told the attendants to wash and dress us with the finest clothes and put us on a horse and they (attendants) must take us around the town for seven days which meant to enjoy our last life in the world for that 7 days, after that he (king) should kill us as we killed his son.[18]

The same relationship of intertwining between the dead and the living is at work here, with the only difference being that the living person must carry the remains of the dead even when he is by no means the murderer. The fissure between death and responsibility is traced by the burden. The bearer of the burden must shoulder the form but not the matter of the murderer. This all unfolds in a field of contrasts, where different experiences are linked not through chaos but through duration. Each *experience* consists first of a conglomeration of heterogeneous elements that can be bound together only in a temporal form, although it itself is often shattered. Life is henceforth but a series of instants and trajectories that are almost parallel, with no overarching unity. There are constant jumps back and forth from one experience to another, from one horizon to another. The entire structure of existence is such that, in order to live, one most constantly escape permanence, which is the bearer of precariousness and vulnerability. Instability, interruption, and mobility, on the other hand, offer possibilities for flight and escape.

But flight and escape are also bearers of danger:

When he was about to catch me or when his hand was touching my head slightly to catch it, then I used the juju which I took from the hidden place that he kept it in before we left his house. And at the same moment that I used it, it changed me to a cow with horns on its head instead of a horse, but I forgot before I used it that I would not be able to change back to the earthly person again. . . . Of course as I had changed to a cow I became more powerful and started to run faster than him, but still, he was chasing me fiercely until he became tired. And when he was about to go back from me I met a lion who was hunting up and down in the bush at that time for his prey as he was very hungry, and without hesitation the lion was also chasing me to kill for his prey, but when he chased me to a distance of about two miles I fell into the cow-men's hands who caught me at once as one of their house which had been lost from them for a long time, then the lion got back at once from the fearful noise of these cow-men. After that they put me among their cows which were eating grass at that time. They thought I was one of their last cows and put me among the cows as I was unable to change myself to a person again.[19]

Three conclusions emerge. First, in the ghostly paradigm, time is neither reversible or irreversible. There is only an unfolding of experience. Things and events roll out on top of each other. If stories and events have a beginning, they do not necessarily have a proper end. They can certainly be interrupted. But a story or an event might continue on in another story or event without there necessarily being a filiation between the two. Conflicts and struggles might be resumed from the points at which they stopped. But they can also be followed upstream, or begun again, without a sensed need for continuity, even if the shadow of the old stories and events always lurks behind the present. Indeed, the same event can have two distinct beginnings. In the process, the life of the subject can pass from phases of loss to phases of enrichment. Everything functions according to a principle of incompletion. As a result, there is no ordered continuity between the present, the past, and the future. And there is no genealogy—only an unfurling of temporal series that are practically disjointed, linked by a multiplicity of slender threads.

Second, to act as a subject within a context haunted by ghostly terror means having the capacity in all circumstances to "rearrange fragments continually in new and different patterns or configurations." In the ghostly realm there can only be schizophrenic subjects. Gilles Deleuze and Félix Guattari write,

It might be said that the schizophrenic passes from one code to another, that he deliberately *scrambles all the codes*, by quickly shifting from one to another, according to the questions asked of him, never giving the same explanation from one day to the next, never invoking the same genealogy, never recording the same event in the same way. When he is more or less forced into it and is not in a touchy mood, he may even accept the banal Oedipal code, so long as he can stuff it full of all the disjunctions that his code was designed to help eliminate.[20]

Under conditions where, according to the Nietzschean expression, "everything divides, but in itself, and where every being is everywhere, on all sides, at all levels, except in terms of intensity," the only way to survive is by living in zigzags.

Third, as a ghostly subject, the slave has neither a unique form nor a content that has been definitively shaped. Form and content change constantly, in relation to life's events. But the deployment of existence can occur only if the subject draws from a reservoir of memories and images that seem to have been fixed once and for all. He leans on them even as he transgresses them, forgets them, places them in dependence on something other than themselves. As a result, the *work for life* consists in distancing oneself time and time again from memory and tradition at the very moment that one depends on them to negotiate the twists and turns of life. With life's contours barely sketched out, the wandering subject must constantly escape from himself and allow himself to be carried away by the flux of time and accidents. He produces himself in the unknown, by means of a chain of effects that is at times calculated but that never materializes exactly in the ways foreseen. It is within the unexpected, and within radical instability, that he creates and invents himself.

Perhaps this is why, in the middle of the night, the subject can allow himself to give in to the song of remembrance. Quite often the song is buried under the rubble of sorrow and thus unable to infuse existence with a sense of ecstasy and eternity. But set free by tobacco, it can suddenly shatter everything that limited the subject's horizon, projecting him into the infinite sea of light that makes it possible to forget misery:

After that he put a kind of smoking pipe which was about six feet long into my mouth. This smoking pipe could contain half a ton of tobacco at a time, then he chose one ghost to be loading this pipe with tobacco whenever it discharged fire. When he lit the pipe with fire then the whole of the ghosts and ghostesses were dancing round me set by set. They were singing, clapping hands, ringing bells and their ancestral drummers were beating the drums in such a way that all the dancers were jumping up with gladness. But whenever the smoke of the pipe was rushing out from my mouth . . . then all of them would laugh at me so that a person 2 miles away would hear them clearly, and whenever the tobacco inside the pipe is near to finishing the ghost who was chosen to be loading it would load it again with fresh tobacco. . . . After some hours that I was smoking this pipe I was intoxicated by the gas of the tobacco as if I drank much hard drink. . . . So at this time I forgot all my sorrow and started to sing the earth the songs which sorrow prevented me from singing about since I entered this bush. But when all these ghosts were hearing the song they were dancing from me to a distance of about five thousand feet and then dancing back to me again as they were much appreciating the song and also to hear my voice was curious to them.[21]

SIX
THE CLINIC
OF THE SUBJECT

Everything, then, starts with an act of identification: "I am Black." The act of identification is based on a question that we ask of ourselves: "Who, then, am I?" Or else it is a response to a question asked of us, a summons: "Who are you?" In both cases identity is unveiled and made public. But to unveil one's identity is also to recognize oneself. It is a form of self-recognition. It is to know who you are and to speak it or, better, to proclaim it—to say it to oneself. The act of identification is also an affirmation of existence. "I am" signifies, from that moment forward, "I exist."

The Master and His Black

But what, in the end, is a "Black"—that *beingness* of which one claims to be a *species*? "Black" is first of all a word—a word that always refers us to something. But the word has its own weight, its own density. A word is meant to evoke something in the conscience of the person to whom it is addressed or in the person who hears it. The more dense and weighty, the more it provokes a sensation, a feeling, or even resentment in the person to whom it refers. There are words that wound. The capacity of words to wound is a part of their particular weight. "Black" seeks above all to be a name. Every name seems to carry a destiny, a more or less generalized condition. "Black" is the name that was given to me by someone else. I did not choose it. I inherited the name because of the position I occupy in the space of the world. Those clothed in the name "Black" are well aware of its external provenance.

They are also well aware that they have no choice but to experience the name's power of falsification. From this point of view, a "Black" is the person who cannot look the Other straight in the eye. To be Black is to be stuck at the foot of a wall with no doors, thinking nonetheless that everything will open up in the end. The Black person knocks, begs, and knocks again, waiting for someone to open a door that does not exist. Many end up getting used to the situation. They start to recognize themselves in the destiny attributed to them by the name. A name is meant to be carried. They take something they did not originally create, and make it their own. Like the word, the name exists only if it is heard and taken on by the person who carries it. Or perhaps there is a name only if the person feels the effect of its weight on their conscience. There are some names carried as a perpetual insult, others as a habit. The name "Black" is both. And though some names can flatter, the name "Black" was from the beginning a mechanism for objectification and degradation. It drew its strength from its capacity to suffocate and strangle, to amputate and emasculate. The name was like death. There has always been an intimate relationship between the name "Black" and death, murder, being buried alive, along with the silence to which the thing necessarily had to be reduced—the order to be quiet and remain unseen.

Black—we cannot forget—aspires also to be a color. The color of obscurity. In this view Black is what lives the night, what lives in the night, whose life is turned into night. Night is its original envelope, the tissue out of which its flesh is made. It is its coat of arms, its uniform. The journey through night and this life as night renders Black invisible. The Other does not see it because, in the end, there is nothing to see. Or, if he does see, he sees only shadows and darkness—almost nothing. Enveloped in a night that was there before he was born, the Black Man cannot even see himself. He does not see that if he strikes his body against a wall with no doors, if he throws himself against it with all his strength and demands that the nonexistent door be opened, sooner or later he will fall out onto the sidewalk. As a thin film of being, he sees nothing. Indeed, because of his color, his sight can only be amniotic and mucosal. Such is the talismanic function of color—that which, surfacing at the end of sight, ultimately imposes itself as symptom and destiny, or as a knot in the conspiracy of power. The color black, from this perspective, has atmospheric properties, the first of which manifests itself in the form of an archaic reminder, a return to a genealogical inheritance that no one can truly alter because the Black Man cannot change his color. The second is an outside in which the Black

Man is imprisoned and in which he becomes transformed into a forever-unrecognizable other. And if the Black Man is unveiled, there is always a price to be paid first: that of a veiling. The color black has no meaning. It exists only in reference to the power that invented it, to an infrastructure that supports it and contrasts it with other colors, and, finally, to a world that makes it a name and an axiom.

The name "Black" is also a kind of link, a relationship to subjection. There is, ultimately, only a "Black Man" in relation to a "master." The "master" possesses his "Black Man." And the "Black Man" belongs to the "master." Every Black person takes form according to the wishes of the master. The master creates the Black Man, and the latter takes on form through the destruction and explosion of what he was before. There is no "Black" as such outside this dialectic of possession, belonging, and dynamiting. Every successful act of subjection is based on a constant relationship of property, appropriation, and belonging to someone other than oneself. In this dialectic of the Black Man and his master, the two most important signs of subjection are the chain and the leash. The leash is that kind of rope attached to a person who is not free. And the one who is not free is the same as the one to whom you cannot extend a hand, and who therefore must be dragged around by the neck. The leash is the ultimate signifier of slave identity, of the slave condition, of the state of servitude. The experience of servitude means being placed forcefully in the zone of undifferentiation between human and animal, in those zones where human life is seen from the posture of the animal—human life taking on the shape of animal life to the point that the two can no longer be distinguished, to the point where it is no longer clear what part of the animal is more human than the human and what part of man is more animal than the animal.

It is this disdained name that was taken up by Marcus Garvey and then Aimé Césaire, among others, with the goal of turning it into the subject of an essentially infinite conversation.

Race War and Self-Determination

Under slavery, the plantation was the central cog in a savage order whose racial violence had three functions. First, it aimed to weaken the capacity of the enslaved to assure their own social reproduction, in the sense that they were never able to unite the means necessary to live a life worthy of the name. This brutality also had a somatic dimension. It aimed to immobilize the body, and to break it if necessary. Finally, it attacked the nervous system and sought to dry up the capacities of its victims to create their own symbolic world. With most of their energies diverted to the basic tasks of survival, they were forced to live their lives only in the mode of repetition. But what characterized the master–slave relation above all was the monopoly the master believed he had on the future. To be Black and therefore a slave was to have no future of one's own. The future of the Black Man was always a delegated future, received from the master as a gift, as emancipation. That is why the question of the future was always at the center of the struggles of the slaves, a future horizon to be reached on their own, and thanks to which it would be possible to constitute themselves as free subjects, responsible for themselves and responsible before the world.

For Garvey, defining oneself through lack was no longer enough. The same was true of secondary or derivative forms of identification (or identification through the intermediary of the master). In the wake of the negative work of destruction, the Black Man had to become someone else, to construct himself as a subject capable of projecting himself into the future and investing in a desire. To give birth to a new human person and confer a modicum of consistency on his existence, he had to produce himself not as repetition but as *indissoluble difference and absolute singularity*. Out of loss and destruction came the power of creation, a living substance capable of giving birth to a new form in the world. Although sensitive to the idea of need, Garvey was careful not to reduce desire to need. He sought, instead, to redefine the very object of Black desire—the desire to govern oneself. Such desire was also a project, and he gave it a name: the African project of "redemption."[1]

To put the project of redemption into practice required a careful reading of the time of the world. The world itself was inhabited by the human species, composed of several races, each of which was called to remain pure. Each race controlled its destiny in the context of a territory over which it fully exercised the rights of sovereignty. Europe belonged to Whites, Asia to those described as "Yellow," and Africa to the Africans. Although distinct, each race was endowed with the same capacities and possibilities. None of them was commanded by nature to exercise control over others. Since the history of world was cyclical, all domination was temporary. At the beginning of the 1920s, Garvey was convinced that a political readjustment of the world was under way. This readjustment was propelled by the rising up of oppressed peoples and dominated races who struggled against the global powers and demanded respect and recognition. A race for life was under way. In this brutal and pitiless process, there was no room for disorganized peoples lacking ambition, incapable of protecting or defending their own interests. If they did not organize themselves, they were simply threatened with extinction. The project of redemption also demanded a theory of the event. For Garvey, the ultimate event was, essentially, called to produce itself in the future, at a time that no one could predict but whose imminence was manifest. For Blacks, the awaited goal was the arrival of the "African empire," without which the Black race could not enjoy political and economic existence in the world. The event was in the air, in the wind. The politics of the sentinel consisted in accompanying, perhaps precipitating, the arrival and preparing for it.[2]

Garvey, then, imagined a vast movement of desertion, or at least an *organized retreat*. He was convinced that the West was in inevitable decline. The development of technology had, paradoxically, opened the way for a civilization determined to destroy itself. With no spiritual foundation, it could not last indefinitely. In the conditions of the time, the Black Man was for Garvey a largely deterritorialized subject. "I know no national boundary where the Negro is concerned," he affirmed. "The whole world is my province until Africa is free." In a geopolitical context deeply shaped by the contest between the races in pursuit of life, these deterritorialized subjects could not guarantee their own protection, or even their survival as a distinct race lacking a homeland. The Black Man could not become an authentic human, that is, a *human like all others*, capable of doing what all humans have the right to do and exercising the kind of authority intrinsic to any human worthy of the name over themselves, others, and nature. The future of any Black person outside of Africa was nothing but ruin and disaster.[3]

Garvey's Africa remained, on many levels, a mythical and abstract entity, a full but also transparent signifier. This, paradoxically, was the source of its strength. In the Garveyite text, to say "Africa" was to start down a path in search of the substance of the sign—a substance that preceded the sign itself, and the form in which it had been called to manifest itself. The history of humanity was a history of race wars. The human race was composed of a race of masters and a race of slaves. Only the race of masters was capable of making laws for itself and imposing those laws on others.

Africa, in Garvey's eyes, was the name of a promise—the promise of a reversal of history. The race of slaves could one day soon become a race of masters again, if it simply gathered its own tools of power. For this distinct possibility to be realized, the Blacks of the Americas and the Caribbean had to desert the inhospitable places to which they had been relegated and return to their natural habitat and occupy it once more. There, far from those who had once placed them in servitude, they would finally recover their own power and nurture their genius. By developing a Black African nationality, they would avoid the hatred of others and the desire for vengeance, both of which would otherwise have consumed them.

The Rise of Humanity

Césaire struggled his entire life—with force and incisiveness, with energy and lucidity, between clarity and obscurity, using the miraculous weapon of poetry along with the no less honorable weapon that is politics. At times he fixed his eyes on the eternal. At other times he fixed them on the ephemeral, on what passes and returns to dust. He sought obstinately to cultivate a place of permanence from which the lie of the name could be aired out and truth resuscitated, where the indestructible would be made manifest. This is why his volcanic thought was simultaneously one of interruption, uprising, and hope. The foundation for his thought on struggle and insurrection was, on one hand, the affirmation of the irreducible plurality of the world, or, as he liked to say, of "civilizations," and, on the other, the conviction that "humans, no matter where they are, have rights as human beings."[4] His thought bore witness to the hope for a humane relationship to difference, an unconditional relationship with humanity. For Césaire, a new relationship was vital to confronting the face without a name and the inexorable violence that pushed us to denude it, to violate it and silence its sound. His thought put racism and colonialism on trial. They were the modern forms of such violation and erasure, two figures of the bestiality within man, of that union between the human and the beast that our world is far from leaving behind. The terror that Césaire inhabited, finally, was one of a slumber from which there was no awakening—with no sun and no tomorrow.

Césaire's obsession went beyond the Antilles, those countries he habitually called not "French" but "Caribbean." It was not only France, whose revolution he considered a completely foundational event, even if one that was incapable of dealing with the "colonial problem," or the possibility of a society without race. It was also Haiti (a land that "had allegedly conquered its liberty" but that was more miserable than a colony). It was Patrice Lumumba's Congo and, through it, Africa (where independence had led to a "conflict among ourselves"). It was Black America (he never stopped recalling and proclaiming his "debt of recognition" to it). It was, as he always repeated, the "fate of the Black Man in the modern world."

How can we take seriously the concern he claimed for what he called the "Black Man"? We must first avoid the temptation to neutralize the polemical charge at its heart, and the unknown to which it points, and accept that it may all be quite disconcerting. We must embrace this concern not to lock Césaire within a carceral conception of identity, nor to relegate his thinking to a form of racial tribalism. Rather, we must embrace it to prevent anyone from shying away from his difficult questions—questions that he never stopped asking and that remain today for the most part unanswered, beginning with questions of colonialism, race, and racism. Did he not still say recently that "what confronts us is racism; the recrudescence of racism throughout the world; the hearths of racism which, here and there, have been lit up once again. That is what confronts us. That is what should preoccupy us. Is now really the time for us to lower our guard and disarm ourselves?" What, then, does Césaire mean when he proclaimed his concern for the fate of the "Black Man" in the modern world? What does he mean by "Black Man"? Why not simply say "human"?[5]

We should underline, first, that in making race the starting point of a critique of politics, modernity, and the very idea of the universal, Césaire inscribed himself in a long line of Black intellectual criticism that can be found among African-American as well as Anglophone Caribbean and African thinkers. But in Césaire's thought, concern for the Black Man does not lead to *secession* from the world but rather to the affirmation of its *plurality* and the necessity of making it thrive. To affirm that the world is plural, and to militate for it to thrive, is to announce that Europe is not the world but only a part of it. It is to offer a counterweight to what Césaire calls "European reductionism"—by which he means "that system of thought, or rather instinctive tendency, on the part of an eminent and prestigious civilization to take advantage of its prestige by creating a vacuum around it that abusively reduces the notion of the universal to its own dimensions, that is to think the universal only on the basis of its own postulations and through its own categories." The result, he explains, is to "amputate man from the human and isolate him, permanently, in a suicidal pride if not in a rational and scientific form of barbarism."[6]

To affirm that the world cannot be reduced to Europe is to rehabilitate singularity and difference. In that, and despite what some say, Césaire is very close to Léopold Sédar Senghor. Both reject abstract visions of the universal. They argue that the universal is always defined through the register of singularity. In their eyes, the universal is precisely the site of a multiplicity of singularities, each of which is only what it is, or what links and separates it from other singularities. For both Césaire and Senghor, there is no absolute universal. The only universal is the community of singularities and differences, a sharing that is at once the creation of something common and a form of separation. Here, the concern for the Black Man makes sense only because it opens the way for a reimagining of the universal community. His critique is relevant today in an age of war without end and the multiple returns of colonialism. Indeed, it is indispensible for contemporary conditions, whether in terms of citizenship, of the presence of foreigners and minorities among us, of non-European forms of human becoming, of the conflict of monotheisms, or else of globalization itself.

On another level, Césaire's critique of race was always inseparable from the critique of colonialism and the thought that sustained it. In his *Discourse on Colonialism* of 1950, Césaire asked: What is the principle of colonialism? It is "neither evangelization, nor a philanthropic enterprise, nor a desire to push back the frontiers of ignorance, disease, and tyranny, nor a project undertaken for the greater glory of God, nor an attempt to extend the rule of law." A dishonest equation, it is the daughter of appetite, cupidity, and violence—lies, violated treaties, punitive expeditions, poison instilled into Europe's veins, transforming people into savages, all of the ways the colonizer decivilizes, dives into brainwashing, learns how to awaken hidden instincts like covetousness, violence, racial hatred, and moral relativism. This is the reason that "no one colonizes innocently, that no one colonizes with impunity; that a nation which colonizes, that a civilization which justifies colonization—and therefore force—is already a sick civilization, a civilization which is morally diseased, which irresistibly, progressing from one consequence to another, one denial to another, calls for its Hitler." And, furthermore, "the colonizer, who in order to ease his conscience gets into the habit of seeing the other man as *an animal,* accustoms himself to treating him like an animal, and tends objectively to transform *himself* into an animal."[7] To take Césaire seriously is to continue to track, in today's world, the signs that mark the return of colonialism, or its reproduction and repetition in contemporary practices—whether practices of war, forms of marginalization and stigmatization of difference, or, more directly, forms of revisionism that, basing themselves on the failures of postcolonial regimes, try to justify retroactively what was above all, as Tocqueville suggested, a rude, venal, and arbitrary form of government.

Finally, it is important to continue to raise questions about the meaning of the term "*Nègre*," which Senghor and Césaire rehabilitated at the height of imperial racism. It is significant that at the end of his life Césaire thought it necessary to remind Françoise Vergès: "Black I am and Black I will stay."[8] He became aware of his Blackness at the beginning of the 1930s, when, in Paris, he met Senghor and the African-American writers Langston Hughes, Claude McKay, Countee Cullen, Sterling Brown, and, later, Richard Wright, as well as many others. His realization was provoked by the anxious and pressing self-questioning that went on among a generation of Black thinkers between the two world wars. It focused on the Black condition, on the one hand, and on the possibilities of the era, on the other. Césaire summarized such concerns in the following manner: "Who are we in this white world? What can we hope for, and what should we do?" In answer to the first question, he offered an unambiguous response: "We are Black." In affirming his "negritude" in such a decisive way, he also affirmed a difference that was not to be simplified, not to be veiled, and from which one should not turn away by claiming that it was inexpressible.[9]

But what did he mean by "Black" ("Nègre"), this return to the name that Frantz Fanon, in *Black Skin, White Masks*, said was only a fiction? And what should we understand by this word today? For him, the name referred not to a biological reality or skin color but to "one of the historical forms of the condition imposed on humans." But the word was also a synonym for "the stubborn struggle for liberty and indomitable hope." For Césaire, the term "Black" communicated something essential that had nothing to do with the idolatry of race. Because it carried the experience of so many trials (which Césaire was absolutely committed to never forgetting) and because it constitutes the ultimate metaphor of being "put to the side," the name best expresses, *a contrario*, the quest for what he calls a "greater fraternity" or "a humanism made to the measure of the world."[10]

That said, this humanism made to fit the world can be articulated only in the language of what-is-to-come, of that which will always be ahead of us and will therefore always be deprived of a name and of memory, but not of reason. As such, it will always escape repetition because of its radical difference. The universalism of the name "Black" depends not on repetition but on the *radical difference without which the dis-enclosure of the world is impossible*. It is in the name of this *radical difference* that we must re-imagine the Black Man as someone on the road, or ready to set out on the road, who experiences being snatched away, being a stranger. But for this experience of travel and exodus to have meaning, it must include Africa as an essential component. It must bring us back to Africa, or at least take a detour through Africa, the double of the world whose time we know will come.

Césaire knew that Africa's time would come, that we had to look ahead to it and prepare ourselves for it. He reinscribed Africa simultaneously onto the registers of neighborliness and extreme distance, of the presence of the Other, thus preventing the possibility of home or residency from being anything other than dreamlike. Yet this manner of inhabiting Africa enabled him to resist the siren call of insularity. In the end it was perhaps Africa that allowed him to understand the existence of a profound strength within humanity that exceeded what is forbidden. And it was this knowledge that lent his thinking its volcanic character.

But how can we reread Césaire without Fanon? The latter witnessed colonial violence, notably in Algeria, and sought to confront its traumatic consequences through his own medical practice. This violence manifested itself in the form of everyday racism, but especially through the torture used by the French army against Algerian resistance fighters.[11] The country for which he had nearly lost his life during World War II reproduced Nazi methods over the course of a savage and nameless war against a people denied the right to self-determination. Fanon often said of the war in Algeria, the "most horrific" of wars, that it had taken on the "look of an authentic genocide" or else an "enterprise of extermination."[12] As he wrote elsewhere, the war was "the most hallucinatory war that any people has ever waged to smash colonial aggression."[13] In Algeria it created a "bloodthirsty and pitiless atmosphere" that led to the widespread "generalization of inhuman prac-tices." As a result, many among the colonized had the impression of being "caught up in a veritable Apocalypse."[14] During this fight to the death, Fanon had taken the side of the Algerian people. From then on, France no longer recognized him as one of its own. He had "betrayed" the nation. He became an "enemy," and long after his death was treated as such.

After its defeat in Algeria and the loss of its colonial empire, France had retreated into the Hexagon. Struck by aphasia, it dove into a kind of postimperial winter.[15] Having suppressed its colonial past, it settled into a phase of "good conscience," forgot Fanon, and subsequently missed out on the new global intellectual journeys that shaped the end of the twenti-eth century—notably postcolonial thought and critical race theory.[16] But Fanon's heretical name was invoked throughout the world by movements struggling for emancipation. For many organizations committed to defend-ing humiliated peoples, fighting for racial justice, or pushing for new psychi-atric practices, to say "Fanon" was to call on a kind of "perennial excess," a "supplement," an "elusive remainder" that made it nevertheless possible to offer "something extremely relevant" to the world.[17]

In our world of hierarchical division, the idea of a common human con-dition is the object of many pious declarations. But it is far from being put into practice. Old colonial divisions have been replaced with various forms of apartheid, marginalization, and structural destitution. Global processes of accumulation and expropriation in an increasingly brutal world eco-nomic system have created new forms of violence and inequality. Their spread has resulted in new forms of insecurity, undermining the capacity of many to remain masters of their own lives. But to read Fanon today is, first of all, to take precise measure of his project with the goal of continu-ing it. For if his thought rang out like a bell, filling its moment with bronze vibration, it is because it countered the brazen law of colonialism with a response that was equally implacable and powerful. His was a *situated thinking*, born of a lived experience that was always in progress, unstable, and changing. An experience at the limits, full of risk, where the thinking subject reflected in full awareness on his history, his very existence, and his own name, and in the name of the people to come, those yet to be born. As a result, in Fanon's logic, to think was to walk with others toward a world created together unendingly, irreversibly, within and through struggle.[18]

For a common world to emerge, critical thought had to be deployed like an artillery shell aimed at smashing, puncturing, and transforming the mineral and rocky wall and interosseous membrane of colonialism. It is this energy that made Fanon's thinking *metamorphic thought*.

The Great Destruction

To reread Fanon today is also to take on for ourselves, in our own conditions, some of the questions he never ceased to ask of his own time, questions related to the possibility for subjects and peoples to stand up, walk with their own feet, use their own hands, faces, and bodies to write their own histories as part of a world that we all share, to which we all have a right, to which we are all heirs.[19] If there is one thing that will never die in Fanon, it is the project of the collective rise of humanity. In his eyes, this irrepressible and implacable quest for liberty required the mobilization of all of life's reserves. Each human subject, and each people, was to engage in a grand project of self-transformation, in a struggle to the death, without reserve. They had to take it on as their own. They could not delegate it to others.

In this quasi-sacrificial aspect of his thought, the duty to revolt, to rise up, became an injunction. It went hand in hand with the duty to violence—a strategic term in the Fanonian lexicon that, as a result of hasty and sometimes casual readings, has led to many misunderstandings. It is therefore worthwhile to return briefly to the historical conditions that served as the background for Fanon's conceptualization of violence. We must remember two things. First, for Fanon, violence was as much a political as a *clinical* concept. It was as much the clinical manifestation of a "sickness" of a political nature as it was a practice of the transformation of symbols. What was at stake was the possibility of reciprocity, and therefore of relative equality in the face of the supreme judgment of death. By choosing violence over becoming its victim, the colonized returns to himself. He discovers that "his life, his breath, his heartbeat are the same as that of the colonizer" and that "the skin of a colonist is not worth any more than that of a native."[20] In the process he reconstitutes himself and redefines himself. He learns anew to weigh and value his life and his own presence to his body, to his word, to the Other, and to the world.

On the conceptual level, Fanonian discourse on violence in general and on the violence of the colonized in particular emerges from the intersection of *the clinic of the subject* and *the politics of the patient*. For Fanon, in effect, politics and the clinic are both psychic sites par excellence.[21] These locations, which a priori are empty, come to be animated by speech. At stake is the relationship to language and the body. Both also expose two events that are decisive for the subject: on the one hand, the radical and nearly irreversible change in the relationship to oneself and to others engendered by the colonial situation; on the other, the extraordinary vulnerability of the psyche in the face of the traumatic experience of the real.[22] But the relationship between these two universes is far from stable. Indeed, Fanon distinguishes clearly between the politics of the clinic and the clinical aspect of politics. He constantly oscillates between the two. At times he sees politics as a form of the clinic, and the clinical as a form of politics. At others he underlines the unavoidable character, the failures, and the impasse of the clinic, especially in situations in which the trauma of war, the ambient destruction and pain and suffering broadly produced by the bestial law of colonialism, weakens the capacity of the subject or patient to enter into the world of human speech.[23] Revolutionary violence is the shock that explodes this ambivalence. But Fanon shows that while violence is a key phase in the acquisition of the status of political subject, violence itself, upon eruption, creates considerable psychic wounds. While the violence carried out by the subject during the war of liberation could become a form of language, it was equally capable of ceasing language, of producing muteness, hallucinatory haunting, and trauma in survivors.

In Algeria, France attempted a "total war" that incited an equally total response on the part of the Algerian resistance. Through his experience of the war and the racism that was one of its driving forces, Fanon became convinced that colonialism was fundamentally a necropolitical force animated by genocidal impulses.[24] The colonial situation was, above all, a situation of potentially exterminating violence that had to be converted into an ontology and a genetics in order to reproduce and perpetuate itself. As a result, the only way to assure its destruction was through an "absolute line of action."[25] Imbued with this realization, Fanon developed his reflections on three forms of violence: colonial violence (whose incandescent moment was the Algerian war), the emancipatory violence of the colonized (whose ultimate stage was the war of national liberation), and violence in international relations. In his eyes, colonial violence had three dimensions. It was a *founding* violence to the extent that it presided over the institutionalization of a mode of subjection whose origins were rooted in violence, and whose function and longevity depended on violence. Colonialism, from this perspective, was unique because it dressed up in the appearance of civil society what was based, at its origin and in its daily functioning, on a state of nature.

Colonial violence was, furthermore, an *empirical* violence. It enclosed the daily life of the colonized using techniques that were at once reticular and molecular. It created a grid of lines and knots that was physical, to be sure—like the barbed wire of the internment and resettlement camps during the high point of the counterinsurgency. But it also worked according to a system of crossed wires, along a spatial and topological axis that included not only surface (horizontality) but also height (verticality).[26] The goal of raids, extralegal assassinations, expulsions, and mutilations was to target individuals whose instincts and very capacity to breathe had to be controlled.[27] This molecular violence even infiltrated language. Its weight crushed all the scenes of life, including the scene of speech. It manifested itself most of all in the everyday behavior of the colonizer toward the colonized: aggressiveness, racism, disdain, unending rituals of humiliation, homicidal behavior—what Fanon called "the politics of hate."[28]

Colonial violence was, finally, a *phenomenal* violence. In this regard it affected not only the domain of the senses but also the psychic and emotional domains. It generated mental disorders that were difficult to treat and heal. It excluded any dialectic of recognition and was indifferent to all moral argumentation. It attacked time, one of the privileged mental contexts of all subjectivity, which placed the colonized in danger of losing the use of all traces of memory, precisely those that might have allowed them "to turn loss into something other than a hemorrhagic abyss."[29] One of its functions was not only to empty the colonized's past of all substance, but also to foreclose on the future. It also attacked the bodies of the colonized, structuring their muscles, provoking stiffening and deformation. And it did not spare the psyche, since violence aims at nothing less than decerebration. The body and conscience of the colonized were striped with cuts, wounds, and injuries. Fanon's practice was to understand them and heal them.[30] We might call this triple violence a sovereign violence, since in reality it was composed of "multiple, diverse, repeated and cumulative violence."[31] The colonized experienced it in their muscles and blood. It required that the colonized perceive their lives as a "permanent struggle against an omnipresent death." It made their lives as a whole seem like an "incomplete death."[32] Above all, it incited within them an interior rage, that of a "pursued man," one forced to contemplate, with his own eyes, the reality of a "truly animal existence."[33]

Fanon's entire oeuvre was a deposition in defense of this bullied and ruined existence. It was an obstinate search for the traces of life that survived this great destruction. New forms of life, he believed, would be born out of this extraordinary state, through hand-to-hand combat with death itself.[34] For him, the role of the critic was as both actor and eyewitness to the events he recounted. He listened to, but also fought alongside, the world emerging from the depths of the struggle. His speech was an incandescent filament, at once testimony and legal declaration. To be a witness to the colonial situation was above all to offer an account of lives plunged into never-ending agony. It meant "walk[ing] step-by-step along the great wound inflicted on the Algerian soil and on the Algerian people." It was necessary, he insisted, "to question the Algerian earth meter by meter," to "measure the fragmentation of the Algerian family, the degree to which it finds itself scattered" as a result of colonial occupation. It was necessary to listen to the "haggard and famished" orphans, to the "husband taken away by the enemy who comes back with his body covered with contusions, more dead than alive, his mind stunned." Doing so meant being attentive to the scenes of mourning, to those sites of loss and heartbreak where new practices had emerged in place of yesterday's lamentations. The ordeal of struggle had put an end to crying and shouting. People did not do what they used to, he noticed. Instead, "one grits one's teeth and one prays in silence. One further step, and it is cries of joy that salute the death of the *moudjahid* who has fallen on the field of honor." And from the transfiguration of suffering and death was born a new "spiritual community."[35]

The Emancipatory Violence of the Colonized

For Fanon, there was a categorical difference between the violence of the colonizer and that of the colonized. The violence of the colonized was not ideological, at least not at first. It was the exact opposite of colonial violence. Before it was consciously turned against colonial oppression during the war of national liberation, it manifested itself in the form of pure rush—ad hoc violence, reptilian and epileptic, a murderous and simple gesture carried out by "the hunted man" with his "back to the wall," the knife "at his throat (or, more precisely, the electrode at his genitals)," seeking desperately "to show that he is prepared to fight for his life."[36]

How to transform this energetic fervor, this banal instinct for survival, into full and complete political speech? How to turn it into an affirmative countervoice in the face of the logic of death deployed by the occupying power? How to turn it into an emancipatory gesture endowed with the attributes of value, reason, and truth? These questions were the starting point for Fanon's reflections on the violence of the colonized. This was no longer the violence that the colonized simply suffered, the violence that was imposed on them and that turned them into resigned victims. Instead, from then on, the colonized chose to *offer* violence to the colonizer. Fanon described this gift in the language of "work," as a "practice of violence," a "reaction to the settler's violence in the beginning." This violence was produced as a kind of circulating energy through which "each individual forms a violent link in a great chain, a part of the great organism of violence" within a "cement which has been mixed with blood and anger."[37] The radical rejection of imposed violence represented a major moment in the transformation of symbols.[38] The goal of work was to produce life. But life could spring forth only from "the rotting corpse of the settler."[39] The goal was truly to *give death* to those who were habituated never to receive it, who had always only submitted others to death without restraint or consequence.

Fanon was conscious of the fact that, by choosing "counter-violence," the colonized were opening the door to a disastrous reciprocity—a "recurring terror." But he believed that in extreme circumstances, circumstances in which all distinction between civil and military power had been eliminated and the rules governing the distribution of weapons within colonial society had been profoundly transformed, the only way for the colonized to restore themselves to life was to use violence to impose a redefinition of the mechanisms through which death was distributed. The resulting exchange nevertheless remained unequal. Did not "machine-gunning from airplanes and bombardments from the fleet go far beyond in horror and magnitude . . . any answer the natives can make?" Moreover, the recourse to violence did not automatically restore the equivalence between the lives of colonizer and colonized. The news of "seven Frenchmen killed or wounded at the Col de Sakamody" incited the "indignation of all civilized consciences," while the "the sack of the douars of Guergour and the dechras of Djerah and the massacre of whole populations—which had merely called for the Sakamody ambush as a reprisal—all of this is of not the slightest importance."[40]

But what gave the violence of the colonized its ethical dimension was its close connection with care and healing: the treatment provided in military hospitals to the injured, including to prisoners that the rebellion refused to kill in their beds the way the colonial troops did; the care offered to torture victims whose personalities had been permanently dislocated, to Algerian women gone mad after being raped, and even to torturers haunted by their terrifying doubles—their victims. In addition to healing the wounds of colonial atrocities, the violence of the colonized had three purposes. It served as a call to a people who were caught in the grip of history and trapped in an untenable situation. They were asked to exercise their freedom, to take charge, to name themselves, to spring to life, and if they refused, they had at least to admit their bad faith in not doing so. They had to make a choice, risk their lives, expose themselves, and "draw on their entire reserves and their most hidden resources."[41] Such was the precondition for achieving liberty. In taking these risks, they counted on an unshakable faith in the power of the masses and on a philosophy of the will to become humans among other humans.

Fanon's theory of violence, however, makes sense only within the context of a more general theory, one of the *rise of humanity*. In the colonial context that was the foundation for Fanon's thought, the rise of humanity meant that the colonized would propel themselves, through their own strength, to a level higher than the one to which they had been consigned as a result of racism or subjugation. The embattled human subject, brought to his knees and subjected to abuse, rallies on his own, scales the ramp, and pulls himself up to his full height and to that of other humans. When necessary, he uses violence—what Fanon called "the absolute line of action."[42] In this way he reopens the possibility—for him and for all of humanity, starting with his executioners—for a new and open dialogue between two equal human subjects, when before there was only an opposition between a man (the colonizer) and his object (the colonized). From this moment on, there is no Black or White. There is only a world finally freed from the burden of race, a world that everyone has the right to inherit.

If Fanon was offering a form of knowledge, it was a situated knowledge—a knowledge of the experience of marginalization and subjection, a knowledge of the dehumanizing colonial situation, and a knowledge of the means to bring it to an end. Whether it was a case of trying to "convey the misery of the black man" in the face of a racist social order or of being aware of the transformation engendered by the war of liberation in Algeria, his knowledge was always openly partisan. It aimed for neither objectivity nor neutrality. "I have not wished to be objective," he declared. "Besides, that would be dishonest: It is not possible for me to be objective."[43] It was, above all, a way of accompanying the struggle of those who were wounded, decerebrated, and driven mad by colonial violence, and—wherever this was still possible—of curing and healing them.

It was also a form of knowledge that joined the critique of human life with the politics of struggle and of the work required to escape death. From this perspective, the goal of struggle was to produce life, with "absolute violence" serving as an agent of de-intoxication and institutionalization. It was, in effect, through violence that "the 'thing' which has been colonized becomes a man" and that new men could be created, along with "a new language and a new humanity." Life as a result took on the appearance of an unending struggle.[44] Strictly speaking, life was what produced struggle. Struggle as such had three dimensions. First, it aimed to destroy that which destroyed, amputated, dismembered, blinded, and provoked fear and rage. Second, it sought to take care of and, eventually, heal those who had been hurt, raped, tortured, imprisoned, or simply driven mad by power. Struggle's function, from then on, was to contribute to the general process of healing. Finally, its goal was to offer a tomb to all who had fallen, "shot in the back."[45] From this perspective, struggle played the role of a burial. Through its three functions, the link between life and power became clear. Power, in this view, was power only to the extent that it shaped life at the intersection of health, sickness, and death (or burial).

The struggle that Fanon wrote about took place in a context in which power—in this case colonial power—tended to reduce what passed as the space of life to an extreme destitution of the body and its needs, which Fanon described in the following terms: "The relations of man with matter, with the world outside, and with history are in the colonial period simply relations with food." For the colonized, he insisted, "living does not mean embodying moral values or taking his place in the coherent and fruitful development of the world." Rather, to live is simply "to keep on existing." To exist is a "triumph for life." And he adds, "The fact is that the only perspective is that belly which is more and more sunken, which is certainly less and less demanding, but which must be contented all the same." In Fanon's eyes, this annexation of human beings by the power of the material, the material of death and of need, constituted the time "before life began," the "heavy darkness"—or the "great night" that had to be escaped.[46] The time before life could be recognized by the fact that, under its empire, there was never a question of the colonized giving meaning to their life, but only of giving meaning "to their death."[47] Fanon gave the escape from the "great night" several different names: "liberation," "rebirth," "restitution," "substitution," "resurgence," "emergence," and "absolute disorder," or "walking constantly, at night and in the day," "making a new man stand up," "finding something else," a new subject emerging whole out of the "cement which has been mixed with blood and anger"—a nearly indefinable subject, always outdoing itself, a kind of difference that resists law, division, and hurt.

As a result, the critique of life, for Fanon, was intertwined with the critique of suffering, fear, and need, of work and law—notably the law of race, or what turns people into slaves by crushing and exhausting both the body and the nervous system. It was also intertwined with a critique of measurement and value—the precondition for a politics of equality and universality. But this politics of equality and universality—another name for truth and reason—was possible only for those who wanted and demanded the "man in front of us" and accepted that such a man was "no longer just a body."[48] To reread Fanon today, then, is partly about learning to resituate his life, work, and language within the history into which he was born and which he tried to transform through struggle and criticism. It also means translating—into the language of our time—the major questions that forced him to stand up, uproot himself, and travel among companions along the new road that the colonized had to build with their own strength, with their own inventiveness, with their irreducible will. We must reactualize this marriage of struggle and criticism in our contemporary world. And so it is inevitable that we must think at once with and against Fanon, the difference between him and some of us being that, for him, to think was first of all to uproot oneself from oneself. It was to put one's life in the balance.

That said, our world is not exactly his world—and yet! Neo- and para-colonial wars are, after all, flourishing once again. The forms of occupation have changed with torture, internment camps, and secret prisons, and with today's mix of militarism, counterinsurgency, and the pillage of resources from a distance. The question of the people's self-determination may have moved to a new location, but it remains as fundamental as it was in Fanon's time. In a world that is rebalkanizing itself within increasingly militarized fences, walls, and borders, where the fury to unveil women remains vehement and the right to mobility is more and more constrained for those in a number of racialized categories, Fanon's great call for an opening up of the world will inevitably find many echoes. We can, in fact, see this in the organization of new forms of struggle—cellular, horizontal, lateral—appropriate for the digital age, which are emerging in the four corners of the world.

If we owe Fanon a debt, it is for the idea that in every human subject there is something indomitable and fundamentally intangible that no domination—no matter what form it takes—can eliminate, contain, or suppress, at least not completely. Fanon tried to grasp how this could be reanimated and brought back to life in a colonial context that in truth is different from ours, even if its double—institutional racism—remains our own beast. For this reason, his work represents a kind of fibrous lignite, a weapon of steel, for the oppressed in the world today.

The Cloud of Glory

For Nelson Mandela, this weapon of steel took on a material form. Apartheid, far from an ordinary form of colonial domination and racial oppression, incited the emergence of a class of extraordinary and fearless men and women who brought about its abolition at the cost of tremendous sacrifice. If, among them all, Mandela came to name the movement, it was because at each crossroads in his life he succeeded—sometimes under pressure from circumstances, but often voluntarily—in following unexpected paths. His life can be summarized in few words: a man constantly on the lookout, a sentinel at the point of departure, whose returns—as unexpected as they were miraculous—only contributed to his mythologization. His myth was founded in part on the desire for the sacred and a thirst for the secret. But it flourished from the beginning because of the proximity of death, that primal form of departure and uprooting.

Mandela experienced uprooting very early on when he converted to nationalism—as others did—as if to a religion. Johannesburg, the city of gold mines, became the main theater of his encounter with destiny. So began a long and painful way of the cross made up of deprivation, repeated arrests, constant harassment, multiple appearances before tribunals, regular stays in prisons (with their string of tortures and rituals of humiliations), periods of clandestine life of varying length, the inversion of the worlds of night and day, more and less successful disguises, a dislocated family life, homes occupied and then deserted; a man in struggle, hunted, a fugitive always about to leave, guided only by the conviction that one day soon he would return.[49]

He took enormous risks, notably with his own life, which he lived intensely—as if everything were to begin again, and as if every moment was his last. But he also took risks with the lives of many others. He barely escaped the death sentence. It was 1964. With the other accused alongside him, he had prepared himself to be condemned, expecting the death sentence: "We discussed it, as I say, and we said that it was necessary for us to think, not only just in terms of ourselves, who were in this situation, but of the struggle as a whole. We should disappear under a cloud of glory, we should fight back. This is the service we can render to our organisation and to our people."[50] This Eucharistic vision was, however, free from any desire for martyrdom. And in contrast to all the others—Ruben Um Nyobé Patrice Lumumba, Amilcar Cabral, Martin Luther King Jr., and so many others—he escaped this fate. It was in the prison camp, in the space of forced labor and exile, that he truly developed his desire for life. Prison became the site of extreme trial, that of confinement and the return of man to his most basic expression. In the place of maximal destitution, Mandela learned to live in a cell as a living being forced to marry a coffin.[51]

Over the course of long and horrible hours of solitude, pushed to the edge of madness, he rediscovered the essential—all that lies in silence and detail. Everything spoke to him anew: the ant going who knows where; the planted seed that dies, then comes to life again, creating the illusion of a garden in the midst of concrete; the gray of the watchtowers and the loud clanging of the heavy metal doors closing; the tiny thing here or there, no matter what it was; the silence of the sad days that all seemed the same and never seemed to pass; time stretching out interminably; the slowness of days, the cold of winter nights, and the wind that screamed of desperation like owls tormented by who knows what; speech becoming so rare; the world outside of the walls of which no murmurs were heard; the abyss that was Robben Island, and the jailer's traces on Mandela's face, which from then on was sculpted by suffering, his eyes faded by the light of the sun refracted on quartz, with tears that never came, the dust of a shroud on a face transformed into a ghostly specter, and on his lungs, toes, and that tramplike envelope that served as his shoes. But above it all was the joyous and brilliant smile, that proud, straight, standing posture, his fist clenched, ready to embrace the world again and raise up a storm.

Stripped of almost everything, he struggled inch by inch, refusing to relinquish the humanity that remained and that his jailers wanted at all costs to rip from him and brandish like a trophy. Reduced to living with almost nothing, he learned to save everything but also to cultivate a profound detachment in relation to the things of profane life. Although he was a prisoner confined between two and a half walls, he was nevertheless no one's slave. A Black Man in bone and flesh, Mandela lived close to disaster. He penetrated into the night of life, close to the shadows, seeking an idea that in the end was quite simple: how to live free from race and the domination that results from it. His choices brought him to the edge of the precipice. He fascinated the world because he became a revenant from the land of shadows, a gushing force on the eve of an aging century that had forgotten how to dream.

Like the worker's movements of the nineteenth century and the struggles of women, our modernity has been haunted by the *desire for abolition* once carried by the slaves. At the beginning of the twentieth century, the dream lived on in the great struggles for decolonization, which from the beginning had a global dimension. Their significance was never only local. It was always universal. Even when anticolonial struggles mobilized local actors, in a circumscribed country or territory, they were always at the origin of solidarities forged on a planetary and transnational scale. It was these struggles that each time allowed for the extension, or rather the universalization, of rights that had previously remained the privilege of a single race.

Democracy and the Poetics of Race

We are, then, far from living in a postracial era in which questions of memory, justice, and reconciliation are irrelevant. Could we, however, speak of a post-Césairian era? We can, if we embrace and retain the signifier "Black" not with the goal of finding solace within it but rather as a way of clouding the term in order to gain distance from it. We must conjure with the term in order to reaffirm the innate dignity of every human being and of the very idea of a human community, a same humanity, an essential human resemblance and proximity. The wellspring for such ascetic work will be found in the best of our Afro-American and South African political, religious, and cultural traditions. These include the prophetic religions of the descendants of slaves and the utopian functions so characteristic of the work of artistic creation. For communities whose history has long been one of debasement and humiliation, religious and artistic creation has often represented the final defense against the forces of dehumanization and death. This twofold creation has deeply shaped political praxis. It has always served as a metaphysical and aesthetic envelope, since one of the functions of art and religion has been precisely to maintain the hope of escaping the world as it has been and as it is, to be reborn into life, to lead the festival once again.

Here the primary function of the work of art has never been to represent, illustrate, or narrate reality. It has always been in its nature simultaneously to confuse and mimic original forms and appearances. As a figurative form, it certainly maintained a relationship of resemblance to the original object. But at the same time it constantly redoubled the original object, deforming it, distancing itself from it, and most of all conjuring with it. In fact, in most Black aesthetic traditions, art was produced only through the work of conjuring, in the space where the optic and tactile functions, along with the world of the senses, were united in a single movement aimed at revealing the double of the world. In this way the time of a work of art is the moment when daily life is liberated from accepted rules and is devoid of both obstacles and guilt.

If there is one characteristic trait of artistic creation, it is that, at the beginning of the act of creation, we always rediscover violence at play, a miming of sacrilege or transgression, through which art aims to free the individual and their community from the world as it has been and as it is. The hope for the liberation of hidden or forgotten energies, the hope for an ultimate reversal of visible and invisible powers, this hidden dream of the resurrection of being and of things—this is the anthropological and political foundation of classic Black art. At its center we find the body, what is fundamentally at stake in the movement of power, the privileged locus for the unveiling of power, and the ultimate symbol of the constitutional debt at the heart of all human community, the debt that we inherit without wanting to and that we can never fully discharge.

The question of debt is another name for life. The central object of artistic creation, and the spirit of its materiality, has always been the critique of life and meditation on what resists death. It is important to clarify that the critique of life is not carried out in the abstract but is rather a meditation on the conditions that make the struggle to live, to stay alive, to survive, in sum, to live a human life, the most important aesthetic—and therefore political—question. Whether in reference to sculpture, music, dance, oral literature, or the worship of divinities, the goal has always been to awaken slumbering powers, once again to lead the celebration, that privileged channel for ambivalence, the provisional theater of luxury, luck, expenditure, and sexual activity, the metaphor for a future to come. There has therefore never been anything traditional in this art, if only because it has always been charged with exposing the extraordinary fragility of the social order. It is a form of art that has constantly reinvented myths and redirected tradition in order to undermine them through the very act that pretended to anchor and ratify them. It has always been an art of sacrilege, sacrifice, and expenditure, multiplying new fetishes in pursuit of a generalized deconstruction of existence precisely through its use of play, leisure, spectacle, and the principle of metamorphosis. It is this utopian, metaphysical, and aesthetic supplement that the radical critique of race brings to democracy.

Struggle as a *praxis of liberation* has always drawn part of its imaginary resources from Christianity. The Christianity in question is not foremost that of the Church, which installed itself from the beginning as a form of dogmatic control precisely where emptiness opened up. Nor is it a certain discourse about God, whose function has often been to translate "the ever expanding powerlessness of man seeking to connect with his own desire."[52] What the enslaved and their descendants mean by Christianity is a space of truth that opens up within an odd scission in a terrain of a truth that it-self is always opening itself up—it is a *be-coming*, a futurity. They understand the declaration of a principle that we might summarize as follows: Some-thing has arrived; an event has occurred; language has unwound; and one can see with one's own eyes, hear with one's own ears, and bear witness with one's own tongue, and for all nations. This event is simultaneously an advent. It is a "here," a "there," a "now" that signifies at once both an instant and a present, but most of all the possibility of Jubilee, a sort of plenitude of time, in which all the peoples of the earth will finally be reunited around something infinite that nothing will be able to limit.

But the part of Christianity that most shapes thought of African ori-gin is the triple pattern of incarnation, crucifixion, and resurrection—of sacrifice and salvation.[53] Meditating on the story of Philip and the eunuch in 1882, Edward W. Blyden saw in the suffering of the Son of God an an-ticipation of the sufferings later experienced by the Black race. The God of salvation gambles by incarnating himself in a Black body subjected to brutality, spoliation, and violence. The gamble is one of a meaning that is open and still to come. In Blyden's eyes, the event of the cross reveals a conception of God and his relationship to suffering humanity that defines the latter as a relationship of justice, freedom, and unconditional recog-nition. The two moments of Christ's violent death and his resurrection reveal the absolute singularity of a human transformation—a transforma-tion into which the Black race is invited. In order to make itself into a sign of salvation, the Black race must become a community of faith, conviction, and reciprocity.[54]

For Martin Luther King Jr., meanwhile, it was through the crucifixion that God acquired his truth as a human confronting his absolute destruc-tion.[55] In return, man and God can henceforth each exist within, and for, the other. By converting the negative into being, Christ undoes death itself. The question that traverses African-American Christianity is whether Christ truly died for the Black Man. Does Christ really deliver him from death and save him from facing it? Or, rather, does Christ give his journey a deep significance that breaks radically from the prosaic char-acter of a nameless life under the cross of racism? In Christ, does death cease to be what is most radically unavoidable? Such is effectively the final meaning of Christ's suffering, the "madness" and "scandal" of which Paul speaks. The proclamation of Christ comes down to a message we can summarize in this way: "I can henceforth be pulled from the concrete experience of my death. Dying for another (the ultimate gift) is no longer an impossibility. Death is no longer irreplaceable. There is no longer anything but the infinite becoming of life, the absolute reconciliation of salvation and the tragic, in absolute reciprocity and the apotheosis of the spirit." In this perspective the final truth of death is in the resurrection—in the infinite possibility of life. The question of the resurrection of the dead, of the return and restitution of the dead to life, of the fact of making life spring forth where death had eliminated it—this is what constitutes the strength of Christianity beyond its formal ecclesial institutions. It is one of the reasons why the figure of Christ, as the ultimate gift to the Other, occupies such a central place in Black political theology. This presence for the Other, alongside the Other, as a witness for the Other, is another name for the politics of the gift, of oblation, of freedom.

But for which rights should Blacks continue to struggle? Everything depends on the locations in which they find themselves, the historical contexts in which they live, and the objective conditions they face. Everything depends as well on the nature of the racial formations in the midst of which they are called to live: either as historical minorities whose presence is not contested but whose entire belonging to the nation remains ambiguous (the case of the United States); as minorities that society chooses neither to see, nor to recognize, nor to listen to as such (the case of France); or else as a demographic majority exercising political power but relatively lacking in economic power (the case of South Africa). Whatever the location, epoch, or context in which they take place, the horizon of such struggles remains the same: how to belong fully in this world that is common to all of us, how to pass from the status of the excluded to the status of the rightholder, how to participate in the construction and the distribution of the world. As long as destructive ideas about the inequality of human races and the differences between human species remain alive, the struggle led by people of African descent for what we can call an "equal share"—or the struggle for rights and responsibilities—will remain a legitimate struggle. It will have to be carried out not with the goal of separating oneself from other humans but in solidarity with humanity itself—a humanity whose multiple faces we seek to reconcile through struggle.

The project of a world in common founded on the principle of "equal shares" and on the principle of the fundamental unity of human beings is a universal project. If we look carefully, we can already see the signs of this world-to-come in the present, although it is true that they are fragile. But exclusion, discrimination, and selection on the basis of race continue to be structuring factors of inequality, the absence of rights, and contemporary domination, notably in our democracies—although the fact is often denied. And we cannot act as if slavery and colonization never took place, or as if we are completely rid of the legacies of such an unhappy period. Although there has been great effort to mask it, the transformation of Europe into a "fortress" and recent legislation against foreigners put into place on the Old Continent are both deeply rooted in the ideology of selection among different human races.

Until we have eliminated racism from our current lives and imaginations, we will have to continue to struggle for the creation of a world-beyond-race. But to achieve it, to sit down at a table to which everyone has been invited, we must undertake an exacting political and ethical critique of racism and of the ideologies of difference. The celebration of difference will be meaningful only if it opens onto the fundamental question of our time, that of sharing, of the common, of the expansion of our horizon. The weight of history will be there. We must learn to do a better job of carrying it, and of sharing its burden. We are condemned to live not only with what we have produced but also with what we have inherited. Given that we have not completely escaped the spirit of a time dominated by the hierarchization of human types, we will need to work with and against the past to open up a future that can be shared in full and equal dignity. The path is clear: on the basis of a critique of the past, we must create a future that is inseparable from the notions of justice, dignity, and the *in-common*.

Along such a path, the new "wretched of the earth" are those to whom the right to have rights is refused, those who are told not to move, those who are condemned to live within structures of confinement—camps, transit centers, the thousands of sites of detention that dot our spaces of law and policing. They are those who are turned away, deported, expelled; the clandestine, the "undocumented"—the intruders and castoffs from humanity that we want to get rid of because we think that, between them and us, there is nothing worth saving, and that they fundamentally pose a threat to our lives, our health, our well-being. The new "wretched of the earth" are the products of a brutal process of control and selection whose racial foundations we well know.

As long as the idea persists that we owe justice only to our own kind and that there are unequal races and peoples, and as long as we continue to make people believe that slavery and colonialism were great feats of "civilization," then the notion of reparation will continue to be mobilized by the historical victims of the brutality of European expansion in the world. In this context we need a dual approach. On the one hand, we must escape the status of victimhood. On the other, we must make a break with "good conscience" and the denial of responsibility. It is through this dual approach that we will be able to articulate a new politics and ethics founded on a call for justice. That said, to be African is first and foremost to be a free man, or, as Fanon always proclaimed, "a man among other men."[56] A man free from everything, and therefore able to invent himself. A true politics of identity consists in constantly nourishing, fulfilling, and refulfilling the capacity for self-invention. Afrocentrism is a hypostatic variant of the desire of those of African origin to need only to justify themselves to themselves. It is true that such a world is above all a form of relation to oneself. But there is no relation to oneself that does not also implicate the Other. The Other is at once difference and similarity, united. What we must imagine is a politics of humanity that is fundamentally a politics of the similar, but in a context in which what we all share from the beginning is difference. It is our differences that, paradoxically, we must share. And all of this depends on reparation, on the expansion of our conception of justice and responsibility.

EPILOGUE
THERE IS ONLY
ONE WORLD

The birth of the racial subject—and therefore of Blackness—is linked to the history of capitalism. Capitalism emerged as a double impulse toward, on the one hand, the unlimited violation of all forms of prohibition and, on the other, the abolition of any distinction between ends and means. The Black slave, in his dark splendor, was the first racial subject: the product of the two impulses, the most visible symbol of the possibility of violence without limits and of vulnerability without a safety net.

Capitalism is the power of capture, influence, and polarization, and it has always depended on *racial subsidies* to exploit the planet's resources. Such was the case yesterday. It is the case today, even as capitalism sets about recolonizing its own center. Never has the perspective of a *Becoming Black of the world* loomed more clearly.

No region of the world is spared from the logics of the distribution of violence on a planetary scale, or from the vast operation under way to devalue the forces of production.

But as long as the retreat from humanity is incomplete, there is a still a possibility of restitution, reparation, and justice. These are the conditions for the collective resurgence of humanity. Thinking through what must come will of necessity be a thinking through of life, of the reserves of life, of what must escape sacrifice. It will of necessity be *a thinking in circulation, a thinking of crossings, a world-thinking.*

The question of the world—what it is, what the relationship is between its various parts, what the extent of its resources is and to whom they belong, how to live in it, what moves and threatens it, where it is going, what its borders and limits, and its possible end, are—has been within us since a human being of bone, flesh, and spirit made its first appearance under the sign of the Black Man, as *human-merchandise, human-metal,* and *human-money*. Fundamentally, it was always *our* question. And it will stay that way as long as speaking the world is the same as declaring humanity, and vice versa.

For, in the end, there is only one world. It is composed of a totality of a thousand parts. Of everyone. Of all worlds.

Édouard Glissant gave this living entity with multiple facets a name: *Tout-Monde,* or *All-World*. It was a way of underscoring the fact that the concept of humanity itself is simultaneously an epiphany and an ecumenical gesture, a concept without which the world, in its thingness, would signify nothing.

It is therefore humanity as a whole that gives the world its name. In conferring its name on the world, it delegates to it and receives from it confirmation of its own position, singular yet fragile, vulnerable and partial, at least in relation to the other forces of the universe—animals and vegetables, objects, molecules, divinities, techniques and raw materials, the earth trembling, volcanoes erupting, winds and storms, rising waters, the sun that explodes and burns, and all the rest of it. There is therefore no world except by way of naming, delegation, mutuality, and reciprocity.

But humanity as a whole delegates itself in the world and receives from the world confirmation of its own being as well as its fragility. And so the difference between the world of humans and the world of nonhumans is no longer an external one. In opposing itself to the world of nonhumans, humanity opposes itself. For, in the end, it is in the relationship that we maintain with the totality of the living world that the truth of who we are is made visible.

In ancient Africa the visible sign of the epiphany that is humanity was the seed that one placed in the soil. It dies, is reborn, and produces the tree, fruit, and life. It was to a large extent to celebrate the marriage of the seed and life that ancient Africans invented speech and language, objects and techniques, ceremonies and rituals, works of art—indeed, social and political institutions. The seed had to produce life in the fragile and hostile environment in the midst of which humanity also had to find space for work and rest—an environment that needed protection and repair. What made most vernacular knowledge useful was the part it played in the endless labor of reparation. It was understood that nature was a force in and of itself. One could not mold, transform, or control nature when not in harmony with it. And this double labor of transformation and regeneration was part of a cosmological assembly whose function was to consolidate the relationships between humans and the other living beings with which they shared the world.

Sharing the world with other beings was the ultimate debt. And it was, above all, the key to the survival of both humans and nonhumans. In this system of exchange, reciprocity, and mutuality, humans and nonhumans were silt for one another.

Glissant spoke of silt as the castoff of matter: a substance made up of seemingly dead elements, things apparently lost, debris stolen from the source, water laden. But he also saw silt as a residue deposited along the banks of rivers, in the midst of archipelagos, in the depths of oceans, along valleys and at the feet of cliffs—everywhere, and especially in those arid and deserted places where, through an unexpected reversal, fertilizer gave birth to new forms of life, labor, and language.

The durability of our world, he insisted, must be thought from the underside of our history, from the slave and the cannibal structures of our modernity, from all that was put in place at the time of the slave trade and fed on for centuries. The world that emerged from the cannibal structure is built on countless human bones buried under the ocean, bones that little by little transformed themselves into skeletons and endowed themselves with flesh. It is made up of tons of debris and stumps, of bits of words scattered and joined together, out of which—as if by a miracle—language is reconstituted in the place where the human being meets its own animal form. The durability of the world depends on our capacity to reanimate beings and things that seem lifeless—the dead man, turned to dust by the desiccated economy; an order poor in worldliness that traffics in bodies and life.

The world will not survive unless humanity devotes itself to the task of sustaining what can be called the *reservoirs of life*. The refusal to perish may yet turn us into historical beings and make it possible for the world to be a world. But our vocation to survive depends on making the desire for life the cornerstone of a new way of thinking about politics and culture.

Among the ancient Dogon people, the unending labor of reparation had a name: the dialectic of meat and seed. The work of social institutions was to fight the death of the human, to ward off corruption, that process of decay and rot. The mask was the ultimate symbol of the determination of the living to defend themselves against death. A simulacrum of a corpse and

substitute for the perishable body, its function was not only to commemo-
rate the dead but also to bear witness to the transfiguration of the body
(the perishable envelope) and to the apotheosis of a rot-proof world. It was
therefore a way of returning to the idea that, as long as the work of reparation continued, life was an imperishable form, one that could not decay.

In such conditions we create borders, build walls and fences, divide,
classify, and make hierarchies. We try to exclude—from humanity itself—
those who have been degraded, those whom we look down on or who
do not look like us, those with whom we imagine never being able to get
along. But there is only one world. We are all part of it, and we all have a right
to it. The world belongs to all of us, equally, and we are all its coinheritors,
even if our ways of living in it are not the same, hence the real pluralism of
cultures and ways of being. To say this is not to deny the brutality and cyn-
icism that still characterize the encounters between peoples and nations.
It is simply to remind us of an immediate and unavoidable fact, one whose
origins lie in the beginnings of modern times: that the processes of mixing
and interlacing cultures, peoples, and nations are irreversible.

There is therefore only one world, at least for now, and that world is
all there is. What we all therefore have in common is the feeling or desire
that each of us must be a full human being. The desire for the fullness of
humanity is something we all share. And, more and more, we also all share
the proximity of the distant. Whether we want to or not, the fact remains
that we all share this world. It is all that there is, and all that we have.

To build a world that we share, we must restore the humanity stolen
from those who have historically been subjected to processes of abstraction and objectification. From this perspective, the concept of reparation
is not only an economic project but also a process of reassembling amputated parts, repairing broken links, relaunching the forms of reciprocity
without which there can be no progress for humanity.

Restitution and reparation, then, are at the heart of the very possibility
of the construction of a common consciousness of the world, which is the
basis for the fulfillment of universal justice. The two concepts of restitution
and reparation are based on the idea that each person is a repository of a
portion of intrinsic humanity. This irreducible share belongs to each of us.
It makes each of us objectively both different from one another and similar
to one another. The ethic of restitution and reparation implies the recognition of what we might call the other's share, which is not ours, but for which

we are nevertheless the guarantor, whether we want to be or not. This share of the other cannot be monopolized without consequences with regard to how we think about ourselves, justice, law, or humanity itself, or indeed about the project of the universal, if that is in fact the final destination.

Reparation, moreover, is necessary because of the cuts and scars left by history. For much of humanity, history has been a process of habituating oneself to the deaths of others—slow death, death by asphyxiation, sudden death, delegated death. These accommodations with the deaths of others, of those with whom we imagine to have shared nothing, these many ways in which the springs of life are dried up in the name of race and difference, have all left deep traces in both imagination and culture and within social and economic relations. These cuts and scars prevent the realization of community. And the construction of the common is inseparable from the reinvention of community.

This question of universal community is therefore by definition posed in terms of how we inhabit the Open, how we care for the Open—which is completely different from an approach that would aim first to enclose, to stay within the enclosure of what we call our own kin. This form of *unkinning* is the opposite of difference. Difference is, in most cases, the result of the construction of desire. It is also the result of a work of abstraction, classification, division, and exclusion—a work of power that, afterward, is internalized and reproduced in the gestures of daily life, even by the excluded themselves. Often, the desire for difference emerges precisely where people experience intense exclusion. In these conditions the proclamation of difference is an inverted expression of the desire for recognition and inclusion.

But if, in fact, difference is constituted through desire (if not also envy), then desire is not necessarily a desire for power. It can also be a desire to be protected, spared, preserved from danger. And the desire for difference is not necessarily the opposite of the project of the *in-common*. In fact, for those who have been subjected to colonial domination, or for those whose share of humanity was stolen at a given moment in history, the recovery of that share often happens in part through the proclamation of difference. But as we can see within certain strains of modern Black criticism, the proclamation of difference is only one facet of a larger project—the project of a world that is coming, a world before us, one whose destination is universal, a world freed from the burden of race, from resentment, and from the desire for vengeance that all racism calls into being.

NOTES

Translator's Introduction

1 When material quoted by Mbembe in the work is originally in English, I have found and incorporated the relevant passages from the original works. I have also tracked down existing English translations of material in French or other languages, and used the relevant passages from those translations. In these cases, the notes in this translation refer to these English versions rather than those referenced in the original work. In all other cases, I have translated the quoted material from French to English myself.

Introduction

1 Dipesh Chakrabarty, *Provincializing Europe: Postcolonial Thought and Historical Difference*, Princeton Studies in Culture/Power/History (Princeton, NJ: Princeton University Press, 2000); Jean Comaroff, *Theory from the South; or, How Euro-America Is Evolving toward Africa* (Boulder, CO: Paradigm, 2011), in particular the introduction; Arjun Appadurai, ed., *The Future as Cultural Fact: Essays on the Global Condition* (London: Verso Books, 2013); Kuan-Hsing Chen, *Asia as Method: Toward Deimperialization* (Durham, NC: Duke University Press, 2010); and Walter Mignolo, *The Darker Side of Western Modernity: Global Futures, Decolonial Options* (Durham, NC: Duke University Press, 2011).

2 On the complexity and tensions inherent in this gesture, see Srinivas Aravamudan, *Enlightenment Orientalism: Resisting the Rise of the Novel* (Chicago: University of Chicago Press, 2012).

3 See François Bernier; and Sue Peabody and Tyler Edward Stovall, eds., *The Color of Liberty: Histories of Race in France* (Durham, NC: Duke University Press, 2003); see also Charles W. Mills, *The Racial Contract* (Ithaca, NY: Cornell University Press, 1997).

4 William Max Nelson, "Making Men: Enlightenment Ideas of Racial Engineering," *American Historical Review* 115, no. 2 (2010): 1364–94; James Delbourgo,

"The Newtonian Slave Body: Racial Enlightenment in the Atlantic World," *Atlantic Studies* 9, no. 2 (2012): 185–207; and Nicholas Hudson, "From Nation to Race: The Origins of Racial Classification in Eighteenth-Century Thought," *Eighteenth-Century Studies* 29, no. 3 (1996): 247–64.

5 Gilles Deleuze, *Deux régimes de fous: Textes et entretiens, 1975–1995* (Paris: Minuit, 2003), 25.

6 Miriam Eliav-Feldon, *The Origins of Racism in the West* (Cambridge: Cambridge University Press, 2009).

7 Frantz Fanon, *Peau noire, masques blancs* (Paris: La Découverte, 2012); and Bloke Modisane, *Blame Me on History* (New York: Dutton, 1963).

8 Walter Johnson, *Soul by Soul: Life inside the Antebellum Slave Market* (Cambridge, MA: Harvard University Press, 1999); and Ian Baucom, *Specters of the Atlantic: Finance Capital, Slavery, and the Philosophy of History* (Durham, NC: Duke University Press, 2005).

9 On these debates, see John W. Blassingame, *The Slave Community: Plantation Life in the Antebellum South* (New York: Oxford University Press, 1972); and Eugene D. Genovese, *Roll, Jordan, Roll: The World the Slaves Made* (New York: Pantheon Books, 1974).

10 Dorothy Porter Wesley, *Early Negro Writing, 1760–1837* (Baltimore: Black Classic Press, 1995); Stephen G. Hall, *A Faithful Account of the Race: African American Historical Writing in Nineteenth-Century America* (Chapel Hill: University of North Carolina Press, 2009), and especially John Ernest, *Liberation Historiography: African American Writers and the Challenge of History, 1794–1861* (Chapel Hill: University of North Carolina Press, 2004). On the Antilles in particular, see Patrick Chamoiseau and Raphaël Confiant, *Lettres créoles: Tracées antillaises et continentales de la littérature; Haïti, Guadeloupe, Martinique, Guyane, 1635–1975* (Paris: Hatier, 1991). For the other areas, see S. E. K. Mabinza Mqhayi, *Abantu Besizwe: Historical and Biographical Writings* (Johannesburg: Wits University Press, 2009); and Alain Ricard, *Naissance du roman africain: Félix Couchoro (1900–1968)* (Paris: Présence Africaine, 1988).

11 Joseph Vogl, *Le spectre du capital* (Paris: Diaphanes, 2013), 152.

12 See Béatrice Hibou, *La bureaucratisation du monde à l'ère néolibérale* (Paris: La Découverte, 2012).

13 Vogl, *Le spectre du capital*, 166ff., 183, 170.

14 Roland Gori and Marie-José Del Volgo, *Exilés de l'intime: La médecine et la psychiatrie au service du nouvel ordre économique* (Paris: Denoël, 2008).

15 On this perspective, see Francesco Masci, *L'ordre règne à Berlin* (Paris: Allia, 2013).

16 See Pierre Laval Dardot and Christian Laval, *The New Way of the World: On Neoliberal Society* (London: Verso, 2013); see also Roland Gori, "Les dispositifs de réification de l'humain (entretien avec Philippe Schepens)," *Semen: Revue sémio-linguistique des textes et discours* 30 (2011): 57–70.

17 Françoise Vergès, *L'homme prédateur: Ce que nous enseigne l'esclavage sur notre temps* (Paris: Albin Michel, 2011).

18 See Stephen Graham, *Cities under Siege: The New Military Urbanism* (London: Verso, 2010); Derek Gregory, "From a View to a Kill: Drones and the Late Modern War," *Theory, Culture and Society* 28, nos. 7–8 (2011): 188–215; Ben Anderson, "Facing the Future Enemy: U.S. Counterinsurgency Doctrine and the Pre-insurgent," *Theory, Culture and Society* 28, nos. 7–8 (2011): 216–40; and Eyal Weizman, *Hollow Land: Israel's Architecture of Occupation* (London: Verso, 2007).

19 Alain Badiou, "La Grèce, les nouvelles pratiques impériales et la ré-invention de la politique," *Lignes*, n. 39 (2012): 39–47; see also Achille Mbembe, "Necropolitics," *Public Culture* 15, no. 1 (2003): 11–40; Naomi Klein, *The Shock Doctrine: The Rise of Disaster Capitalism* (New York: Metropolitan Books, 2007); Adi Ophir, Michal Givoni, and Sari Ḥanafi, *The Power of Inclusive Exclusion: Anatomy of Israeli Rule in the Occupied Palestinian Territories* (New York: Zone Books, 2009); and Weizman, *Hollow Land*.

20 David H. Ucko, *The New Counterinsurgency Era: Transforming the U.S. Military for Modern Wars* (Washington, DC: Georgetown University Press, 2009); Jeremy Scahill, *Blackwater: The Rise of the World's Most Powerful Mercenary Army* (New York: Nation Books, 2007); John A. Nagl, *Learning to Eat Soup with a Knife: Counterinsurgency Lessons from Malaya and Vietnam* (Chicago: University of Chicago Press, 2005); and Grégoire Chamayou, *Théorie du drone* (Paris: La Fabrique, 2013).

21 Maurizio Lazzarato, *The Making of the Indebted Man: An Essay on the Neoliberal Condition*, trans. J. D. Jordan (Los Angeles: Semiotext(e), 2012).

22 Didier Anzieu, *The Skin Ego* (New Haven, CT: Yale University Press, 1989).

23 See in particular the poetry of Aimé Césaire. On the thematic of the salt of the earth, see Édouard Glissant and Patrick Chamoiseau, *L'intraitable beauté du monde: Adresse à Barack Obama* (Paris: Galaade, 2009).

24 Éric Fassin, *Démocratie précaire: Chroniques de la déraison d'état* (Paris: La Découverte, 2012); and Didier Fassin, ed., *Les nouvelles frontières de la société française* (Paris: La Découverte, 2010).

One The Subject of Race

1 James Baldwin, *Nobody Knows My Name* (New York: First Vintage International, 1993).

2 Frantz Fanon, *Black Skin, White Masks*, trans. Richard Philcox (New York: Grove Press, 2008). See also Richard Wright, *Native Son* (New York: Harper and Brothers, 1940).

3 Joseph C. Miller, *Way of Death: Merchant Capitalism and the Angolan Slave Trade, 1730–1830* (Madison: University of Wisconsin Press, 1988).

4 Karen E. Fields and Barbara Jeanne Fields offer a useful distinction between "race" (the idea that nature has produced distinct groups of humans recognizable through inherent traits and specific characteristics that consecrate their

difference while placing them on a hierarchical ladder), "racism" (the complex of social, juridical, political, institutional, and other practices founded on the refusal of the presumption of equality between humans), and what they call "racecraft" (the repertoire of maneuvers that aim to place human beings differentiated in this way within an operational grid). Fields and Fields, *Racecraft: The Soul of Inequality in American Life* (London: Verso, 2012); see also W. J. T. Mitchell, *Seeing through Race* (Cambridge, MA: Harvard University Press, 2012).

5 On this topic, see Josiah C. Nott, *Types of Mankind* (London: Trubner, 1854); and the three volumes by James Bryce: *The American Commonwealth* (New York: Macmillan, 1888), *The Relations of the Advanced and the Backward Races of Mankind* (London: Clarendon, 1902), and *Impressions of South Africa* (London: Macmillan, 1897). See also Charles H. Pearson, *National Life and Character: A Forecast* (London: Macmillan, 1893); and Lowe Kong Meng, Cheok Hong Cheong, and Louis Ah Mouy, eds., *The Chinese Question in Australia, 1878–79* (Melbourne: F. F. Bailliere, 1879).

6 Pierre Larousse, *Nègre, négrier, traite des nègres: Trois articles du "Grand dictionnaire universel du XIXe siècle"* (Paris: Bleu Autour, 2007), 47.

7 G. W. F. Hegel, *Phenomenology of Spirit*, trans. A. V. Miller, foreword by J. N. Findlay (Oxford: Oxford University Press, 1977), 420.

8 Larousse, *Nègre, négrier, traite des nègres*, 68.

9 Christopher Leslie Brown, *Moral Capital: Foundations of British Abolitionism* (Chapel Hill: University of North Carolina Press, 2006).

10 See Igor Kopytoff and Suzanne Miers, eds., *Slavery in Africa: Historical and Anthropological Perspectives* (Madison: University of Wisconsin Press, 1979).

11 On these developments, see Thomas Benjamin, Timothy Hall, and David Rutherford, eds., *The Atlantic World in the Age of Empire* (Boston: Houghton Mifflin, 2001); and Wim Klooster and Alfred Padula, eds., *The Atlantic World: Essays on Slavery, Migration, and Imagination* (Upper Saddle River, NJ: Pearson/Prentice Hall, 2005).

12 Jorge Fonseca, "Black Africans in Portugal during Cleynaert's Visit (1533–1538)," in *Black Africans in Renaissance Europe*, ed. T. F. Earle and K. J. P. Lowe (Cambridge: Cambridge University Press, 1995), 113–21; see also C. M. Saunders, *A Social History of Black Slaves and Freedmen in Portugal, 1441–1555* (Cambridge: Cambridge University Press, 1982).

13 Frédéric Mauro, *Le Portugal et l'Atlantique au XVIIᵉ siècle* (Paris: SEVEPEN, 1960).

14 Ben Vinson, *Bearing Arms for His Majesty: The Free-Colored Militia in Colonial Mexico* (Stanford, CA: Stanford University Press, 2001).

15 Matthew Restall, "Black Conquistadors: Armed Africans in Early Spanish America," *The Americas* 57, no. 2 (2000): 171–205.

16 Michelle Ann Stephens, *Black Empire: The Masculine Global Imaginary of Caribbean Intellectuals in the United States, 1914–1962* (Durham, NC: Duke University Press, 2005).

17 David Eltis, ed., *Coerced and Free Migration: Global Perspectives* (Stanford, CA: Stanford University Press, 2002).

18 Alexander X. Byrd, *Captives and Voyagers: Black Migrants across the Eighteenth-Century British Atlantic World* (Baton Rouge: Louisiana State University Press, 2008); Philip D. Morgan, "British Encounters with Africans and African-Americans, circa 1600–1780," in *Strangers within the Realm: Cultural Margins of the First British Empire*, ed. Bernard Bailyn and Philip D. Morgan, 157–219 (Chapel Hill: University of North Carolina Press, 1991); Stephen J. Braidwood, *Black Poor and White Philanthropists: London's Blacks and the Foundation of the Sierra Leone Settlement, 1786–1791* (Liverpool: Liverpool University Press, 1994); and Ellen Gibson Wilson, *The Loyal Blacks* (New York: G. P. Putnam's Sons, 1976).

19 Restall, "Black Consquistadors."

20 Lester D. Langley, *The Americas in the Age of Revolution, 1750–1850* (New Haven, CT: Yale University Press, 1996); John Lynch, *The Spanish American Revolutions, 1808–1826*, 2nd ed. (New York: Norton, 1986); and J. H. Elliott, *Empires of the Atlantic World: Britain and Spain in America, 1492–1830* (New Haven, CT: Yale University Press, 2006).

21 Kim D. Butler, *Freedoms Given, Freedoms Won: Afro-Brazilians in Post-abolition São Paulo and Salvador* (New Brunswick, NJ: Rutgers University Press, 1998); João José Reis, *Slave Rebellion in Brazil: The Muslim Uprising of 1835 in Bahia* (Baltimore: Johns Hopkins University Press, 1995); and Colin A. Palmer, *Slaves of the White God: Blacks in Mexico, 1570–1650* (Cambridge, MA: Harvard University Press, 1976).

22 John K. Thornton, "African Soldiers in the Haitian Revolution," *Journal of Caribbean History* 25, nos. 1–2 (1991): 58–80.

23 David P. Geggus, ed., *The Impact of the Haitian Revolution in the Atlantic World* (Columbia: University of South Carolina, 2001); Laurent Dubois, *A Colony of Citizens: Revolution and Slave Emancipation in the French Caribbean, 1787–1804* (Chapel Hill: Published for the Omohundro Institute of Early American History and Culture, Williamsburg, Virginia, by the University of North Carolina Press, 2004); Robin Blackburn, *The Overthrow of Colonial Slavery, 1776–1848* (London: Verso, 2011); and Robin Blackburn, "Haiti, Slavery, and the Age of the Democratic Revolution," *The William and Mary Quarterly*, 3rd ser., 63, no. 4 (2006): 643–74.

24 Sidney Kaplan and Emma Nogrady Kaplan, *The Black Presence in the Era of the American Revolution* (Amherst: University of Massachusetts Press, 1989).

25 Edmund S. Morgan, *American Slavery, American Freedom: The Ordeal of Colonial Virginia* (New York: Norton, 1975).

26 See Michel Foucault, *Les mots et les choses: Une archéologie des sciences humaines* (Paris: Gallimard, 1966), especially chap. 5.

27 Éric Vogelin, *Race et état* (Paris: Vrin, 2007), 265.

28 On the development of the spirit of curiosity despite this closing of the mind, see Lorraine Daston and Katharine Park, *Wonders and the Order of Nature, 1150–1750* (New York: Zone Books, 1998).

29 Georges-Louis Leclerc, Comte de Buffon, "Variétés dans l'espèce humaine," in *Histoire naturelle, générale et particulière, avec la description du Cabinet du Roy* (Paris: Imprimerie Royale, 1798), 3:371–530.

30 Hegel, *Reason in History*, trans. Robert S. Hartman (Indianapolis: Bobbs-Merrill, 1953).

31 Friedrich W. Schelling, *Introduction à la philosophie de la mythologie* (Paris: Aubier, 1945).

32 Michel Foucault, *The Order of Things: An Archaeology of the Human Sciences*, ed. and trans. R. D. Laing (New York: Random House, 1973), 156–57.

33 On the dilemmas resulting from this mixing, see Doris Lorraine Garraway, *The Libertine Colony: Creolization in the Early French Caribbean* (Durham, NC: Duke University Press, 2005), particularly chaps. 4 and 5. On the United States, see Ira Berlin, *Slaves without Masters: The Free Negro in the Antebellum South* (New York: Free Press, 2007), xiii–xxiv; and Caryn Cossé Bell, *Revolution, Romanticism, and the Afro-Creole Protest Tradition in Louisiana, 1718–1868* (Baton Rouge: Louisiana State University Press, 1997).

34 Edwin Black, *War against the Weak: Eugenics and America's Campaign to Create a Master Race* (New York: Thunder's Mouth, 2003).

35 Étienne Balibar writes on "the return of race." "Le retour de la race," March 29, 2007, originally published in the online journal *Mouvements des idées et des luttes*, http://www.mouvements.info. Available at http://1libertaire.free.fr/RetourRaceBalibar.html (consulted June 26, 2016).

36 Peter Wade, *Blackness and Race Mixture: The Dynamics of Racial Identity in Colombia* (Baltimore: Johns Hopkins University Press, 1993); France Winddance Twine, *Racism in a Racial Democracy: The Maintenance of White Supremacy in Brazil* (New Brunswick, NJ: Rutgers University Press, 1998); and Livio Sansone, *Blackness without Ethnicity: Constructing Race in Brazil* (New York: Palgrave Macmillan, 2003).

37 David Theo Goldberg, *The Racial State* (Malden, MA: Blackwell, 2002).

38 Troy Duster, "Lessons from History: Why Race and Ethnicity Have Played a Major Role in Biomedical Research," *Journal of Law, Medicine and Ethics* 34, no. 3 (2006), 2–11.

39 Richard S. Cooper, Jay S. Kaufman, and Ryk Ward, "Race and Genomics," *New England Journal of Medicine* 348, no. 12 (2003): 1166–70.

40 Alondra Nelson, "Bioscience: Genetic Genealogy Testing and the Pursuit of African Ancestry," *Social Studies of Science* 38, no. 5 (2008): 759–83; and Ricardo Ventura Santos and Marcos Chor Maio, "Race, Genomics, Identities and Politics in Contemporary Brazil," *Critique of Anthropology* 24, no. 4 (2004): 347–78.

41 Barbara A. Koenig, Sandra Soo-Jin Lee, and Sarah S. Richardson, *Revisiting Race in a Genomic Age* (New Brunswick, NJ: Rutgers University Press, 2008); Nikolas S. Rose, *The Politics of Life Itself: Biomedicine, Power, and Subjectivity in the Twenty-First Century* (Princeton, NJ: Princeton University Press, 2007); Michal Nahman, "Materializing Israeliness: Difference and Mixture in Transnational Ova Donation," *Science as Culture* 15, no. 3 (2006): 199–213.

42 David Theo Goldberg, *The Threat of Race: Reflections on Racial Neoliberalism* (Malden, MA: Wiley-Blackwell, 2009).

43 On these discussions, see Amade M'charek, *The Human Genome Diversity Project: An Ethnography of Scientific Practice* (Cambridge: Cambridge University Press, 2005); Jenny Reardon, *Race to the Finish: Identity and Governance in an Age of Genomics* (Princeton, NJ: Princeton University Press, 2005); and Sarah Franklin, *Embodied Progress: A Cultural Account of Assisted Conception* (London: Routledge, 1997).

44 On these mutations, see Tamara Vukov and Mimi Sheller, "Border Work: Surveillant Assemblages, Virtual Fences, and Tactical Counter-media," *Social Semiotics* 23, no. 2 (2013): 225–41.

45 Michael Crutcher and Matthew Zook, "Placemarks and Waterlines: Racialized Cyberscapes in Post-Katrina Google Earth," *Geoforum* 40, no. 4 (2009): 523–34.

46 See Louise Amoore, "Biometric Borders: Governing Mobilities in the War on Terror," *Political Geography* 25 (2006): 336–51; and Chad Harris, "The Omniscient Eye: Satellite Imagery, 'Battlespace Awareness,' and the Structures of the Imperial Gaze," *Surveillance and Society* 4, nos. 1–2 (2006): 101–22.

47 Grégoire Chamayou, *Théorie du drone* (Paris: La Fabrique, 2013).

48 Caren Kaplan and Raegan Kelly, "Dead Reckoning: Aerial Perception and the Social Construction of Targets," *Vectors Journal* 2, no. 2 (2006).

49 Peter M. Asaro, "The Labor of Surveillance and Bureaucratized Killing: New Subjectivities of Military Drone Operators," *Social Semiotics* 23, no. 2 (2013): 196–224.

50 Ayse Ceyhan, "Technologie et securité: Une gouvernance libérale dans un context d'incertitudes," *Cultures et Conflits* 64 (winter 2006).

51 Lara Palombo, "Mutations of the Australian Camp," *Continuum: Journal of Media and Cultural Studies* 23, no. 5 (2009): 613–27.

52 Paul Silverstein, "Immigrant Racialization and the New Savage Slot: Race, Migration, and Immigration in the New Europe," *Annual Review of Anthropology* 34 (2005): 363–84.

53 Carolyn Sargent and Stephanie Larchanche, "The Muslim Body and the Politics of Immigration in France: Popular and Biomedical Representations of Malian Migrant Women," *Body and Society* 13, no. 3 (2007): 79–102.

54 Ernst Junger, *L'état universel suivi de La Mobilisation Totale* (Paris: Gallimard, 1962), 107–10.

55 Wendy Brown, *Walled States, Waning Sovereignty* (New York: Zone Books, 2010).

56 Balibar, "Le retour de la race"; and Federico Rahola, "La forme-camp: Pour une généalogie des lieux de transit et d'internement du présent," *Cultures et Conflits* 68 (winter 2007): 31–50.

57 Ira Reid, *The Negro Immigrant: His Background, Characteristics, and Social Adjustment, 1899–1937* (New York: Columbia University Press, 1939).

58 See Winston James, *Holding aloft the Banner of Ethiopia: Caribbean Radicalism in Early Twentieth-Century America* (London: Verso, 1998).

59 See Baldwin, *Nobody Knows My Name*, 13–55; as well as Kwame Anthony Appiah, *In My Father's House: Africa in the Philosophy of Culture* (New York: Oxford University Press, 1992); see also Fanon, *Peau noire, masques blancs*.

60 Martin Robison Delany and Robert Campbell, *Search for a Place: Black Separatism and Africa, 1860* (Ann Arbor: University of Michigan Press, 1969).

61 *The Collected Essays of Ralph Ellison*, ed. John F. Callahan (New York: Modern Library, 2003); *Trading Twelves: The Selected Letters of Ralph Ellison and Albert Murray*, ed. Albert Murray and John F. Callahan (New York: Modern Library, 2000); and Ellison, *Invisible Man* (New York: Random House, 2002).

62 Kevin Gaines, *American Africans in Ghana: Black Expatriates and the Civil Rights Era* (Chapel Hill: University of North Carolina Press, 2006); Ibrahim Sundiata, *Brothers and Strangers: Black Zion, Black Slavery, 1914–1940* (Durham, NC: Duke University Press, 2003); more recently, Maryse Condé, *La vie sans fards* (Paris: J. C. Lattès, 2012); and Saidiya V. Hartman, *Lose Your Mother: A Journey along the Atlantic Slave Route* (New York: Farrar, Straus and Giroux, 2007).

63 Richard Wright, *Black Power: A Record of Reactions in a Land of Pathos* (New York: Harper, 1954); Margaret Walker, *Richard Wright, Daemonic Genius: A Portrait of the Man, a Critical Look at His Work* (New York: Warner Books, 1988); Kwame Anthony Appiah, "A Long Way from Home: Wright in the Gold Coast," in *Richard Wright: Modern Critical Views*, ed. Harold Bloom (New York: Chelsea House, 1987), 173–90; and Jack B. Moore, "Black Power Revisited: In Search of Richard Wright," *Mississippi Quarterly* 41 (1988): 161–86.

64 On the ambiguities of this process, see James Sidbury, *Becoming African in America: Race and Nation in the Early Black Atlantic* (Oxford: Oxford University Press, 2007); and Clare Corbould, *Becoming African Americans: Black Public Life in Harlem, 1919–1939* (Cambridge, MA: Harvard University Press, 2009).

65 Crummell, *The Future of Africa, Being Addresses, Sermons, etc., etc., Delivered in the Republic of Liberia* (New York: Charles Scribner, 1862), especially chaps. 2 and 7.

66 Nietzsche, *On the Use and Abuse of History for Life*, trans. Ian Johnston (Arlington, VA: Richer Resources, 2010), 8.

67 Mary Ann Shadd Cary, *A Plea for Emigration; or, Notes of Canada West in Its Moral, Social, and Political Aspect: With Suggestions Respecting Mexico, W. Indies and Vancouver's Island* (Detroit: George W. Pattison, 1852); and Martin Robison Delany, *The Condition, Elevation, Emigration, and Destiny of the Colored People of the United States: Politically Considered* (Philadelphia, 1852).

68 On the complexity of what was at stake, see Robert S. Levine, *Martin Delany, Frederick Douglass, and the Politics of Representative Identity* (Chapel Hill: University of North Carolina Press, 1997).

69 Henry Blanton Parks, *Africa: The Problem of the New Century; The Part the African Methodist Episcopal Church Is to Have in Its Solution* (New York: A.M.E. Church, 1899).

70 Michele Mitchell, *Righteous Propagation: African Americans and the Politics of Racial Destiny after Reconstruction* (Chapel Hill: University of North Carolina Press, 2004).

71 Engelbert Mveng, *Les sources grecques de l'histoire négro-africaine* (Paris: Présence Africaine, 1995); Cheikh Anta Diop, *Nations nègres et culture* (Paris: Présence Africaine, 1954); Cheikh Anta Diop, *The African Origin of Civilization: Myth or Reality*, trans. Mercer Cook (New York: L. Hill, 1974); and Theophile Obenga, *Africa in Antiquity: Pharaonic Egypt—Black Africa* (London: Karnak House, 1997).

72 For examples of this kind of discourse, see Evelyn Baring Cromer, "The Government of Subject Races," *Edinburg Review*, January 1908, 1–27; and Evelyn Baring Cromer, *Modern Egypt* (New York: Macmillan, 1915).

73 On the various formulations of these questions in African-American historiography, see Stephen G. Hall, *A Faithful Account of the Race: African American Historical Writing in Nineteenth-Century America* (Chapel Hill: University of North Carolina Press, 2009); on the African side, see Diop, *Nations nègres et culture*.

74 Alain Locke, "The Negro Spirituals," in *The New Negro: An Interpretation* (New York: Arno, 1968); W. E. B. Du Bois, *The Souls of Black Folk* (New York: Library of America, 1990); Samuel A. Floyd, *The Power of Black Music: Interpreting Its History from Africa to the United States* (New York: Oxford University Press, 1995); Paul Gilroy, *The Black Atlantic: Modernity and Double Consciousness* (Cambridge, MA: Harvard University Press, 1993); and Paul Gilroy, *Darker Than Blue: On the Moral Economies of Black Atlantic Culture* (Cambridge, MA: Harvard University Press, 2010). See also Paul Allen Anderson, *Deep River: Music and Memory in Harlem Renaissance Thought* (Durham, NC: Duke University Press, 2001).

75 David Walker, *David Walker's Appeal, in Four Articles; Together with a Preamble, to the Coloured Citizens of the World, but in Particular, and Very Expressly, to Those of the United States of America* (Boston, 1830); James W. Pennington, *Text Book of the Origin and History, &c. &c. of the Colored People* (Hartford, CT: L. Skinner, 1841); Robert Benjamin Lewis, *Light and Truth; Collected from the Bible and Ancient and Modern History* (Boston, 1844); and Maria W. Stewart, "Productions of Mrs. Maria W. Stewart, 1835," in *Spiritual Narratives*, ed. Sue E. Houtchins, 51–56 (Oxford: Oxford University Press, 1988).

76 Alexander Crummell, *Civilization and Black Progress: Selected Writings of Alexander Crummell on the South*, ed. J. R. Oldfield (Charlottesville: University Press of Virginia, 1995).

77 Certain aspects of this terror are analyzed in detail in W. E. B. Du Bois, *Black Reconstruction in America: An Essay toward a History of the Part Which Black Folk Played in the Attempt to Reconstruct Democracy in America, 1860–1880* (New

York: Oxford University Press, 2007); see also Steven Hahn, *A Nation under Our Feet: Black Political Struggles in the Rural South, from Slavery to the Great Migration* (Cambridge, MA: Harvard University Press, 2003); and Crystal Nicole Feimster, *Southern Horrors: Women and the Politics of Rape and Lynching* (Cambridge, MA: Harvard University Press, 2009).

78 Fanon, *Black Skin, White Masks.*

79 Fabien Eboussi Boulaga, *La crise du Muntu: Authenticité africaine et philosophie* (Paris: Présence Africaine, 1977), 184.

80 Brent Hayes Edwards, *The Practice of Diaspora: Literature, Translation, and the Rise of Black Internationalism* (Cambridge, MA: Harvard University Press, 2003); and Roderick D. Bush, *The End of White World Supremacy: Black Internationalism and the Problem of the Color Line* (Philadelphia: Temple University Press, 2009).

81 Gilroy, *Black Atlantic.*

82 Bill Schwarz, ed., *West Indian Intellectuals in Britain* (Manchester: Manchester University Press, 2003).

83 Peter Linebaugh and Marcus Rediker, *The Many-Headed Hydra: Sailors, Slaves, Commoners, and the Hidden History of the Revolutionary Atlantic* (Boston: Beacon, 2000); Claude McKay, *Banjo: A Story without a Plot* (New York: Harpers, 1929); and Robin D. G. Kelley, *Freedom Dreams: The Black Radical Imagination* (Boston: Beacon, 2002).

84 Gilroy, *Black Atlantic.*

85 Cedric J. Robinson, *Black Marxism: The Making of the Black Radical Tradition* (Chapel Hill: University of North Carolina Press, 2000).

86 See, in reference to the state, Michel Foucault, *Naissance de la biopolitique: Cours au Collège de France, 1978–1979*, ed. Michel Senellart (Paris: Gallimard, 2004), 79.

87 Fanon, *Black Skin, White Masks.*

88 Foucault, *Society Must Be Defended: Lectures at the Collège de France, 1975–76*, trans. David Macey (New York: Picador, 2003), 254–56.

89 Vogelin, *Race et état.*

90 On this, see John Ernest, *Liberation Historiography: African American Writers and the Challenge of History, 1794–1861* (Chapel Hill: University of North Carolina Press, 2004), especially chaps. 1–4.

91 This is explained well by Frederick Douglass in *My Bondage and My Freedom*, in *Frederick Douglass, Autobiographies* (New York: Library of America, 1994), 149; see also Hortense J. Spillers, "Mama's Baby, Papa's Maybe: An American Grammar Book," in *Black, White, and in Color: Essays on American Literature and Culture* (Chicago: University of Chicago Press, 2003); a synthesis is provided by Nancy Bentley, "The Fourth Dimension: Kinlessness and African American Narrative," *Critical Inquiry* 35, no. 2 (2009): 270–92.

92 Césaire, *Cahier d'un retour au pays natal* (Paris: Présence Africaine, 2008).

93 See in particular Marcus Garvey, *Philosophy and Opinions of Marcus Garvey; or, Africa for the Africans* (Dover, MA: Majority Press, 1986).

94 This thematic infuses many of the major texts of the nineteenth century. See in particular Edward W. Blyden, *Liberia's Offering* (New York, 1862).

95 Nancy, *La communauté désœuvrée* (Paris: C. Bourgois, 1986), 39.

96 Georges Bataille and Michel Leiris, *Correspondence*, ed. Louis Yvert, trans. Liz Heron (London: Seagull Books, 2008), 73.

Two The Well of Fantasies

1 Frédéric Godefroy, *Dictionnaire de l'ancienne langue française: Et de tous ses dialectes du IXe au XVe siècle* (Paris: H. Champion, 1902), vol. 10; *Dictionnaire de Trévoux*, 1728; and Simone Delesalle and Lucette Valensi, "Le mot 'nègre' dans les dictionnaires de l'Ancien Régime: Histoire et lexicographie," *Langue Française* 15 (September 1972): 79–104.

2 See the remarks of Pliny the Elder, *Histoire Naturelle*, vol. 6-2 (Paris: Les Belles Lettres, 1980); and Al-Mas'udi, *Les prairies d'or*, vol. 1 (Paris: Imprimerie Impériale, 1861).

3 Georg Wilhelm Friedrich Hegel, *Reason in History*, trans. Robert S. Hartman (Indianapolis: Bobbs-Merrill, 1953).

4 Fanon, *Black Skin, White Masks*, trans. Richard Philcox (New York: Grove, 2008), 93.

5 Ian Baucom, *Specters of the Atlantic: Finance Capital, Slavery, and the Philosophy of History* (Durham, NC: Duke University Press, 2005).

6 Georges Hardy, *L'art nègre: L'art animiste des noirs d'Afrique* (Paris: H. Laurens, 1927).

7 Pablo Picasso quoted in William Rubin, *Le primitivisme dans l'art du XXe siècle: Les artistes modernes devant le tribal* (Paris: Flammarion, 1992).

8 Breton, *Entretiens, 1913–1952* (Paris: Gallimard, 1973), 237.

9 Jean-Claude Blachère, *Le modèle nègre: Aspects littéraires du mythe primitiviste au XXe siècle chez Apollinaire, Cendrars, Tzara* (Dakar: Nouvelles Éditions Africaines, 1981).

10 See, for instance, Filippo Tommaso Marinetti, *Mafarka the Futurist: An African Novel* (London: Middlesex University Press, 1998); and Clément Pansaers, *Le pan pan au cul du nu nègre* (Brussels: Alde, Collection Aio, 1920).

11 See Carole Reynaud Paligot, *Parcours politique des surréalistes, 1919–1969* (Paris: CNRS, 1995).

12 Lucien Lévy-Bruhl, *Les fonctions mentales dans les sociétés inférieures* (Paris: F. Alcan, 1910). See also Lévy-Bruhl, *La mentalité primitive* (Paris: Presses Universitaires de France, 1922); and Lévy-Bruhl, *L'âme primitive* (Paris: Presses Universitaires de France, 1928).

13 Arthur Gobineau, "Essai sur l'inégalité des races humaines," in *Œuvres complètes*, (Paris: Gallimard, 1983), 1:623, 1146.

14 Gobineau, "Essai sur l'inégalité des races humaines," 472–74.

15 See Roger Shattuck, *The Banquet Years: The Origins of the Avant-Garde in France, 1885 to World War I* (New York: Vintage Books, 1968).

16 Césaire, *The Collected Poetry*, trans. Clayton Eshleman and Annette Smith (Berkeley: University of California Press, 1983), 97, 121, 141.

17 Fanon, *Black Skin, White Masks*, 91.

18 On the contradictions of this process and the role of women within it, see Angela Davis, "Reflections on the Black Woman's Role in the Community of Slaves," in *The Angela Y. Davis Reader*, ed. Joy James (Oxford: Blackwell, 1996), 111–28.

19 Raymond Roussel, *New Impressions of Africa/Nouvelles impressions d'Afrique*, trans. Mark Ford (Princeton, NJ: Princeton University Press, 2011).

20 Hegel summarizes this better than anyone in *Reason in History*.

21 Michel Leiris, *L'Afrique fantôme* (Paris: Gallimard, 1990), 225.

22 Leiris, *Miroirs de l'Afrique* (Paris: Gallimard, 1996), 230.

23 Deleuze, *The Logic of Sense*, trans. Mark Lester (New York: Columbia University Press, 1990), 13.

24 Foucault, *Death and the Labyrinth: The World of Raymond Roussel*, trans. Charles Ruas (Garden City, NY: Doubleday, 1986), 163–64.

25 Deleuze, *The Logic of Sense*, 29.

26 Foucault, *Death and the Labyrinth*, 165.

27 See the first chapter of Fanon, *Black Skin, White Masks*.

28 Vernant, "Figuration de l'invisible et catégorie psychologique du double: Le Kolossos," in *Œuvres: Religions, rationalités, politique* (Paris: Seuil, 2007), 534.

29 See, notably, chapter 6 of Arendt, *The Origins of Totalitarianism* (New York: Harcourt Brace Jovanovich, 1976).

30 Arendt, *Origins of Totalitarianism*, 185.

31 Carl Schmitt, *The Nomos of the Earth in the International Law of the Jus Publicum Europaeum*, trans. G. L. Ulmen (New York: Telos, 2003), 86.

32 Arendt, *Origins of Totalitarianism*, 176–77, 183.

33 Arendt, *Origins of Totalitarianism*, 189.

34 Schmitt, *Nomos of the Earth*, 94.

35 See Thomas Hobbes, *Leviathan*, ed. Marshall Missner (New York: Pearson Longman, 2008); and Hobbes, *Behemoth; or, The Long Parliament*, ed. Paul Seaward (Oxford: Oxford University Press, 2010).

36 Schmitt, *Nomos of the Earth*, 74. Schmitt quotes Trier, "Zaun und Mannring," *Beiträge zur Geschichte der deutschen Sprache und Literatur* 66 (1942): 232.

37 Schmitt, *Nomos of the Earth*, 199.

38 See the works of Carole Reynaud Paligot: *La République raciale: Paradigme racial et idéologie républicaine (1860–1930)* (Paris: Presses Universitaires de France, 2006) and *Races, racisme et antiracisme dans les années 1930* (Paris: Presses Universitaires de France, 2007).

39 Judith Surkis, *Sexing the Citizen: Morality and Masculinity in France, 1870–1920* (Ithaca, NY: Cornell University Press, 2006).

40 See Christopher M. Andrew and Alexander S. Kanya-Forstner, "The French Colonial Party: Its Composition, Aims and Influence, 1885–1914," *Historical*

Journal 14, no. 1 (1971): 99–128; and Raoul Girardet, *L'idée coloniale en France de 1871 à 1962* (Paris: La Table Ronde, 1972).

41 Charles Richet, *La sélection humaine* (Paris: F. Alcan, 1919).

42 Sean Quinlan, "Colonial Bodies, Hygiene and Abolitionist Politics in Eighteenth-Century France," *History Workshop Journal* 42 (1996): 106–25.

43 William H. Schneider, *Quality and Quantity: The Quest for Biological Regeneration in Twentieth-Century France* (Cambridge: Cambridge University Press, 2001).

44 Jean Pluyette, *La doctrine des races et la sélection de l'immigration en France* (Paris: Bossuet, 1930); Arsène Dumont, *Dépopulation et civilisation: Étude démographique* (Paris: Lecrosnier et Babé, 1890); and Paul Leroy-Beaulieu, *La question de la population* (Paris: F. Alcan, 1913).

45 Denis Provencher and Luke Eilderts, "The Nation According to Lavisse: Teaching Masculinity and Male Citizenship in Third Republic France," *French Cultural Studies* 18, no. 1 (2007): 31–57.

46 Hélène d' Almeida-Topor, "L'histoire de l'Afrique occidentale enseignée aux enfants de France," in *L'Afrique occidentale au temps des Français: Colonisateurs et colonisés, 1860–1960*, ed. Catherine Coquery-Vidrovitch (Paris: La Découverte, 1992), 49–56.

47 Declaration to the Chamber of Deputies, July 9, 1925.

48 *Conférence de Jean Jaurès, maître de conferences à la Faculté des Lettres de Toulouse*, brochure of l'Alliance Française, association nationale pour la propagation de la langue française dans les colonies et à l'étranger (Albi, France: Imprimérie Pezous, 1884), 9.

49 See, for example, Émile Fournier-Fabre, *Le choc suprême; ou, La mêlée des races* (Paris: G. Ficker, 1921); and Maurice Muret, *Le crépuscule des nations blanches* (Paris: Payot, 1925).

50 Leroy-Beaulieu, *De la colonisation chez les peuples modernes* (Paris: F. Alcan, 1908), 605–6.

51 Mérignhac, *Précis de législation et d'économie coloniales* (Paris: Sirey, 1912), 205.

52 Sue Peabody and Tyler Edward Stovall, eds., *The Color of Liberty: Histories of Race in France* (Durham, NC: Duke University Press, 2003).

53 Christopher L. Miller, *The French Atlantic Triangle: Literature and Culture of the Slave Trade* (Durham, NC: Duke University Press, 2008).

54 See Ulrike Schneebauer, "Le personage de l'esclave dans la littérature franco-phone contemporaine à travers trois œuvres de Maryse Condé, Mahi Binebine et Aimé Césaire" (master's thesis, University of Vienna, 2009).

55 See Petrine Archer Straw, *Negrophilia: Avant-Garde Paris and Black Culture in the 1920s* (New York: Thames and Hudson, 2000).

56 George E. Brooks, "Artists' Depiction of Senegalese Signares: Insights Concerning French Racist and Sexist Attitudes in the Nineteenth Century," *Journal of the Swiss Society of African Studies* 18, no. 1 (1979): 75–89.

57 Chalaye, *Du noir au nègre: L'image du noir au théâtre de Marguerite de Navarre à Jean Genet (1550–1960)* (Paris: L'Harmattan, 1998).

58 Elvire Jean-Jacques Maurouard, *Les beautés noires de Baudelaire* (Paris: Karthala, 2005).

59 Chateaubriand, *Les Natchez* (Paris: G. Chinard, n.d.), 398–99.

60 Phyllis Rose, *Jazz Cleopatra: Josephine Baker in Her Time* (New York: Doubleday, 1989), 8.

61 Tocqueville, *De la colonie en Algérie* (Brussels: Editions Complexe, 1988), 38. He is speaking here of the first moments of French presence in Algeria.

62 Labat, *Nouvelle relation de l'Afrique occidentale*, vol. 1 (Paris: G. Cavalier, 1728), quoted in Andrew Curran, "Imaginer l'Afrique au siècle des lumières," *Cromohs: Cyber Review of Modern Historiography* 10 (2005).

63 Victor Hugo, "Discours sur l'Afrique," in *Actes et paroles*, edited by Jean-Claude Fizaine (Paris: Laffont, 1985), 4:1010.

64 Hugo, "Discours sur l'Afrique," 4: 1010.

65 Swift, *Poems*, ed. Harold Herbert Williams (Oxford: Oxford University Press, 1958), 2:645–46.

66 François Le Vaillant: *Voyage de M. Le Vaillant dans l'Intérieur de l'Afrique par Le Cap de Bonne Espérance, dans les années 1783, 84 & 85* (Paris: Leroy, 1790).

67 Cournot, *Martinique* (Paris: Gallimard, 1949), 13.

68 Dapper, *Description de l'Afrique* (Amsterdam: W. Waesberge, 1686), 5.

69 See the selections in Stanley Engerman, Seymour Drescher, and Robert Paquette, eds., *Slavery* (Oxford: Oxford University Press, 2001).

70 See Marcel Dorigny, *La Société des Amis des Noirs 1788–1799: Contribution à l'histoire de l'abolition de l'esclavage* (Paris: UNESCO, 1998).

71 Yves Bénot, *La révolution française et la fin des colonies* (Paris: La Découverte, 2004).

72 On this subject, see Roxann Wheeler, *The Complexion of Race: Categories of Difference in Eighteenth-Century British Culture* (Philadelphia: University of Pennsylvania Press, 2000), 256.

73 Voltaire, *Œuvres complètes* (Paris: Garnier Frères, 1878), 11:6.

74 Hugo, "Discours sur l'Afrique," 4: 1010.

75 Quoted in Gilles Manceron, *1885, le tournant colonial de la République* (Paris: La Découverte, 2007), 60–61.

76 Henri Brunschwig, *Mythes et réalités de l'impérialisme colonial français, 1871–1914* (Paris: A. Colin, 1960), 173–74; and Charles Robert Ageron, *L'anticolonialisme en France, de 1871 à 1914* (Paris: Presses Universitaires de France, 1973).

77 Harvey Goldberg, *The Life of Jean Jaurès* (Madison: University of Wisconsin Press, 1962), 202–3.

78 Pierre Mille and Félicien Challaye, *Les deux Congo devant la Belgique et devant la France* (Paris: Cahiers de la Quinzaine, 1906).

79 Paul Louis, *Le colonialisme* (Paris: G. Bellais, 1905); and Paul Vigné d'Octon, *Les crimes coloniaux de la Troisième République*, vol. 1, *La sueur du burnous* (Paris: Editions de la Guerre Sociale, 1911).

Three Difference and Self-Determination

1 Whether through the vocabulary of alienation or that of deracination, Francophone criticism has probably conceptualized this process of the "exit from oneself" best. See in particular Aimé Césaire, *Discourse on Colonialism*, trans. Joan Pinkham (New York: Monthly Review Press, 2000); Frantz Fanon, *Black Skin, White Masks*, trans. Charles Lam Markmann (New York: Grove, 1967); Hamidou Kane, *Ambiguous Adventure* (London: Heinemann, 1972); Fabien Eboussi Boulaga, *La crise du Muntu: Authenticité africaine et philosophie* (Paris: Présence Africaine, 1977); and Fabien Eboussi Boulaga, *Christianity without Fetishes: An African Critique and Recapture of Christianity* (Maryknoll, NY: Orbis Books, 1984).

2 This applies in particular to Anglophone work in Marxist political economy. See, for example, Walter Rodney, *How Europe Underdeveloped Africa*, rev. ed. (Washington, DC: Howard University Press, 1982); or the works of authors such as Samir Amin, *Le développement inégal: Essai sur les formations sociales du capitalisme périphérique* (Paris: Minuit, 1973).

3 On falsification and the necessity to "re-establish historical truth," see, for example, the work of nationalist historians: Joseph Ki-Zerbo, *Histoire de l'Afrique noire, d'hier à demain* (Paris: Hatier, 1972); and Cheikh Anta Diop, *The African Origin of Civilization: Myth or Reality*, trans. Mercer Cook (New York: L. Hill, 1974).

4 On the problematic of slavery as social death, see Orlando Patterson, *Slavery and Social Death: A Comparative Study* (Cambridge, MA: Harvard University Press, 1982).

5 Foucault, *The Birth of Biopolitics: Lectures at the Collège de France, 1978–79*, trans. Graham Burchell (New York: Palgrave Macmillan, 2008), 64, 66.

6 Foucault, *Birth of Biopolitics*, 67.

7 Tocqueville, *Democracy in America: Historical-Critical Edition of "De la démocratie en Amérique,"* ed. Eduardo Nolla, trans. James T. Schleifer (Indianapolis: Liberty Fund, 2012), 516–17.

8 Tocqueville, *Democracy in America*, 517–18.

9 Tocqueville, *Democracy in America*, 549, 551.

10 Tocqueville, *Democracy in America*, 552.

11 Tocqueville, *Democracy in America*, 555, 566.

12 Tocqueville, *Democracy in America*, 572, 578.

13 On the centrality of the body as the ideal unity of the subject and the locus of recognition of its unity, its identity, and its value, see Umberto Galimberti, *Les raisons du corps* (Paris: Grasset, 1998).

14 On this point and those that precede it, see, among others, Pierre Pluchon, *Nègres et Juifs au XVIIIᵉ siècle: Le racisme au siècle des lumières* (Paris: Tallandier, 1984); Charles de Secondat, Baron de Montesquieu, *De l'esprit des lois*, vol. 1 (Paris: Garnier/Flammarion, 1979); Voltaire, "Essais sur les mœurs et l'esprit

des nations et sur les principaux faits de l'histoire depuis Charlemagne jusqu'à Louis XIV," in *Œuvres complètes* (Paris: Imprimerie de la Société Littéraire et Typographique, 1784), vol. 16; and Immanuel Kant, *Observations sur le sentiment du beau et du sublime*, trans. Roger Kempf (Paris: Vrin, 1988).

15 Thomas R. Metcalf, *Ideologies of the Raj* (Cambridge: Cambridge University Press, 1994).

16 The most developed institutional form of this economy of alterity was the apartheid regime, in which hierarchies were of a biological order. It was an expanded version of indirect rule. See Lucy P. Mair, *Native Policies in Africa* (London: Routledge and Kegan Paul, 1936); and Frederick D. Lugard, *The Dual Mandate in British Tropical Africa* (London: W. Blackwood and Sons, 1980).

17 See the texts gathered in Henry S. Wilson, *Origins of West African Nationalism* (London: Macmillan, 1969).

18 See, for example, Nicolas de Condorcet, "Réflexions sur l'esclavage des Nègres (1778)," in *Œuvres* (Paris: Firmin-Didot, 1847), vol. 7.

19 Edward W. Blyden, *Christianity, Islam and the Negro Race* (Baltimore: Black Classic Press, 1994); and Edward W. Blyden, *Liberia's Offering* (New York: John A. Gray, 1862).

20 See, for example, the texts gathered in Aquino de Bragança and Immanuel Wallerstein, eds., *The African Liberation Reader*, 3 vols. (London: Zed, 1982).

21 See Immanuel Kant, *Anthropology from a Pragmatic Point of View* (Chicago: Southern Illinois Press, 1978).

22 On this point, see Pierre Guiral and Emile Temime, eds., *L'idée de la race dans la pensée politique française contemporaine* (Paris: Editions du CNRS, 1977).

23 You can see the centrality of this theme in Fanon, *Black Skin, White Masks*; Césaire, *Discourse on Colonialism*; and, in a general sense, the poetry of Léopold Sédar Senghor.

24 W. E. B. Du Bois, *The World and Africa: An Inquiry into the Part Which Africa Has Played in World History* (New York: International Publishers, 1946).

25 To this effect, see the final pages of Fanon, *Black Skin, White Masks*.

26 This is the thesis of Léopold Sédar Senghor, "Negritude: A Humanism in the Twentieth Century," in *Colonial Discourse and Postcolonial Theory: A Reader*, ed. Patrick Williams and Laura Chrisman (New York: Harvester Wheatsheaf, 1994), 27–35.

27 In this regard, see the critique of the texts of Alexander Crummell and W. E. B. Du Bois in Kwame Anthony Appiah, *In My Father's House: Africa in the Philosophy of Culture* (New York: Oxford University Press, 1992), chaps. 1 and 2. See also Kwame Anthony Appiah, "Racism and Moral Pollution," *Philosophical Forum* 18, nos. 2–3 (1986–1987): 185–202.

28 Léopold Sédar Senghor, *Liberté I: Négritude et humanisme* (Paris: Seuil, 1964); and Senghor, *Liberté III: Négritude et civilisation de l'universel* (Paris: Seuil, 1977).

29 Georg Wilhelm Friedrich Hegel, *Reason in History*, trans. Robert S. Hartman (Indianapolis: Bobbs-Merrill, 1953).

30 In the Francophone world, see in particular the works of Diop and, in the Anglophone world, the theses on Afrocentricity offered by Molefi Kete Asante, *Afrocentricity* (Trenton, NJ: Africa World Press, 1988).

31 See, among others, Théophile Obenga, *L'Afrique dans l'Antiquité: Égypte pharaonique, Afrique noire* (Paris: Présence Africaine, 1973)

32 Paradoxically, we find the same impulse and the same desire to conflate race and geography in the racist writings of White colonists in South Africa. For details on this, see John M. Coetzee, *White Writing: On the Culture of Letters in South Africa* (New Haven, CT: Yale University Press, 1988). See especially the chapters on Sarah Gertrude Millin, Pauline Smith, and Christiaan Maurits van den Heever.

33 They must "return to the land of [their] fathers and be at peace," as writes Blyden in *Christianity*, 124.

34 Africa as a subject of racial mythology can be found as much in the works of Du Bois as those of Diop or else Wole Soyinka; for the latter, see Soyinka, *Myth, Literature, and the African World* (Cambridge: Cambridge University Press, 1976).

35 Joseph C. Miller, *Way of Death: Merchant Capitalism and the Angolan Slave Trade, 1730–1830* (Madison: University of Wisconsin Press, 1988).

36 Alexander Crummell, *Africa and America: Addresses and Discourses* (New York: Negro Universities Press, 1969 [1885]), 14–36.

37 What follows is abundantly inspired by Boulaga's reflections on "tradition." See Boulaga, *La crise du Muntu*, 152–72.

38 Boulaga, *La crise du Muntu*, 152.

39 Boulaga, *La crise du Muntu*, 156, 158.

40 V. Y. Mudimbe, *The Invention of Africa: Gnosis, Philosophy, and the Order of Knowledge* (Bloomington: Indiana University Press, 1988); and Mudimbe, *The Idea of Africa* (Bloomington: Indiana University Press, 1994).

41 Appiah, *In My Father's House*. In a later study Appiah denounced the narrowness of nationalist positions, emphasized the value of double ancestrality, and proclaimed himself a cosmopolitan liberal. See Appiah, "Cosmopolitan Patriots," *Critical Inquiry* 23, no. 3 (1997): 617–39.

42 Oscar Bimwenyi-Kweshi, *Discours théologique négro-africain: Problème des fondements* (Paris: Présence Africaine, 1981).

43 John L. Comaroff and Jean Comaroff, *Of Revelation and Revolution*, vol. 2, *The Dialectics of Modernity on a South African Frontier* (Chicago: University of Chicago Press, 1991).

Four The Little Secret

1 Jean-Pierre Vernant, *Figures, idoles, masques* (Paris: Julliard, 1990), 29.

2 Frantz Fanon, "Pourquoi nous employons la violence," in *Œuvres* , eds. Magali Bessone and Achille Mbembe (Paris: La Découverte, 2011), 414.

3 Michel Foucault, *"Il faut défendre la société": Cours au Collège de France (1975–1976)* (Paris: Seuil/Gallimard, 1997), 51. It needs to be understood that, for Foucault, the term "race" does not have a stable biological meaning. It sometimes designates historico-political splits, at others differences in origin, language, or religion, but above all a kind of link that is established only through the violence of war.

4 Fanon, "Pourquoi," 414.

5 Fanon, "Pourquoi," 414.

6 Fanon, *The Wretched of the Earth* (New York: Grove, 1968), 57.

7 Césaire, *Discourse on Colonialism*, trans. Joan Pinkham (New York: Monthly Review Press, 2000), 33, 41. Fanon speaks, in turn, of "this Europe where they are never done talking of Man, yet murder men everywhere they find them, at the corner of every one of their own streets, in all the corners of the globe." Or, again, "that same Europe where they were never done talking of Man, and where they never stopped proclaiming that they were only anxious for the welfare of Man: today we know with what sufferings humanity has paid for every one of their triumphs of the mind." Fanon, *Wretched of the Earth*, 311–12.

8 Georges Bataille, *La part maudite, précédé de La notion de dépense* (Paris: Minuit, 1967); Hannah Arendt, *The Origins of Totalitarianism* (New York: Harcourt Brace Jovanovich, 1976), especially the chapter "Race and Bureaucracy"; Ernst Junger, *L'état universel suivi de La mobilisation totale* (Paris: Gallimard, 1962); and Emmanuel Levinas, *Quelques réflexions sur la philosophie de l'hitlérisme* (Paris: Payot and Rivages, 1997).

9 Guy Rosolato, *Le sacrifice: Repères psychanalytiques* (Paris: Presses Universitaires de France, 1987), 30.

10 Fanon expresses the impossibility of community in the following manner: "Colonialism is not a thinking machine, nor a body with reasoning faculties. It is violence in its natural state and it will only yield when confronted with an even greater violence." Or: "For the native, life can only spring up again out of the rotting corpse of the settler." Fanon, *Wretched of the Earth*, 39, 61.

11 Fanon, *Black Skin, White Masks*, trans. Charles Lam Markmann (New York: Grove, 1967), 220; Fanon, *Wretched of the Earth*, chap. 5; and Fanon, *A Dying Colonialism* (New York: Grove, 1965), chap. 4.

12 Jean-François Bayart, *Le gouvernement du monde: Une critique politique de la globalisation* (Paris: Fayard, 2005), 208; see also Françoise Vergès, *Abolir l'esclavage: Une utopie coloniale; Les ambiguïtés d'une politique humanitaire* (Paris: Albin Michel, 2001).

13 Fanon, *Black Skin, White Masks*.

14 Saidiya V. Hartman, *Scenes of Subjection: Terror, Slavery, and Self-Making in Nineteenth-Century America* (New York: Oxford University Press, 1997); and Todd L. Savitt, *Medicine and Slavery: The Diseases and Health Care of Blacks in Antebellum Virginia* (Urbana: University of Illinois Press, 2002).

15 Megan Vaughn, *Curing Their Ills: Colonial Power and African Illness* (Cambridge: Polity, 1990); and Nancy Rose Hunt, *A Colonial Lexicon of Birth Ritual, Medicalization, and Mobility in the Congo* (Durham, NC: Duke University Press, 1999).

16 Achille Mbembe, *On the Postcolony* (Berkeley: University of California Press, 2001), chap. 4.

17 Arendt, *Origins of Totalitarianism*; see also Olivier Lecour Grandmaison, *Coloniser, exterminer: Sur la guerre et l'état colonial* (Paris: Fayard, 2005).

18 Fanon, *Toward the African Revolution: Political Essays*, trans. Haakon Chevalier (New York: Monthly Review Press, 1967), 66.

19 Fanon, *Dying Colonialism*, 99.

20 Fanon, *Wretched of the Earth*, 58; see also Fanon, *Dying Colonialism*, particularly the chapter "Medicine and Colonialism."

21 Fanon, *Toward the African Revolution*, 67.

22 Fanon, *Wretched of the Earth*, 36.

23 Fanon, *Wretched of the Earth*, 250.

24 See, for example, the narrative of the assassination of the national leader of Cameroon, Ruben Um Nyobè, and of the desecration of his cadaver, in Achille Mbembe, *La naissance du maquis dans le Sud-Cameroun (1920–1960): Histoire des usages de la raison en colonie* (Paris: Karthala, 1986), 13–17; see also Ludo de Witte, *The Assassination of Lumumba* (London: Verso, 2001).

25 Alexis de Tocqueville, *De la colonie en Algérie* (Brussels: Editions Complexe, 1988), 39.

26 Regarding the colony as an experience of subjectification, see Bayart, *Le gouvernement du monde*. See also John L. Comaroff and Jean Comaroff, *Of Revelation and Revolution*, vol. 2, *The Dialectics of Modernity on a South African Frontier* (Chicago: University of Chicago Press, 1991), in particular chaps. 3–8.

27 Nietzsche, *The Birth of Tragedy*, trans. Douglas Smith (Oxford: Oxford University Press, 2002), 25.

28 Fanon, *Wretched of the Earth*, 45.

29 Francis Jeanson, "Préface à l'édition de 1952 de *Peau noir, masques blancs*," in *Œuvres*, by Frantz Fanon (Paris: La Découverte, 2011), 49.

30 Fanon, *Black Skin, White Masks*, 89–90.

31 Fanon, *Black Skin, White Masks*, 91–92.

32 Fanon, *Wretched of the Earth*, 42.

33 Fanon, *Black Skin, White Masks*; see the chapters on interracial sexuality.

34 Maurice Merleau-Ponty, *Le visible et l'invisible* (Paris: Gallimard, 1964), 17.

35 Friedrich Nietzsche, *La volonté de puissance* (Paris: Gallimard, 1935), 2:219.

36 Fanon, *Black Skin, White Masks*, 137–38.

37 Fanon, *Black Skin, White Masks*, 142–43, 147.

38 Tocqueville, *De la colonie en Algérie*, 38–40.

39 Ferdinand Oyono, *Une vie de boy* (Paris: Julliard, 1960); and Mongo Beti, *Perpétue et l'habitude du malheur* (Paris: Buchet/Chastel, 1974).

40 Tocqueville, *De la colonie en Algérie*, 46, 74–75.

41 William Pietz, *Le fétiche: Généalogie d'un problème* (Paris: Kargo et l'Éclat, 2005), 105.

42 Heusch, *Sacrifice in Africa: A Structuralist Approach* (Bloomington: Indiana University Press, 1985), 101, and generally the chapter "King on the Sacrificial Scene"; see also Heusch, *Le roi de Kongo et les montres sacrés* (Paris: Gallimard, 2000).

43 Joseph C. Miller, *Way of Death: Merchant Capitalism and the Angolan Slave Trade, 1730–1830* (Madison: University of Wisconsin Press, 1988).

44 Freud, *The Uncanny*, trans. David McLintock (London: Penguin Books, 2003).

45 Gérard Guillerault, *Le miroir et la psyché* (Paris: Gallimard, 2003), 142.

46 Merleau-Ponty, *Phénomologie de la perception* (Paris: Gallimard, 1945), 469.

47 Freud, *Uncanny*, 142.

48 Catherine Coquery-Vidrovitch includes sacred forests, the tombs of Muslim saints, mosques, and certain masks and dances among other vectors of memory. Coquery-Vidrovitch, "Lieux de mémoire et occidentalisation," in *Histoire d'Afrique: Les enjeux de mémoire*, ed. Jean-Pierre Chrétien and Jean-Louis Triaud (Paris: Karthala, 1999), 378–79.

49 Sami Tchak, *Place des fêtes* (Paris: Seuil, 2001).

50 Ahmadou Kourouma, *En attendant le vote des bêtes sauvages* (Paris: Seuil, 1998).

51 Amos Tutuola, *The Palm-Wine Drinkard and My Life in the Bush of Ghosts* (New York: Grove, 1994).

52 See especially Sony Labou Tansi, *La vie et demie* (Paris: Seuil, 1979); Tansi, *Les yeux du volcan* (Paris: Seuil, 1988); Tansi, *L'état honteux* (Paris: Seuil, 1981); and Tansi, *Le commencement des douleurs* (Paris: Seuil, 1995).

53 Mia Couto, *Les baleines de Quissico* (Paris: Albin Michel, 1996).

54 Sony Labou Tansi, *L'anté-peuple* (Paris: Seuil, 1983).

55 Tutuola, *Palm-Wine Drinkard and My Life*.

56 Ahmadou Kourouma, *Allah n'est pas obligé* (Paris: Seuil, 2000).

57 Sony Labou Tansi, *Les sept solitudes de Lorsa Lopez* (Paris: Seuil, 1985).

58 Hamidou Kane, *Ambiguous Adventure* (London: Heinemann, 1972).

59 See, for example, Yvonne Vera, *Papillon brûle* (Paris: Fayard, 2002); Tansi, *Le commencement des douleurs*; and Tansi, *L'autre monde: Écrits inédits* (Paris: Revue Noire, 1997).

60 Achille Mbembe, "Politiques de la vie et violence spéculaire dans la fiction d'Amos Tutuola," *Cahiers d'Études Africaines* 172 (2003): 791–826.

61 Alain Mabanckou, *Verre cassé* (Paris: Seuil, 2005).

62 Kossi Efoui, *La Polka* (Paris: Seuil, 1998), 9.

63 Efoui, *La Polka*, 11–12.

64 Efoui, *La Polka*, 54, 111.

65 Efoui, *La Polka*, 58–65.

66 Laurence Bertrand Dorléac, *L'ordre sauvage: Violence, dépense et sacré dans l'art des années 1950–1960* (Paris: Gallimard, 2004).

67 Didier Nativel and Françoise Raison-Jourde, "Rapt des morts et exhibition monarchique: Les contradictions de la République colonisatrice à Madagascar," in Chrétien and Triaud, *Histoire d'Afrique*, 173–95; and Odile Goerg, "Le site du Palais du gouverneur à Conakry: Pouvoirs, symbôles et mutations de sens," in Chrétien and Triaud, *Histoire d'Afrique*, 389–404.

68 Achille Mbembe, "La 'chose' et ses doubles dans la caricature camerounaise," *Cahiers d'Études Africaines* 36, no. 141–42 (1996): 143–70.

69 Catherine Coquery-Vidrovitch, "Fêtes et commemorations en Afrique Occidentale au XXème siècle," in Odile Goerg, ed., *Fêtes urbaines en Afrique: Espaces, identités et pouvoirs* (Paris: Karthala, 1999), 201–12.

70 Mbembe, *La naissance du maquis*.

71 René Pélissier, *Les guerres grises: Résistance et révoltes en Angola, 1845–1941* (Orgeval, France: Pélissier, 1978); Pélissier, *La colonie du Minotaure: Nationalismes et révoltes en Angola, 1926–1961* (Orgeval, France: Pélissier, 1979); Pélissier, *Les campagnes coloniales du Portugal, 1844–1941* (Paris: Pygmalion, 2004); and David Anderson, *Histories of the Hanged: The Dirty War in Kenya and the End of Empire* (New York: Norton, 2005).

72 For a theorization of this terror, see Tocqueville, *De la colonie en Algérie*.

73 Nasser Hussain, *The Jurisprudence of Emergency: Colonialism and the Rule of Law* (Ann Arbor: University of Michigan Press, 2003); and Sidi Mohammed Barkat, *Le corps d'exception: Les artifices du pouvoir colonial et la destruction de la vie* (Paris: Editions d'Amsterdam, 2005).

Five Requiem for the Slave

1 Gilles Deleuze, *Francis Bacon, logique de la sensation* (Paris: Seuil, 2002), chap. 4.

2 Tansi, *Life and a Half* (Bloomington: Indiana University Press, 2011), 24.

3 Gérard Guillerault, *Le miroir et la psyché* (Paris: Gallimard, 2003), 142.

4 Tansi, *Life and a Half*, 8–9.

5 Tansi, *Life and a Half*, 23–24.

6 Tansi, *Life and a Half*, 6.

7 Tansi, *Life and a Half*, 6–7.

8 Tansi, *Life and a Half*, 8.

9 Tutuola, *The Palm-Wine Drinkard and My Life in the Bush of Ghosts* (New York: Grove, 1994).

10 Melchior-Bonnet, *Histoire du miroir* (Paris: Imago, 1994), 113–14.

11 Tutuola, *Palm-Wine Drinkard and My Life*, 248–49.

12 Tutuola, *Palm-Wine Drinkard and My Life*, 109.

13 Tutuola, *Palm-Wine Drinkard and My Life*, 29.

14 Tutuola, *Palm-Wine Drinkard and My Life*, 24–25.

15 Tutuola, *Palm-Wine Drinkard and My Life*, 263–64.

16 Tutuola, *Palm-Wine Drinkard and My Life*, 36.

17 Tutuola, *Palm-Wine Drinkard and My Life*, 90–92.

18 Tutuola, *Palm-Wine Drinkard and My Life*, 271–72.

19 Tutuola, *Palm-Wine Drinkard and My Life*, 42.

20 Deleuze and Guattari, *Anti-Oedipus: Capitalism and Schizophrenia*, trans. Robert Hurley, Mark Seem, and Helen R. Lane (Minneapolis: University of Minnesota Press, 1983), 7, 15.

21 Tutuola, *Palm-Wine Drinkard and My Life*, 74–75.

Six The Clinic of the Subject

1 Marcus Garvey, *Philosophy and Opinions of Marcus Garvey; or, Africa for the Africans* (Dover, MA: Majority Press, 1986).

2 Garvey, *Philosophy and Opinions*, 10–14.

3 Garvey, *Philosophy and Opinions*, 37, 53.

4 Aimé Césaire, *Nègre je suis, nègre je resterai*, interviews by Françoise Vergès (Paris: Albin Michel, 2005), 69.

5 Césaire, "Discours sur la négritude," speech, University of Florida, February 26, 1987, http://blog.ac-versailles.fr/1erelnerval/public/LA_2_Cesaire_Discours_sur_la_Negritude.pdf.

6 Césaire, "Discours sur la négritude."

7 Césaire, *Discourse on Colonialism*, trans. Joan Pinkham (New York: Monthly Review Press, 2000), 32, 36, 39, 41. What the West cannot forgive Hitler for, he argues, "is not *the crime* itself, the crime against man, it is not *the humiliation of man as such*, it is the fact that he applied to Europe colonialist procedures which until then had been reserved exclusively for the Arabs of Algeria, the 'coolies' of India, and the 'niggers' of Africa" (36).

8 Césaire and Vergès, *Nègre je suis*.

9 Césaire, *Discours sur la négritude*.

10 Césaire, *Discourse on Colonialism*, 73.

11 Fanon, *The Wretched of the Earth* (New York: Grove, 1968), chap. 5

12 Fanon, "Les damnés de la terre," in *Œuvres*, eds. Magali Bessone and Achille Mbembe (Paris: La Découverte, 2011), 627, 493.

13 Fanon, *A Dying Colonialism* (New York: Grove, 1965), 23.

14 Fanon, *The Wretched of the Earth* (New York: Grove, 1968), 251.

15 Ann Stoler, "Colonial Aphasia: Race and Disabled Histories in France," *Public Culture* 23, no. 1 (2011): 121–56.

16 Achille Mbembe, "Provincializing France?" *Public Culture* 23, no. 1 (2011): 85–119.

17 Miguel Mellino, "Frantz Fanon, un classique pour le présent," *Il Manifesto*, May 19, 2011, http://frantz-fanon.blogspot.com/2011/05/frantz-fanon-un-classique-pour-le.html.

18 "We have risen to our feet and we are now moving forward. Who can settle us back into servitude?" Fanon, *Dying Colonialism*, 32.

19 "I am a man, and I have to rework the world's past from the very beginning." Fanon, *Black Skin, White Masks*, 201.

20 Bernard Doray, "De notre histoire, de notre temps: À propos de Frantz Fanon, portrait, d'Alice Cherki," *Sud/Nord*, no. 14 (2001): 145–66.

21 Jacques Postel and Claudine Razanajao, "La vie et l'œuvre psychiatrique de Frantz Fanon," *L'Information Psychiatrique* 51, no. 10 (1975): 147–74.

22 On the paradoxes and possibilities of a politics of love in Fanon, see Matthieu Renault, "'Corps à corps': Frantz Fanon's Erotics of National Liberation," *Journal of French and Francophone Philosophy* 19, no. 1 (2011): 49–55.

23 Olivier Douville, "Y a-t-il une actualité clinique de Fanon," *L'Évolution Psychiatrique* 71, no. 4 (2006): 709.

24 Fanon, *Dying Colonialism*, 28–29; and Fanon, "Pourquoi nous employons la violence," in *Œuvres*, 413ff.

25 Fanon, *Wretched of the Earth*, 85.

26 Fanon, *Wretched of the Earth*, 92.

27 "It is not the land that is occupied. . . . Colonialism . . . has installed itself in the very center of the individual . . . and has carried out a sustained labor of sweeps, of the expulsion of oneself, of rationally pursued mutilation. . . . It is the country as a whole, its history, its daily heartbeat, that are challenged. . . . In these conditions, the individual's breathing is observed, occupied. It is breathing as combat." Fanon, "L'an V de la révolution, Annexe: Les femmes dans la révolution," in *Œuvres*, 300.

28 Fanon, "Pourquoi nous employons la violence," 414. Or sometimes the "circle of hate," in Fanon, *Wretched of the Earth*, 89.

29 Fanon, "Pourquoi nous employons la violence," 414.

30 Fanon, *Wretched of the Earth*, 249.

31 Fanon, "Pourquoi nous employons la violence," 414.

32 Fanon, *Dying Colonialism*, 128.

33 Fanon, "Pourquoi nous employons la violence," 414.

34 Mathieu Renault, "Vie et mort dans la pensée de Frantz Fanon," *Cahiers Sens Public* 10 (2009), https://www.cairn.info/revue-cahiers-sens-public-2009-2-p-133.htm.

35 Fanon, *Dying Colonialism*, 118–20.

36 Fanon, *Wretched of the Earth*, 58; and Fanon, "Pourquoi nous employons la violence," 415.

37 Fanon, *Wretched of the Earth*, 93.

38 Bernard Doray, *La dignité: Les debouts de l'utopie* (Paris: La Dispute, 2006).

39 Fanon, *Wretched of the Earth*, 93.

40 Fanon, *Wretched of the Earth*, 89.

41 Fanon, *Dying Colonialism*, 23.

42 Fanon, *Wretched of the Earth*, 85.

43 Fanon, *Black Skin, White Masks*, 86.

44 Fanon, *Wretched of the Earth*, 36–37, 92.

45 Fanon, "Pourquoi nous employons la violence," 417.

46 Fanon, *Wretched of the Earth*, 308–9, 31. For the "great night" the phrase in the original is "la grande nuit."

47 Fanon, "Pourquoi nous employons la violence," 415.

48 Fanon, "Pourquoi nous employons la violence," 415.

49 Mandela, *Conversations with Myself* (London: Macmillan, 2010).

50 Mandela, *Conversations with Myself*, 122–24.

51 See Sarah Nuttall and Achille Mbembe, "Mandela's Mortality," in *The Cambridge Companion to Mandela*, ed. Rita Bernard, 267–89 (Cambridge: Cambridge University Press, 2014).

52 Jacques Lacan, "La psychanalyse est-elle constituante pour une éthique qui serait celle que notre temps nécessite?" *Psychoanalyse* 4 (1986).

53 See James Baldwin, *The Cross of Redemption* (New York: Pantheon, 2010).

54 Blyden, *Liberia's Offering* (New York: John A. Gray, 1862), 174–97.

55 King, *Letter from the Birmingham Jail* (San Francisco: Harper San Francisco, 1994).

56 Fanon, *Black Skin, White Masks*, 112. *Peau noire, masques blancs* (Paris: La Découverte, 2012), 151.

INDEX